The American
Civil War

The American Civil War

COLE C. KINGSEED

Greenwood Guides to Historic Events 1500–1900
Linda S. Frey and Marsha L. Frey, Series Editors

GREENWOOD PRESS
Westport, Connecticut • London

Library of Congress Cataloging-in-Publication Data

Kingseed, Cole C. (Cole Christian), 1949–
    The American Civil War / Cole C. Kingseed.
        p. cm. — (Greenwood guides to historic events 1500–1900, ISSN 1538–442X)
    Includes bibliographical references and index.
    ISBN 0–313–31638–4 (alk. paper)
        1. United States—History—Civil War, 1861–1865. I. Title. II. Series.
E468.K56 2004
973.7—dc22   2004052651

British Library Cataloguing in Publication Data is available.

Library of Congress Catalog Card Number: 2004052651
ISBN: 0–313–31638–4
ISSN: 1538–442X

First published in 2004

Greenwood Press, 88 Post Road West, Westport, CT 06881
An imprint of Greenwood Publishing Group, Inc.
www.greenwood.com

Printed in the United States of America

The paper used in this book complies with the
Permanent Paper Standard issued by the National
Information Standards Organization (Z39.48–1984).

10 9 8 7 6 5 4 3 2 1

To Mary

CONTENTS

Photo essay follows page 126.

SERIES FOREWORD

American statesman Adlai Stevenson stated that "We can chart our future clearly and wisely only when we know the path which has led to the present." This series, Greenwood Guides to Historic Events 1500–1900, is designed to illuminate that path by focusing on events from 1500 to 1900 that have shaped the world. The years 1500 to 1900 include what historians call the Early Modern Period (1500 to 1789, the onset of the French Revolution) and part of the Modern Period (1789 to 1900).

In 1500, an acceleration of key trends marked the beginnings of an interdependent world and the posing of seminal questions that changed the nature and terms of intellectual debate. The series closes with 1900, the inauguration of the twentieth century. This period witnessed profound economic, social, political, cultural, religious, and military changes. An industrial and technological revolution transformed the modes of production, marked the transition from a rural to an urban economy, and ultimately raised the standard of living. Social classes and distinctions shifted. The emergence of the territorial and later the national state altered man's relations with and view of political authority. The shattering of the religious unity of the Roman Catholic world in Europe marked the rise of a new pluralism. Military revolutions changed the nature of warfare. The books in this series emphasize the complexity and diversity of the human tapestry and include political, economic, social, intellectual, military, and cultural topics. Some of the authors focus on events in U.S. history such as the Salem Witchcraft Trials, the American Revolution, the abolitionist movement, and the Civil War. Others analyze European topics, such as the Reformation and Counter Reformation and the French Revolution. Still others bridge cultures and continents by examining the voyages of discovery, the Atlantic slave trade, and the Age of Imperialism. Some focus on intellectual questions that have shaped the modern world, such as Darwin's *Origin of Species,* or on turning points, such as the Age of Romanticism. Others examine defining economic, religious, or legal events or issues such as the building of the railroads, the Second Great Awakening, and abolitionism. Heroes (e.g., Lewis and Clark), scientists (e.g., Darwin), military leaders (e.g., Napoleon), poets (e.g., Byron), stride across its pages. Many of these events were seminal in that they marked profound changes or turning points. The Scientific Revolution, for example, changed the way individuals viewed themselves and their world.

The authors, acknowledged experts in their fields, synthesize key events, set developments within the larger historical context, and, most important, present a well-balanced, well-written account that integrates the most recent scholarship in the field.

The topics were chosen by an advisory board composed of historians, high school history teachers, and school librarians to support the curriculum and meet student research needs. The volumes are designed to serve as resources for student research and to provide clearly written interpretations of topics central to the secondary school and lower-level undergraduate history curriculum. Each author outlines a basic chronology to guide the reader through often confusing events and a historical overview to set those events within a narrative framework. Three to five topical chapters underscore critical aspects of the event. In the final chapter the author examines the impact and consequences of the event. Biographical sketches furnish background on the lives and contributions of the players who strut across this stage. Ten to fifteen primary documents ranging from letters to diary entries, song lyrics, proclamations, and posters cast light on the event, provide material for student essays, and stimulate a critical engagement with the sources. Introductions identify the authors of the documents and the main issues. In some cases a glossary of selected terms is provided as a guide to the reader. Each work contains an annotated bibliography of recommended books, articles, CD-ROMs, Internet sites, videos, and films that set the materials within the historical debate.

These works will lead to a more sophisticated understanding of the events and debates that have shaped the modern world and will stimulate a more active engagement with the issues that still affect us. It has been a particularly enriching experience to work closely with such dedicated professionals. We have come to know and value even more highly the authors in this series and our editors at Greenwood, particularly Kevin Ohe. In many cases they have become more than colleagues; they have become friends. To them and to future historians we dedicate this series.

Linda S. Frey
University of Montana

Marsha L. Frey
Kansas State University

INTRODUCTION

The Civil War is the central event in American history. More than any other, the war defined us as a nation and as a people. What we are today, how we view the role of the national government within our daily lives, how we interpret our relations within our diverse population, and how we evolved as a world power are largely the results of the cataclysmic struggle that shook the American republic in the mid-nineteenth century. For better or worse, the irrepressible conflict that gripped this country nearly 150 years ago also formed our national character.

This volume is intended to offer an introduction to the American Civil War to the general public and to students at the secondary school and college level. It seeks to be informative and interesting and to present a broad background to the events that precipitated the war, the principal personalities who waged the conflict, and the social, economic, and political dimensions that gave the Civil War its unique character. I have placed a special emphasis on refuting many of the popular myths surrounding the conflict and on examining the interaction between strategy and policy on the national level. Naturally the conduct of battles and campaigns constitutes a central theme of this volume, but in no sense is this work to be considered strictly a military history.

This book begins with a chronology of events of the Civil War, followed by an introductory essay that provides an overview of the war, examining the roots of the conflict, then progressing to a more detailed study of the major military and political events and their consequences. Next four topical essays illuminate specific aspects of the war. Chapter 2 challenges "The Myth of Southern Martial Superiority." Traditional historians give the Confederacy the initial advantage with respect to martial prowess. Robert E. Lee and Thomas J. "Stonewall" Jackson have long since been immortalized in the pantheon of Civil War military heroes, but recent interpretations suggest that Union commanders were as talented as their Southern counterparts and that the Lee of legend and myth committed serious errors from which the Confederacy never fully recovered. Chapter 3, "The Transformation of Abraham Lincoln," examines the social and political transformation of the nation's sixteenth president from a unionist to an abolitionist to a nationalist. Through its drawing upon Lincoln's speeches and actions, the reader will gain a broader understanding of Lincoln as a war leader and an emancipator. Next, "Could the South Have Won the Civil War?" This question has intrigued historians for generations. Examining the concept of contingencies and determining what factors might have contributed to a Confederate victory forms the basis for chapter 4. In 1863 Southern hopes for independence reached their apogee, a prospect that rested solely on the shoulders of General Robert E. Lee and the Army of Northern Virginia. Chapter 5 analyzes the Confederate defeat at the Battle of Gettysburg, often called the turning point of the war. A contemporary perspective on the consequences of the American Civil War constitutes the concluding chapter.

The final section of the book presents biographical profiles of the major political and military figures involved in the war. Each biographical sketch includes a brief background of the individual's life and then summarizes the individual's role in the Civil War. Next a glossary provides the reader with the terms necessary to comprehend the terminology associated with the conflict. Of special significance are the primary documents that show the war from a unique perspective. These documents include diaries, political speeches, memoirs, and the official records of the War of the Rebellion. The selected works of Abraham Lincoln and Jefferson Davis shed light on the political aspects of the war, while soldiers' accounts provided by Joshua Lawrence Chamberlain and George Stevens give insights on human behavior in the midst of battle. Generals Robert E. Lee and Ulysses S. Grant also present their observations on the war's climactic battles and campaigns. Of particular interest are Edward Vollum's account of the transportation of wounded and Henry Wirz's spirited defense of his actions as commandant of Andersonville Prison, the most notorious of all Civil War prison camps.

More literature has been written on the Civil War than any other event in American history. Hence, the annotated bibliography must be selective. The works listed address a broad range of political, social, economic, cultural, and military issues and have been universally accepted by the leading scholars of the war. The bibliography includes contemporary accounts, general histories, biographies of the key figures of the war, personal memoirs, and recommended Web sites to provide readers with a range of sources to enhance their ability to investigate specific features of the nation's greatest conflict.

In writing this book, I wish to acknowledge a personal debt to the series' editors, Professors Linda and Marsha Frey. Both have been extremely supportive and have offered constructive criticism throughout the enterprise. I have been associated with both professors for a number of years, and have always found them extremely encouraging and helpful in a number of literary projects. I would also like to express my personal appreciation to Mr. Kevin Hymel for his assistance in researching photographs for this project. Additionally, Frank Martini, cartographer for the Department of History, U.S. Military Academy at West Point, provided technical advice in obtaining the map that the Department of History graciously permitted me to use.

My personal association with Civil War history dates to the centennial of the Civil War, which brought me into contact with the works of such noted historians as Bruce Catton and Douglas S. Freeman. The transition to more modern scholars such as James McPherson, Thomas Connelly, William C. Davis, and Russell F. Weigley was an easy jump. Three historians merit special consideration. While preparing for my doctoral degree at The Ohio State University, Professor Allan R. Millett trained me to view documents with a critical eye and then guided my research and writing. At the U.S. Military Academy at West Point, where I served two tours of duty, Colonels Paul L. Miles and Robert A. Doughty refined my skills and exhibited the highest forms of professionalism and character. My military duties also brought me into close contact with Mr. Dave Sherman, an elementary school teacher at West Point. Probably the finest history teacher whom I have had the pleasure to know, Dave has annually taken his students to the Gettysburg battlefield to help them discover America's past and to extol the heroism and selfless service of the generation who waged the Civil War. Last, and surely not least, my heartfelt thanks to my wife, Mary, to whom this book is dedicated, and to my children, John and Maura, who accompanied me to Gettysburg and rekindled my interest in the Civil War.

To those named above, and to all others whom I may have unintentionally omitted, I express my gratitude and thanks.

I alone am responsible for any errors that appear in this narrative. Such deficiencies are sins of omission rather than commission.

CHRONOLOGY OF EVENTS

1860

November 6	Election of Abraham Lincoln
December 20	South Carolina secedes

1861

January 9	Mississippi secedes
January 10	Florida secedes
January 11	Alabama secedes
January 19	Georgia secedes
January 26	Louisiana secedes
February 1	Texas secedes
February 4	Confederate States of America formed in Montgomery, Alabama
February 9	Jefferson Davis elected provisional president of CSA
February 18	Davis and Alexander Stephens inaugurated
March 4	Abraham Lincoln inaugurated as president
April 12	Confederates fire on Fort Sumter
April 14	Fort Sumter surrenders
April 15	Lincoln calls for 75,000 volunteers
April 17	Virginia secedes
April 20	Robert E. Lee resigns from the U.S. Army
May 6	Arkansas and Tennessee secede
May 20	North Carolina secedes
July 21	First Battle of Bull Run/Manassas
July 27	Major General George B. McClellan assumes command of Union forces around Washington

November 1	McClellan appointed general-in-chief, replacing Winfield Scott
November 8	Confederate agents Slidell and Mason seized from British steamer *Trent*
December 9	Joint Committee on the Conduct of the War created

1862

January 1	Mason and Slidell released
January 15	Congress confirms Edwin Stanton as Secretary of War
February 6	U. S. Grant captures Fort Henry
February 16	Grant captures Fort Donelson
March 8	*CSS Virginia*, formerly the *USS Merrimack*, attacks Union blockading fleet at Hampton Roads
March 9	Battle between the *CSS Virginia* and the *USS Monitor*
April 6–7	Battle of Shiloh
April 25	Admiral David Farragut captures New Orleans
June 1	Lee assumes command of the Army of Northern Virginia
June 26–July 1	Seven Days' Campaign outside Richmond
July 11	Major General Henry Halleck appointed general-in-chief of Union Army
August 29–30	Second Battle of Bull Run/Manassas
September 4	Lee invades Maryland
September 17	Battle of Antietam/Sharpsburg
September 22	Lincoln issues preliminary Emancipation Proclamation
October 8	Battle of Perryville, Kentucky
November 9	Ambrose Burnside replaces McClellan as commander of the Army of the Potomac
December 13	Battle of Fredericksburg
December 30–31 January 3, 1863	Battle of Stones River/Murfreesboro

1863

| January 1 | Emancipation Proclamation takes effect |
| January 26 | Joseph Hooker assumes command of Army of the Potomac |

April 17	Benjamin Grierson begins his raid through Mississippi
May 1–4	Battle of Chancellorsville
May 10	Stonewall Jackson dies
May 19–July 4	Grant lays siege to Vicksburg
June 28	George Meade succeeds Hooker to command the Army of the Potomac
July 1–3	Battle of Gettysburg
July 4	Grant captures Vicksburg
July 13	New York draft riots begin
September 19–20	Battle of Chickamauga
September 22	Confederate siege of Chattanooga begins
November 19	Lincoln delivers Gettysburg Address
November 24–25	Battle of Lookout Mountain and Missionary Ridge
November 26	Bragg retreats from Chattanooga

1864

February 17	*USS Housatonic* sunk by Confederate submarine *CSS Hunley*
March 9	Grant receives commission as lieutenant general
May 4	Grant's Overland Campaign begins
May 5–6	Battle of the Wilderness
May 8–19	Battle of Spotsylvania Courthouse
June 1–3	Battle of Cold Harbor
June 12	Army of the Potomac crosses the James River
June 19	*CSS Alabama* sunk by *USS Kearsarge*
July 18	Davis replaces Joseph Johnston with John Bell Hood as William T. Sherman approaches Atlanta
July 30	Battle of the Crater at Petersburg, Virginia
August 1	Sherman begins siege of Atlanta
August 5	Admiral Farragut captures Mobile Bay
August 30	George B. McClellan accepts Democratic Party's nomination for president
September 2	Sherman occupies Atlanta
October 19	Philip Sheridan defeats Jubal Early at Battle of Cedar Creek
November 8	Lincoln reelected president
November 16	Sherman begins March to the Sea

November 30	Battle of Franklin, Tennessee
December 16	George Thomas destroys Confederate Army of Tennessee at Nashville
December 21	Sherman captures Savannah, Georgia

1865

January 15	Fort Fisher, North Carolina, falls to Union forces
January 19	Sherman's army begins leaving Savannah
January 31	House of Representatives passes Thirteenth Amendment
February 3	Lincoln meets Confederate representatives at Hampton Roads
February 6	Lee assumes command of all Confederate forces
February 17	Confederate forces evacuate Charleston
March 3	Congress establishes Freedmen's Bureau
March 4	Lincoln inaugurated as president
March 25	Lee launches final offensive against Fort Stedman
April 2	Lee evacuates Petersburg
April 3	Union forces occupy Richmond
April 4	Lincoln visits Richmond
April 9	Lee surrenders Army of Northern Virginia to Grant at Appomattox Courthouse
April 14	Lincoln assassinated by John Wilkes Booth at Ford's Theater
April 15	Lincoln dies at the Peterson house
April 26	Johnston surrenders to Sherman at Durham Station, North Carolina
April 26	John Wilkes Booth killed by federal troops
May 4	Lincoln buried in Springfield, Illinois
May 10	Jefferson Davis captured at Irwinville, Georgia
May 12–13	Battle at Palmito Ranch, Texas, last battle of the Civil War
May 23–24	Grand review of the Armies of the Republic
May 29	President Andrew Johnson issues Pardon and Amnesty Proclamation
July 7	Lincoln conspirators hanged
November 6	*CSS Shenandoah* surrenders in Liverpool, England

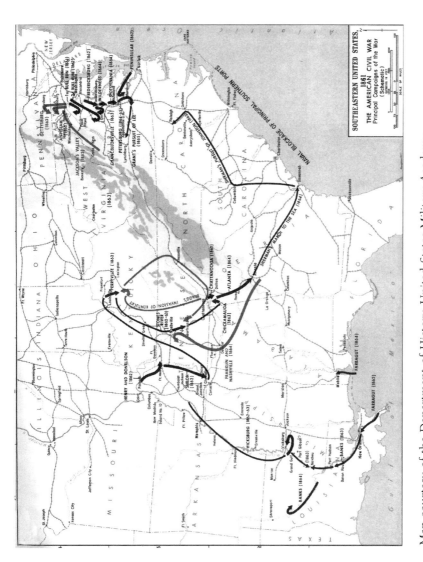

Map courtesy of the Department of History, United States Military Academy.

CHAPTER 1

OVERVIEW OF THE WAR

The Civil War was the central event in American history. Moreover, it was the central event in the lives of the men and women who experienced the tumultuous upheaval that shook the American republic between 1861 and 1865. Placing the conflict in perspective, Shelby Foote, the plain-speaking Southern historian whose three-volume narrative history remains a definitive examination of the Civil War, remarked for the Public Broadcasting Service:

> Any understanding of this nation has to be based, and I mean really based, on an understanding of the Civil War. I believe that firmly. It defined us. The Revolution did what it did. Our involvement in European wars, beginning with the First World War, did what it did. But the Civil War defined us as what we are and it opened us to being what we became, good and bad things. And it is very necessary, if you're going to understand the American character in the twentieth century, to learn about this enormous catastrophe of the nineteenth century. It was the crossroads of our being, and it was a hell of a crossroads: the suffering, the enormous tragedy of the whole thing.[1]

Over the course of the conflict, 620,000 Americans perished; double that number carried the scars of war for the remainder of their lives. More Americans died in the Civil War than any other conflict in American history. Until the latter stages of the Vietnam War, the Civil War had claimed more American lives than all the previous wars combined that the United States had fought. One hundred forty years after the war, the Battle of Antietam/Sharpsburg still is the bloodiest single day in American history.

It is no small wonder that one can scarcely pass through any town of the states that were in the Union at the outset of the Civil War without coming across a monument to the residents who perished in the conflict. Such was the extent of the conflagration that consumed North and South in the middle of the nineteenth century. But in a larger sense the war culminated over eight decades of sectional strife that threatened the continued existence of American democracy. Fought in 10,000 places, with 2,000 engagements large enough to be called battles, this irrepressible conflict served as a rite of passage from an imperfect union of disparate states to a single national entity. In the process one civilization passed from the national scene and a significantly more united country emerged, based on a stronger "government of the people, by the people, and for people."

As has been the case throughout our history, crisis brings forth the very best in American society. The Civil War was no exception. Countless millions from every walk in life answered their country's call; both sides considered themselves the legitimate heirs of the nation's Founding Fathers and Mothers. On both sides of the Mason–Dixon Line, armies were led by perhaps the most formidable array of political and military leaders that this nation has ever produced. For the North, Abraham Lincoln, the son of an itinerant farmer who could hardly write his name, reversed two decades of presidential inactivity and became the greatest chief executive in American history. Commanding Lincoln's army was Ulysses S. Grant, a failure in every profession but war, but a general who developed the military strategy that shattered the Confederate armies and won the war for the North. At his side was William T. Sherman, whose march through Georgia in 1864 came to symbolize the indescribable horror and total destruction of modern warfare. Opposing this trio of Union leaders were Confederate President Jefferson Davis and General Robert E. Lee. Davis, a graduate of the U.S. Military Academy at West Point and a former secretary of war, faced the unenviable task of guiding a nascent nation to obtain its independence against overwhelming resources. And through four years of conflict, Lee, whose military prowess and personal sense of duty made him the most beloved commander in either army, bequeathed a legacy of honor and conciliation to a united nation that had been torn apart by the unspeakable horror of civil war.

Eighty-five years after the delegates of the Second Continental Congress affixed their names to the Declaration of Independence in 1776, the very symbol of the nation to which they had pledged their lives, their property, and their sacred honor, flew atop a flagpole inside Fort Sumter in Charleston Harbor. Commanding the federal garrison was Major Robert Anderson, a former artillery instructor at West Point. A Kentucky-born officer who had married a Georgian, Anderson was torn between loyalty to his native state and the nation whose flag he had served all his adult life. In charge of the Confederate forces that ringed Fort Sumter and that were awaiting orders to reduce the fort was Anderson's former student at the U.S. Military Academy, General Pierre G. T. Beauregard. Beauregard had been appointed superintendent of West Point when his state had passed its ordinance of secession and left the Union. Consequently he never assumed the office and offered his sword to the newly formed Confederate States of America. The telegraph office soon gave Beauregard his orders from the Confederate capital in Montgomery, Alabama. At precisely 4:30 in the morning of April 12, 1861, sixty-seven-year-old Edmund Ruffin, an ardent secessionist whose hatred for the Union was second only to his loyalty for the South, pulled the lanyard that sent the first shot careening toward Fort Sumter. The war which so many statesmen had struggled for several decades to avoid had begun.

The Road to War

War erupted in 1861 because each side accepted armed conflict as the only means to settle the divergence of interests that had gradually split the United States into two competing economic, social, and political camps. Whatever similarities existed, and there were many—Americans North and South spoke the same language, they used a common currency, they relished democratic institutions—one principal difference divided the two sections: the issue of slavery. From 1619, when the first indentured servants arrived in Jamestown, Virginia, the peculiar institution of slavery drove a wedge between North and South. At the time of the American Revolution, slavery was recognized by each of the thirteen British colonies, but it gradually died out in the North. By the Constitutional Convention of 1787, five Northern states had already abolished slavery, but the issue was paramount enough to play an integral role in the formation of the U.S. Constitution. Compromise with the Southern delegates over counting slaves as population to determine representation in the U.S. House of Representatives was required to ensure ratification by the Southern states. Six years later, in Connecticut Eli Whitney invented the cotton gin, which reversed the decline of slavery in the South by providing the incentive to bring additional acreage under cotton production. Two decades later, ex-President Thomas Jefferson was sufficiently alarmed to recognize that the growing sectional strife over slavery would inevitably increase. Though a slave owner himself, Jefferson deplored the institution of slavery as inhumane and strongly believed that the contradiction between those inalienable rights expressed in the Declaration of Independence and the existence of human bondage could be resolved only by the eventual abolition of legalized slavery. As sectional differences surfaced over the admission of Missouri as a slave state in 1820, Jefferson told fellow ex-President John Adams that the current crisis was "more serious that that which they had faced during the American Revolution." A few weeks later, he described the Missouri question as "a firebell in the night."[2] Though Henry Clay successfully negotiated a compromise in which Missouri was admitted as a slave state and Maine admitted as a free state, the political lines were clearly drawn. According to the compromise, those territories above 36 degrees, 30 minutes north latitude would be admitted as free states; those south of the line would enter the Union as slave states. It was a temporary fix at best. In the decade following Jefferson's death in 1826, sectional differences took the form of states' rights and nullification, but the underlying foundation was clearly slavery. Indeed, the issue of slavery became so contentious that Congress instituted a gag rule by which the subject could not even be addressed in the halls of government.

The Mexican–American War

What brought the problem to the surface again was the expansionist war with Mexico by which the United States acquired two-fifths of Mexican territory in the Treaty of Guadalupe Hidalgo in 1848. President James K. Polk's victory was clearly a tremendous victory for the adherents of Manifest Destiny, but the newly acquired territory provided the seeds for ultimate disunion. Would the new territories be slave or free? Polk himself thought there was "no probability that any territory will ever be acquired from Mexico in which slavery would ever exist." He was wrong. Pro-slavery legislators demanded the expansion of slavery into the former Mexican provinces, but anti-slavery congressman David Wilmot of Pennsylvania then introduced a proviso to the appropriations bill that slavery not be permitted to extend into any territory acquired from Mexico. The proviso passed in the House of Representatives by a sectional vote, but failed in the Senate. Southerners, fearing the growing political influence of the North, sought to solidify their political power, and they took umbrage with what they perceived as a growing political alliance between the northern and western states that would eventually lead to their loss of political and economic liberty. Polk attempted to defuse the increasing contentiousness between the adherents and opponents of slavery by extending the Missouri Compromise line west to the Pacific. Congress would have none of it, and the ten years prior to the outbreak of the American Civil War were marked by weak chief executives, growing sectional strife, and irreconcilable differences. War could just as easily have erupted in 1850, but first veteran Senator Henry Clay engineered a final compromise that would postpone armed conflict for another decade, a decade in which a former one-term Illinois congressman reached his political maturity.

The Great Compromise

In the Senate, emerging leaders of the next generation listened as the legislative giants of the Jacksonian era brokered a final compromise. Jefferson Davis, Stephen A. Douglas, and William H. Seward sat intently as Henry Clay, Daniel Webster, and John C. Calhoun, too weak to present his own speech in support of Southern rights, carried the day. The Compromise of 1850 had something for every side, but no one was completely satisfied. Clay presented a series of resolutions that maintained a precarious peace for eleven years. These resolutions included (1) the immediate admission of California as a free state; (2) organization of territorial governments in New Mexico and Utah on the basis of popular sovereignty, the right of territorial residents to decide if they would be free or slave; (3) a much stronger Fugitive Slave Act by which escaped slaves would be forcibly returned to their Southern owners; and (4) the abolition of the slave trade within the District of Columbia.[3] Clay and Webster vigorously advocated passage of the compromise, but Calhoun, haggard and worn, warned the Senate that "The cords that bind the States together" were snapping one by one. The North must "do justice by conceding to the South an equal right in the acquired territory" by doing her duty as to fugitive slaves; by restoring to the South, through constitutional amendment, the equilibrium of power she once possessed in the federal government.[4] With the able intervention of Senator Stephen A. Douglas, who carefully directed the senatorial debate to pass Clay's resolutions individually instead of collectively, the Compromise of 1850 passed and was signed into law by President Millard Fillmore, who had succeeded Zachary Taylor on the latter's death in July 1850. The senators breathed a sigh of relief, but Calhoun had identified the central problems: the South was dissatisfied by the continual Northern attacks against slavery, and the South also feared that it was losing power and that the balance in the federal government was being tipped in favor of the North. Since the birth of the republic, Southerners or pro-Southern Northern Democrats and Whigs had dominated the executive branch of government. The same was true in the judicial branch, where Southerners or their sympathizers had held the office of chief justice of the U.S. Supreme Court. Northerners held the majority in the House of Representatives, but the South could offset that advantage in the legislative branch as long as it maintained a precarious balance in the Senate. Now, pending the fate of the territories obtained from Mexico, that equilibrium was jeopardized.

The Sectional Crisis Escalates

The Great Compromise ushered in a decade of prosperity and averted civil war, but within two years, those who had originated it and ensured its passage had passed from the political scene. By 1852, Clay, Webster, and Calhoun were all dead, and their successors, though statesmen of great ability, proved unable to halt the inexorable slide toward civil strife. Equally disturbing to Southern congressmen was the arrival of a new breed of Northern politician on the national scene, men like Thaddeus Stevens of Pennsylvania, Charles Sumner of Massachusetts, and Benjamin Wade of Ohio, radical anti-slavery men ambitious enough to challenge the entrenched bureaucracy of the Democratic Party for party leadership. Once again the question of slavery dominated the national agenda, though this time the debate was not confined to the halls of Congress. By the end of the decade, a new political party had been founded whose principal platform called for the restriction of slavery at first and eventually its total abolition. The 1850s also witnessed anti-slavery sentiment reaching epic proportions throughout the North, legislators and federal judges muddling the mix by contradictory policies and decisions, and the nation's chief executives failing to provide decisive leadership as the country drifted toward war. Complicating the problem was the fact that sectional differences had now turned violent, first in the territory of Kansas and then in Virginia, where diehard abolitionist John Brown seized a federal arsenal at Harpers Ferry in an abortive attempt to foster a slave insurrection throughout the South. There would be several halfhearted attempts to compromise; however, the final decision as to whether there would be war or peace rested with the presidential election of 1860 and whether Northern and Southern Democrats could set aside their political differences and unite their forces against the increasing power of the Republican Party in the North.

Uncle Tom's Cabin

Onto the scene came Harriet Beecher Stowe, a Connecticut woman who penned one of the most influential books in history. The daughter of a Congregational clergyman, Stowe published *Uncle Tom's Cabin* in the spring of 1852. The book had first appeared in extract, but now, in hard cover, *Uncle Tom's Cabin* was an immediate success. The book sold 300,000 copies in the United States alone, and within a decade it sold in excess of 2 million copies, with similar sales in Great Britain. Stowe chronicled the evils of slavery through the events she had witnessed when she lived in Cincinnati, Ohio, for eighteen years. With slaveholding Kentucky directly across the Ohio River, Stowe had observed runaway slaves in the streets of the Queen City and was aware of the Fugitive Slave Act, which required their forceful return to their masters. Inspired by God, or so she said, Stowe sought to describe the inhumanity of human bondage to an evangelical generation that had just experienced the Second Great Awakening. She found a ready audience. Moreover, the literary success of *Uncle Tom's Cabin* captivated not only prominent political leaders but also the general public, North and South. Northerners hailed her book as a literary masterpiece; a "coup de main," said Henry Wadsworth Longfellow, who joined his fellow Yankees in condemning the South. For their part, incensed Southerners decried Stowe's "falsehoods" and "distortions." And when Lincoln finally met Stowe in 1862, he allegedly greeted her, "So you're the little woman who wrote the book that made this great war."[5]

The Kansas–Nebraska Act

Next the legislators had their turn. Stephen A. Douglas, who had proved so instrumental in the passage of the Compromise of 1850, introduced a bill in Congress to organize the territory of Nebraska along the lines of popular sovereignty. Since Nebraska lay north of the Missouri Compromise line, the bill should never have gained momentum. Douglas's plan called for the division of the territory into two sections, Kansas and

Nebraska, one territory each for North and South. Such a scheme would render the Missouri Compromise obsolete as squatters of both sides of the slavery question flooded the newly formed Kansas Territory to establish a popular majority to influence the territorial legislature. Douglas was playing with legislative fire, and he touched off a conflagration. On May 25, 1854, the Kansas–Nebraska Act became law with President Franklin Pierce's signature, and widespread violence erupted across the Kansas prairie. Pro-slavery advocates crossed the border from Missouri, and radical abolitionists, including John Brown and his sons, committed wanton acts of violence against "intruders" from the South. At Pottawatomie Creek, Brown butchered a number of innocent people whom he proclaimed were Southern sympathizers. In the hallowed chambers of the U.S. Senate, a cousin of South Carolinian Senator Benjamin Butler clubbed Massachusetts Senator Charles Sumner, who had recently delivered an invective oration titled "The Crime Against Kansas," within inches of his life. "Bleeding Kansas" also ushered in the formation of a new political party, whose leaders first met in a school house in Ripon, Wisconsin, on February 28, 1854, resolved to prevent the extension of slavery into the territories. Within two years the Republican Party would offer one of their own, Western pathfinder John C. Frémont, as a candidate for the presidency. With a slogan of "Free soil, free speech, and Frémont," the Republican Party grew so rapidly that by 1860, it would elect Abraham Lincoln to the highest office in the land. Such spectacular political growth was testament to the Northern disgust surrounding the Kansas–Nebraska Act.

Dred Scott

Now it was the Supreme Court's turn to play its hand. Dred Scott was a slave who had been taken by his master from Missouri to Illinois, a free state, then returned to Missouri. Upon his return to Missouri, Scott sued for his freedom, stating that his temporary residence in a free slave invalidated his former status as a slave. The case made its way through the appellate process and reached the Supreme Court in 1856. Headed by Chief Justice Roger B. Taney, a Marylander with strong sympathies toward the South, the court ruled against Scott on March 6, 1857. In delivering the majority opinion, Taney stated that (1) as a Negro, Dred Scott could not be a citizen of the United States and could not sue in a federal court; (2) as a resident of Missouri, the laws of Illinois had no effect on Scott's status; and (3) as a resident of the territory north of the Missouri

Compromise line, Scott had not been emancipated because Congress had no right to deprive citizens of their property without due process of law. Moreover, since Congress had no right to regulate slavery in the territories, the Missouri Compromise was unconstitutional. The division of North and South along even sharper lines hastened the rapid rise of the Republican Party across the North.

In Illinois, a onetime Whig Party congressman who was also one of the most prominent lawyers of his day was rejuvenated by the Dred Scott Decision. Speaking out against the extension of slavery into the territories, Abraham Lincoln delivered a speech in Peoria, Illinois, on October 16, 1854, in which he stated emphatically that "A house divided against itself cannot stand. I believe this government cannot endure, permanently half slave and half free. I do not expect the Union to be dissolved—I do not expect the house to fall—but I do expect it will cease to be divided."[6] Four years later, Lincoln, now a nationally known politician, challenged incumbent Senator Stephen A. Douglas for the U.S. Senate seat of Illinois. In a series of debates that attracted national attention, Lincoln reiterated his "House Divided" speech, striking directly to the heart of the anti-slavery movement. Though he was defeated, Lincoln emerged with an increased stature that in 1860 would propel him to the presidency.

John Brown's Raid

With the Union sliding toward disunion, it only took a spark to ignite the powder keg of civil war, and that spark was provided by old John Brown. On the night of October 16, 1859, John Brown, accompanied by thirteen white men and five blacks, seized the federal arsenal at Harpers Ferry, Virginia. Holding some of the town's most prominent citizens hostage, Brown intended to arm the slaves and foment an insurrection across the South. It was what white Southerners most feared, and they reacted with speedy alarm. Within hours telegraph lines brought the news to Richmond and Washington, D.C. Commanding General of the U.S. Army Winfield Scott dispatched Colonel Robert E. Lee, who was home on leave from Texas, with a detachment of U.S. Marines to Harpers Ferry to capture Brown and his followers. The Marines stormed the fire house where Brown was holed up and apprehended the entire lot. Eight days later, Brown was brought to trial on charges of treason against the state of Virginia, rapidly convicted, and hanged in Charles Town, Virginia, on December 2, 1859. Extremists on both sides now took up the cause.

Vilified in the South as a symbol of Northern radicals, Brown was canonized in the North as a modern prophet and liberator. Regardless, the lines were clearly drawn. Southerners were more adamant that the Union had become radicalized and that their continued association within that union was predicated on the forthcoming presidential election the following November.

The Election of Abraham Lincoln

As the presidential election loomed on the political horizon, Southerners made it clear that the election of a "Black Republican" would lead to the dissolution of the Union. To any casual observer, it was evident that the North was united behind the Republican Party candidate, whoever he might be. The question was answered in Chicago in mid-May when the Republican delegates assembled to nominate a candidate. On the first ballot, William H. Seward, Lincoln's future secretary of state, garnered more support than Lincoln, but the Illinois lawyer gained considerable support on the second ballot. Lincoln was nominated on the third ballot, after several delegates switched their votes to the candidate who just six years earlier was relatively unknown outside Illinois. The party platform, now less radical than in 1854, called for the restriction of slavery to the new territories, but no abolition of slavery in the states where slavery legally existed.

The Democratic Party was far less united. Douglas, who had alienated Southern Democrats over the issue of popular sovereignty, took the nomination in June, but only after Southern Democrats had withdrawn their delegations and held their own nominating convention, nominating John C. Breckinridge of Kentucky as their candidate. To further complicate matters, John Bell of Tennessee received the nomination of the National Constitutional Union Party, which advocated the U.S. Constitution, the Union, and law enforcement. In retrospect, one ponders in astonishment the political ineptitude of the Southern Democrats. The only way to prevent the election of a Republican president was to unify their own political party. Hopelessly divided, the Democratic Party split along regional lines, with Abraham Lincoln receiving the majority in the Electoral College, even though he received a minority of the popular vote. In retrospect a united Democratic Party would not have won the election because Lincoln's electoral majority was so great. He carried every free state. The slave states split among his various opponents.

Lincoln's election on November 6 produced the predictable results. As the North celebrated the election of its new political hero, the Southern states, led by South Carolina, called for special sessions of their state legislatures to consider secession. South Carolina led the way on December 20 and unanimously passed an ordinance of secession, severing South Carolina's ties to the Union. Six states of the Lower South quickly followed suit. Georgia was next, followed in rapid succession by Alabama, Florida, Mississippi, Louisiana, and Texas. On February 8, 1861, delegates assembled in Montgomery, Alabama, and formed the Confederate States of America. The next day they nominated former U.S. Senator Jefferson Davis of Mississippi as provisional president of the Confederacy. Within weeks Confederates seized all federal territory within their borders, leaving the U.S. government in possession of only Fort Pickens off the Florida coast and Fort Sumter in Charleston Harbor. Whether the Buchanan administration would reinforce and resupply the two forts was the question of the day. In the end Buchanan did nothing, which is why he is universally regarded as the nation's most inept chief executive. What really mattered was what President-elect Lincoln would do after taking the oath of office as president on March 4, 1861.

Historians View the Origins of the War

Considering the divisiveness that characterized the American Civil War, it is no surprise that historians have failed to reach a consensus on its origins. No one disputes, however, that slavery was a principal cause of the conflict. The institution of slavery, with its complementary social, economic, and political consequences, was the cornerstone on which states' rights, secession, and nullification rested. In his recent analysis of the forging of the Confederacy, William Davis argues that slavery was the "single motive force that drove the flood toward war."[7] In the immediate postwar era, the histories of the recent conflict generally fell along regional lines. The Unionists, led by Henry Adams and Henry Cabot Lodge, concluded that the North fought the war for the preservation of the Union. Southerners, led by Wade Hampton and Jefferson Davis (*Rise and Fall of the Confederate Government*), concluded that the South was justified, morally and constitutionally, to secede from the Union. They concentrated on states' rights, not the defense of slavery, as the principal reason that they took up arms in 1861. Davis underscored the justice and righteousness of the Southern cause that he had so eloquently addressed in his inaugural address in Montgomery, Alabama, in February 1861. At the turn of the twentieth century, historians began taking a more economic and legalistic approach to the commencement of the war. Charles Beard espoused this view in his economic interpretation of the U.S. Constitution. Such views held sway until the centennial of the Civil War, when historians including James McPherson (*Battle Cry of Freedom*) and Allan Nevins (*Ordeal of the Union*) offered a more nationalistic interpretation. Kenneth Stampp (*And the War Came*) argues that leaders failed to avert the crisis because firebrands on both sides demanded war as the only resolution to the sectional crisis. In *The Imperiled Union: Essays on the Background of the Civil War*, Stampp also posits that "Lincoln accepted the possibility of war, which in retrospect, was the almost certain consequence" of his desire to preserve the Union.[8] In any event, both sides reacted swiftly to Lincoln's election. The North heralded the election of a Republican president, and the South moved swiftly to secede from the Union which they felt jeopardized its continued existence as an independent society.

The Outbreak of War

When Abraham Lincoln took the oath of office as president of the United States on March 4, 1861, he faced a crisis without parallel in the nation's history. Confronted with the secession of seven states in the Lower South and the confiscation of federal property in those states, the new president emphasized that he would not tolerate secession. Promising to respect slavery where it already existed, he reminded the secessionists that in their hands, not his, lay the "momentous issue of civil war." The federal government, he informed the South, would not attack. There would be no conflict unless the South became the aggressor. Then came the caveat: "You [the South] have no oath registered in heaven to destroy the government, while I shall have the most solemn one to 'preserve, protect, and defend' it."[9]

The first question awaiting Lincoln was whether to provision Fort Sumter. In his first cabinet meeting the majority of the cabinet agreed with General-in-Chief Winfield Scott that any attempt to provision Fort Sumter would probably initiate civil war. Lincoln considered all alternatives, including the possible defection of the Upper South (Virginia, North Carolina, Tennessee, and Arkansas), and decided to send a relief expedition as soon as possible. At the same time Confederate emissaries were in Washington, D.C., attempting to negotiate a surrender of the fort's beleaguered garrison. Lincoln would have none of it, and refused to meet with the envoys. Directing his secretary of the navy to prepare the relief expedition, Lincoln patiently awaited news from Major Robert Anderson, Fort Sumter's commander. If the South wanted war, then the Confederate States of America must initiate hostilities. The ball was definitely in Jefferson Davis's court.

Having telegraphed the governor of South Carolina that he intended to provision Fort Sumter, Lincoln anticipated war. For his part Jefferson Davis convened a war council on April 9, and after intense debate, cabled Beauregard, commanding the Confederate forces in Charleston, to reduce the fort before the relief fleet arrived. The Civil War began on April 12 at 4:30 A.M., when Confederate forces began a two-day bombardment of the fort. After a token resistance to display his personal and his country's honor, Anderson surrendered the fort on April 14. The South had its war.

The news electrified both North and South. On the day following the surrender, Lincoln issued a call for 75,000 volunteers to put down the rebellion and to cause the laws of the United States to be duly executed. Four days later, Lincoln proclaimed a blockade of all Confederate ports. Within a week Virginia delegates convened and prepared for war. On April 25, Virginia joined the Confederacy, quickly followed by Arkansas, North Carolina, and Tennessee. In the western counties of Virginia, pro-Union sentiment was strong; these counties seceded from the Confederacy and were admitted to the Union in 1863 as the state of West Virginia.

Across the land, volunteers flocked to their colors. The North answered enthusiastically; 150,000 volunteers responded to Lincoln's summons. The response was similar in the South, where in excess of 100,000 men answered Davis's call to arms on March 6. One Virginian, Colonel Robert E. Lee, the greatest "military genius in America," according to Winfield Scott, was offered command of the Union armies to subdue the South, but Lee refused to draw his sword against his native state. Resigning his commission with a heavy heart, he offered his services to the Confederacy, whose capital was now transferred from Montgomery, Alabama, to Richmond, Virginia. Most Americans anticipated a short war, probably no longer than ninety days. They were mistaken. Federal troops marched to Washington, arriving to Lincoln's immense relief on April 19, but not before blood was shed in Baltimore, when the new recruits were attacked by an angry pro-Southern mob.

On the surface, it seemed the South had little chance of success. Outnumbered twenty-three to eleven states, the Confederacy's white, homogeneous population was generally united on the cause of independence. Though outnumbered in white population 18.9 million to 5.5 million, the South could maintain interior lines to offset the Northern numerical advantages in population, industry, railroad mileage, and virtually every other sinew of war. Most Southerners, to say nothing of the majority of Europeans, did not expect the North to fight to preserve the Union. To mobilize the North to wage modern war would take two years, and nobody expected the war to last that long. Southerners could also point to the experience of the Founding Fathers, who had successfully waged war against Great Britain in 1776 and had achieved American independence. What the South failed to anticipate was how aggressively Lincoln would fight the war and how committed the Northern population was to the preservation of the Union. By firing on the American flag, the Confederacy galvanized the Northern population every bit as much as the Japanese attack on Pearl Harbor on December 7, 1941, and the terrorist attack on the United States by Islamic militants on September 11, 2001, galvanized the entire U.S. population. How effectively both sides would wage war lay in the hands of their political and military leaders.

Civilian and Military Leadership

The presidents of the United States and the Confederate States could not have been more different, both in temperament and in personality. Any casual observer would have undoubtedly considered Davis the abler of the two to lead his nation in war. Both Lincoln and Davis hailed from Kentucky, Davis from Christian County and Lincoln from a log cabin outside Hodgenville.

Davis, the youngest of ten children, was born in 1808, less than 100 miles from where Lincoln was born a year later. Davis's father secured his son an appointment to West Point in 1824, a typical profession for the youngest son of a well-to-do Southern family. At the U.S. Military Academy, Davis befriended future Confederate generals Robert E. Lee, Joseph J. Johnston, Albert S. Johnston, and Leonidas Polk. He served in the army for seven years, then married the daughter of General Zachary Taylor, one of the army's most distinguished warriors. Forsaking a military career for that of a farmer, Davis became a successful plantation owner before he became enmeshed in politics in the mid-1840s. Elected to Congress as a representative-at-large on the coattails of James Knox Polk, Davis resigned his seat and raised a volunteer regiment, the Mississippi Rifles, for the war with Mexico, in which he served brilliantly. Hailed as a hero of the South, Davis was appointed U.S. senator from Mississippi. A strong advocate of the extension of slavery into the territory acquired from Mexico, he served as secretary of war in Franklin Pierce's administration, then returned to the Senate in 1857. By all accounts he was one of that body's most distinguished members. He resigned from the Senate in 1861 and returned to Brierfield, his Mississippi plantation, where he stayed until he received notice that he had been unanimously elected president of the provisional Confederate States of America.

Abraham Lincoln lacked Davis's sophistication. Born in a single-room, dirt-floor cabin, Lincoln spent his early years in Indiana. Receiving what education was available, he became an itinerant worker. The early 1830s found him in central Illinois, where he raised a company of volunteers to fight in the Black Hawk War. Unlike his future adversary, he saw no action and shortly thereafter entered local politics. He moved to Springfield, Illinois, now the state capital, and practiced law. He evolved into a superb trial lawyer, married Mary Todd in 1842, and then began a lucrative law practice. Always interested in politics, young Lincoln successfully ran in 1846 for the U.S. Congress, where he became a vocal opponent of Polk's war with neighboring Mexico. Defeated for reelection in 1848, Lincoln returned to Springfield, where he intended to spend the remainder of his life. The passage of the Kansas–Nebraska Act of 1854 and the Dred Scott Decision rekindled his love of politics, and he ran unsuccessfully against incumbent Stephen A. Douglas for the U.S. Senate seat from Illinois in 1858. Now a well-respected and renowned public figure, Lincoln became a leading spokesman for the Republican Party platform. In 1860, he received the party's presidential nomination because he was the only candidate likely to carry the states of Illinois and Indiana. When he finally arrived in Washington to assume the nation's highest office, he brought with him the firm commitment that secession lacked legal justification and that the Union must be preserved at all costs.

With respect to military leaders, both sides drew upon graduates of the U.S. Military Academy at West Point. The Regular Army, which numbered 16,257 officers and men, remained on the American frontier to protect settlers and to combat the Native American tribes. The Civil War was to be fought with volunteer regiments. Consequently, state governors sought West Point graduates to command the volunteers from their respective states. Governors appointed officers in the rank of colonel, while soldiers elected their junior officers in the rank of captain and below. Hence a West Point graduate who had resigned his commission as a junior officer at the end of the Mexican War might find himself appointed a colonel in command of a regiment at the beginning of the Civil War. This was the case with the majority of officers who achieved renown on the battlefield, leaders like U. S. Grant, William T. Sherman, Thomas J. Jackson, George B. McClellan, and George G. Meade. There were a few notable exceptions. Robert E. Lee, Joseph J. Johnston, Albert S. Johnston, and Pierre G. T. Beauregard were members of the Regular Army who cast their fortunes with the South. President Davis knew them well and immediately assigned them to positions of increased responsibility at the outset of the war.

Thus the initial clashes of arms generally went in the Confederates' favor. The Union commanders who rose to prominence first served in the Mississippi River Valley, where they made their share of mistakes but were not summarily removed from command after losing a single engagement. Far from the direct reach of Washington, D.C., and the eyes of Lincoln and his politicians, these officers, including Grant, Sherman, and later Philip Sheridan, had time to develop their distinctive command styles. By late 1862 they proved more than a match for their Confederate counterparts. By 1863 the Northern commanders were vastly superior to those commanding the Southern armies, with the single exception of Lee. Battlefield attrition also exacted a severe toll on commanders from both armies. Over the course of the war only a few of the senior commanders escaped injury or death.

The War Plans

Now that war had erupted, both Lincoln and Davis developed military and political strategies to achieve their national objectives: Lincoln to preserve the Union, Davis to achieve independence. Geography would undoubtedly play a part in whatever strategy was adopted. The Appalachian Mountain chain divided the South into two distinct regions, what became the Eastern and Western theaters of operations. Though most of the fighting occurred east of the Mississippi River, there also existed a trans-

Mississippi River theater to which Lincoln and Davis gave varying degrees of attention. In addition, the Mississippi River and its tributaries, principally the Tennessee and Cumberland Rivers, offered the armies operating in the West access to the entire Confederacy. In the east, the two warring capitals were separated by a mere 100 miles, but in Virginia the rivers acted as impediments to an army's advance because they flowed in an easterly direction. Any Union army intent on marching toward Richmond would first have to cross a series of waterways that were heavily defended by a Confederate army.

In order to suppress the rebellion, Lincoln's strategy had to be offensive. The blockade would ensure the South was cut off from foreign trade, which had proven invaluable in the American Revolution. Lincoln complemented the blockade by appointing his most skilled diplomats to serve as ambassadors to Great Britain and France. Their mission was to ensure that no major European power offered diplomatic recognition and foreign aid to the Confederacy. From the military perspective, he asked General Winfield Scott to develop a strategy to force the Confederate states back into the Union and to defeat Southern armies. Such a strategy would entail an invasion of the Confederacy, most likely directed at seizing the capital at Richmond.

Davis's challenge was defensive. In his inaugural address, he had reminded the North "that all we wish is to be left alone." The South sought no territorial aggrandizement or conquest. It would wait the advancement of Northern armies while sending diplomats to Europe to encourage foreign recognition. Davis immediately employed an economic tool and embargoed the sale of cotton, feeling that, cut off from its source of cotton to fuel its textile industry, Great Britain would be compelled to recognize the South and break the federal blockade. The real question confronting Confederate military leaders was how to defend 3,500 miles of coastline and inland waterways, as well as a 1,000-mile border with the Northern states. Davis had to decide early whether it was prudent to defend the entire boundary or to concentrate his forces to defend a few strategic cities and vital economic areas. With no navy and only a nascent army, such a task would prove challenging, with or without foreign aid.

Winfield Scott's Anaconda Plan

In 1861, General Winfield Scott, the commanding general of the U.S. Army, was seventy-five years old. The aging hero of the War of 1812 and the conquest of Mexico was no longer able to exercise direct command of the nation's field armies, but his strategic sense was hardly lacking. To conquer the South, Scott predicted that the North would require 300,000 men and that the war would require a minimum of two years. No one in Washington, including the president, was prepared for a prolonged war of the nature that Scott was describing. Next he urged Lincoln to adopt a maritime strategy that included a naval blockade of the Confederate coast and the seizure of the Mississippi River Valley. Seizing the Mississippi River would divide the Confederacy in two and allow federal armies access to the Lower South and its railway centers of Atlanta and Chattanooga. Such a strategy made sense militarily, but not politically. Lincoln wanted a quick war; a maritime strategy produces results over a prolonged period. Thus Lincoln adopted Scott's strategy for the long term, but insisted that the federal army that was around Washington, D.C., must first advance and capture Richmond. Scott urged caution and advised the president to train the army first and not be controlled by politicians and newspapers that urged the "On to Richmond" strategy before the army was ready for combat.

The Confederate Dilemma

Davis, too, had to consider political pressure from the firebrands who had first urged war. The Confederate president also had another problem. Militarily, the defense of the entire northern boundary of the Confederacy was impossible with the resources on hand. At the same time, Davis felt that he could not abandon any territory to the invader. Thus he dispersed what forces he had along the entire border, on what he considered the most likely avenues of approach into the heart of the Confederacy, thereby surrendering the initiative to the enemy, much as the Continental Congress and George Washington had done during the American Revolution.

1861: End of the Short War

By July 1861 both armies in the Eastern Theater were poised for action. At sea the forty-ship U.S. Navy had already blockaded the larger Confederate ports, but the blockade leaked like a sieve until the North built sufficient ships to surround the major ports. Along the border of the Confederacy, small Union armies had already entered Missouri, the western counties of Virginia, and Kentucky. Commanding the Union forces outside the federal capital was Major General Irwin McDowell. Under his command were roughly 35,000 men. Most were recruited from Lincoln's initial call for volunteers, whose period of service expired in mid-July. Opposing McDowell were two smaller armies commanded by Generals Beauregard and Joseph Johnston. McDowell's plan was to defeat Beauregard first, outside Manassas Junction in Virginia, then turn on Johnston's forces in the Shenandoah Valley. Following the destruction of these armies, McDowell would then march and seize Richmond. Lincoln forced McDowell to move before he was ready.

The Opening Campaigns

The first major battle of the war occurred along Bull Run Creek, just thirty miles from Washington, D.C., when McDowell's army clashed with Beauregard's Confederates astride Manassas Junction on July 21, 1861. At first the battle went well for the North, but when Confederate reinforcements arrived from the Shenandoah Valley and a Virginia regiment under command of Thomas J. Jackson stood "like a stone wall" on a prominent hill, the Union army was forced to retreat. Before long, the retreat turned into a rout as Union soldiers fled in complete panic. Within twenty-four hours, the army was cowering within the defenses of Washington. The Southerners, more disorganized by their victory than the Union soldiers were by their defeat, did not pursue. Casualties were high by contemporary standards, the Union suffering nearly 3,000 killed, wounded, and missing; the Confederates, about 1,000 less. The first major battle of the Civil War was thus a major Confederate victory. Foreign observers predicted that Confederate independence was now a matter of weeks, if not days, but they did not reckon with Abraham Lincoln. Unfazed by this initial military disaster, Lincoln called for additional volunteers to serve for three years. There was no longer talk of a ninety-day war. Scott had been correct, and for the remainder of 1861 the Union prepared for a prolonged conflict. So did the Confederacy, though it missed a golden opportunity to end the war by marching on Washington. Davis preferred remaining on the defensive, both East and West, and calmly awaited the next Northern advance.

Lincoln Retains the Border States

Though he had lost the Battle of Bull Run/Manassas (the North generally named battles and armies after waterways and rivers; the South named theirs after regions, towns, and cities), Lincoln did win an important victory in the summer and fall of 1861. Had the South controlled the slaveholding border states of Maryland, Kentucky, Missouri, and Delaware, Lincoln's task of suppressing the rebellion would have been infinitely more complicated, if not impossible. Consequently, Lincoln moved rapidly and employed powers far beyond those granted by the U.S. Constitution. Delaware posed no threat because the population was decidedly pro-Union. Maryland was a different matter. Over the course of the war, Maryland provided thousands of soldiers to both North and South. If Maryland cast its lot with the Confederacy, Washington, D.C., would be a Union island in a Confederate sea. Lincoln immediately arrested prominent Southern sympathizers, suspended habeas corpus, and declared martial law. Critics and the U.S. Supreme Court condemned his actions as unconstitutional, but Lincoln dismissed their criticisms, justifying his actions as the exercise of wartime emergency powers as commander-in-chief. Maryland was secured and remained so throughout the war. In Kentucky, Lincoln forbade any invasion until the Confederate army moved first. When it did, the Northern army moved into the state to protect the citizens from the unwarranted invasion from the South. In Missouri a small Union army under Nathaniel Lyon fought a short battle against local Confederate forces at Wilson's Creek on August 10. Lyon perished in the battle, but a Confederate retreat left Missouri in Union hands, though partisan warfare remained a fact of life in Missouri for the remainder of the war. Meanwhile, another Union army under command of Brigadier General George B. McClellan invaded the western counties of Virginia, rapidly defeated several Confederate armies, including one commanded by Robert E. Lee, and secured that section of Virginia for the North. Newspapers labeled McClellan the "new Napoleon," and Lincoln summoned McClellan to Washington in the wake of the First Manassas disaster. McClellan assumed command of the Union army around Washington and named it the Army of the Potomac. For the remainder of the year, McClellan prepared his army for the next campaign.

1862: Ebb and Flow

As 1861 turned into 1862, a million men congregated along the Confederacy's northern border and prepared for the inevitable onslaught once the ground permitted the advance of large armies. In Washington,

D.C., Julia Ward Howe listened to soldiers singing a familiar refrain and wrote new lyrics to "John Brown's Body." The result, "The Battle Hymn of the Republic," was destined to be the unofficial anthem of the North. At the War Department, McClellan was preparing the Army of the Potomac to fight the Confederate army at Manassas Junction, while Winfield Scott, forced into retirement, quietly observed the war from his home near West Point. In the West an unknown general by the name of Ulysses S. Grant intended to strike at the Confederate forts along the border of Tennessee. The year began with Robert E. Lee advising Jefferson Davis on the best manner to counter the anticipated Northern attack. Within five months, Lee assumed command of the main Confederate army outside Richmond and gave it a new name, the Army of Northern Virginia. The year would also introduce the American public to the unspeakable horror of modern war. Even before the spring thaw, the Northern armies advanced first, both in the West and in the East.

War in the West

Along the Mississippi River, in both Kentucky and Tennessee, General Henry Halleck prepared his forces to penetrate the Confederate defenses commanded by Albert S. Johnston, Jefferson Davis's handpicked commander for the Western Theater. Even before Johnston marshaled his forces, one of Halleck's best commanders, U. S. Grant, teamed up with naval forces and forced the surrender of Fort Henry, a Confederate bastion on the Tennessee River. Ten days later, Grant demanded the unconditional surrender of Fort Donelson on the Cumberland River. Now known as "Unconditional Surrender" Grant, he moved into southwestern Tennessee, where Johnston attacked him at Pittsburg Landing. The resulting Battle of Shiloh was a Union victory, but casualties were so horrendous—five times those of Bull Run/Manassas, that both North and South were shocked at the carnage. For the remainder of the year, Union forces concentrated on capturing Vicksburg, the last Confederate fortress on the Mississippi River, now that a federal fleet had seized New Orleans in February 1862. The South did launch an offensive into Kentucky in October, but the year's end brought the fighting back to central Tennessee and the Mississippi River.

War in the East

While Northern armies attacked in the West, General McClellan led the Army of the Potomac against Richmond in March 1862. Transported to the peninsula between the York and James Rivers, McClellan battled his way to the gates of Richmond by late May. Following a short engagement in which Confederate General Joseph E. Johnston was wounded, President Davis appointed Robert E. Lee to command the army outside Richmond. Within a month, Lee raised the siege of Richmond, defeated another Union army on the old Manassas battlefield, and in September launched his first invasion of the North. Turned back at Sharpsburg/Antietam, Lee retreated to Virginia, only to halt another Northern army at Fredericksburg in mid-December. Following every victory by Lee, Lincoln relieved the commander of the Army of the Potomac, still searching for an officer who could defeat Lee in a pitched battle. Lincoln, however, did deliver a mortal blow to the Confederacy following the Battle of Antietam. Five days after the battle, he announced a preliminary Emancipation Proclamation, liberating the slaves in the states still opposed to the Union. The proclamation was to take effect on January 1, 1863. Lincoln's action, designed as a war measure, undercut all attempts at foreign recognition of the South. In announcing his proclamation, Lincoln now provided the North with a new war aim. No longer was the war being fought simply to preserve the Union; Lincoln now had made the conflict a moral crusade against slavery.

1863: The Turning Point

The Confederate high-water mark of the war came in 1863. During the first two years of the war, the Confederacy enjoyed a string of victories in the Eastern Theater, mostly due to the superior generalship of Lee and Stonewall Jackson. Along the Mississippi River, the South still held Vicksburg, having thwarted several attempts by Grant to capture the city. If the South's star was ascendant during the first half of the year, it was decidedly descendant as the war wore on. In both East and West, the Confederacy suffered catastrophic reverses at Gettysburg and Vicksburg, and in late November the North captured the strategic railway center of Chattanooga, Tennessee. More important, the Lower South now lay open to invasion. For the remainder of the war, the South fought on the defensive, valiantly resisting the Northern armies as they prepared to strike at the heart of the Confederacy. As the year neared its conclusion, Abraham Lincoln delivered what was perhaps the greatest speech in American history. Speaking at Gettysburg on November 19, he reenergized the North and reminded the nation that the struggle would be costly but necessary if a democratic nation "of the people, by the people and for the people" were to survive.

High Tide at Gettysburg

Robert E. Lee began 1863 on the heels of a great victory at Fredericksburg. In May he faced an army twice his size, commanded by Major General Joseph Hooker. At the Battle of Chancellorsville, Lee split his army in three parts and defeated Hooker in what was likely Lee's tactical masterpiece. Unfortunately, Lee lost the able services of Stonewall Jackson, who was mistakenly shot by his own men while conducting a night reconnaissance. Flush with victory, Lee now led the Army of Northern Virginia into Pennsylvania for his second invasion of the North. In the largest battle ever fought on the North American continent, Lee was defeated at Gettysburg after three days. The climax of the battle occurred on July 3, when "Pickett's Charge" was thrown back with tremendous loss. Lee remained on the battlefield the next day, July 4, and then began the slow, arduous retreat to Virginia. Gettysburg was both a strategic and tactical reversal for the Confederacy, and Lee never recovered. Having lost so many key leaders, the Army of Northern Virginia was basically confined to the defensive for the remainder of the war. Never again was Lee strong enough to launch large offensive operations against his enemy, and never again was he able to invade the North. Any chance of real success for Southern independence disappeared in the open ground in front of Cemetery Ridge, over which the Confederates had made their grand assault. That the army did not disintegrate and that it prolonged the war for an additional two years by defeating subsequent Northern advances is a tribute to the military genius of Robert E. Lee.

Vicksburg and the West

While Lee fought at Gettysburg, the noose was slowly tightening around Vicksburg. For six months Grant had tried a variety of schemes to capture the Confederate stronghold. In May he devised a masterful plan. Bypassing the city's defenses, Grant marched his army east of the Mississippi River and lived off the land. By May he had successfully driven the Confederate army within the city and laid siege. The end came on July 4, one day after Lee's defeat at Gettysburg. With the fall of Vicksburg, the Union now commanded the entire Mississippi River Valley. Lincoln heard the news of Vicksburg's surrender and proudly proclaimed, "The Father of Waters now flows unvexed to the sea."[10] Once again Grant was the hero of the Union, and Lincoln promoted him to commander of all federal armies in the Western Theater. In November, Lincoln directed Grant to Chattanooga, where Confederate General Braxton Bragg was besieging a Union army, following his victory at Chickamauga. Grant arrived in early November and immediately reversed the tide. He first opened a supply route to the besieged army, then launched concentrated attacks on Lookout Mountain and Missionary Ridge. By late November, Bragg's army was in total retreat and Lincoln now summoned Grant east to take command of all Union armies in the field.

1864: War of Attrition

The year 1864 produced the most severe fighting and the greatest number of casualties since the war began in 1861. So many casualties arrived in Washington, D.C., from the Virginia battlefields that literally every cemetery in the city was filled. Consequently, the War Department looked across the Potomac River and directed that future Union dead were to be buried in the front yard of Lee's Arlington, Virginia mansion; thus was born Arlington National Cemetery. At sea the Confederate commerce raider, the *CSS Alabama*, was finally caught and sunk off the coast of Cherbourg, France.

On the battlefront, the Confederate forces held firm against Grant and William T. Sherman's advances, and although the naval blockade was strangling the South, two ports—Mobile, Alabama, and Wilmington, North Carolina—remained in Confederate hands. Unless the North could close those ports and win a significant battle, Lincoln feared his reelection was in doubt. Appalled by the mounting toll of war, Northern citizens and politicians began to question Lincoln's administration of the war effort. By year's end Lincoln, now safely elected for a second term, was comfortable in the White House as the combined forces of Grant and Sherman prepared to deliver a fatal blow to the fortunes of the Confederacy.

Lincoln Finds His General

During the first week in March 1864, Ulysses S. Grant, accompanied by his son, checked in to the Willard Hotel, Washington, D.C.'s most prestigious lodging. The next day Grant joined Lincoln in the White House and received his appointment as lieutenant general, a rank that had previously been held only by George Washington. Grant's mission was to direct all Union armies and to win the war. In selecting Grant, Lincoln had finally found his general. The victor of Forts Henry and Donelson, Shiloh, Vicksburg, and Chattanooga presented the president with a master plan. Unlike previous Union attacks over the first three years of the war, Grant directed that all Union armies advance simultaneously. "It is my design," stated Grant, that "if the enemy keeps quiet and allows me to take the initiative in the spring campaign, to work all parts of the army together, and somewhat towards a common center."[11] For the first time since General Winfield Scott's Anaconda Plan, a Union commander had provided Lincoln with a blueprint for victory.[12] No longer were Southern cities the objectives of the armies; now the Confederate armies were the objective. "Where Lee goes, you go, too," he informed Major General George Meade, commanding the Army of the Potomac. Once the Southern armies were destroyed, the Confederacy would collapse. Next he gave Sherman command of all the Western armies and directed Sherman to move "against [Joseph E.] Johnston's army, to break it up, and to get into the interior of the enemy's country as far as you can, inflicting all the damage you can against their war resources."[13]

Lee vs. Grant

In the ensuing campaign, Grant accompanied Meade as the Army of the Potomac crossed the Rapidan River and engaged Lee's Army of Northern Virginia. Lee, only too aware of the disparity of forces, attacked Grant in the tangled region known as the Wilderness on May 5. From that day until mid-June, the Union and Confederate armies were in daily contact. Fighting from trenches and behind earthen walls, the Confederates inflicted 55,000 casualties on Grant's forces in the Battles of the Wilderness, Spotslyvania Courthouse, the North Anna, Cold Harbor, and Petersburg. Grant was labeled a butcher, but he refused to let Lee's army escape. "I propose to fight it out on this line if it takes all summer," he informed Lincoln.[14] The grand campaign not only took all summer, but all autumn and all winter, too. Finally, in mid-June Grant gave Lee the slip, crossed the James River, and laid siege to Petersburg, the major Southern link to the Confederate capital of Richmond. Now locked in the trenches before Petersburg, Lee could no longer maneuver. Denied the ability to commence offensive operations, he realized it was only a matter of time before Grant accumulated sufficient forces to overwhelm Petersburg's defenders.

Sherman and the March to the Sea

On the day that the Army of the Potomac crossed the Rapidan to battle Lee, William T. Sherman marched his army southeast in the direction of Atlanta. Contesting every inch was Johnston's Army of Tennessee. Late summer found Sherman outside Atlanta. Dissatisfied that Johnston had not halted Sherman's advance, President Davis relieved him and appointed General John B. Hood in his place. While Johnston was unduly cautious, Hood was extremely reckless. In a series of battles in which he took a horrible beating, Hood was forced to abandon Atlanta to Sherman on September 2, 1864. It was precisely the victory Lincoln needed to garner support for the presidential campaign. A month earlier newly promoted Admiral David Farragut had attacked and captured Mobile Bay, thus closing the last Confederate port on the Gulf of Mexico. With the fall of Atlanta, the way was now open for Sherman to march into the interior of the Confederacy. He ushered in a new era of warfare by forcing the evacuation of Atlanta's citizens, then burned the city to the ground. While he and Grant debated as to what course of action Sherman should now take, Sherman proposed "to abandon Atlanta, and the railroad back to Chattanooga, to sally forth to ruin Georgia and bring up on the seashore."[15] Thus began Sherman's "March to the Sea" in mid-November 1864. Christmas found Sherman outside Savannah, which promptly surrendered without a fight to avoid Atlanta's fate. Presenting Savannah to Lincoln as "a Christmas present," Sherman then turned his army north and attacked through South Carolina. Leaving total devastation in his wake, Sherman halted only long enough to destroy the state capital of Columbia, before proceeding into the interior of North Carolina.

1865: The War's Conclusion

With Lincoln's reelection assured by Union victories in the field, it was only a matter of time before the Confederacy collapsed. Grant geared his forces for a final spring offensive that would overwhelm the remnants of the enemy's armies. In far-off Tennessee, John B. Hood had sacrificed his Army of Tennessee in fruitless attacks against Franklin and Nashville, which resulted in the complete disintegration of his forces. The Confederate Army of Tennessee simply ceased to exist as an effective fighting force by mid-December. In Virginia, Lee still held Grant at bay in the trenches of Petersburg, while a second Union army had recently devastated the Shenandoah Valley, the breadbasket of the South. On the high seas, the blockade had effectively strangled the South, with the Confederacy's last port of Wilmington, North Carolina, now in Union hands. In Richmond, President Davis still hoped against hope for Confederate military success. In February 1865 he belatedly appointed Lee as commanding general of all Confederate armies. As usual, it was too little, too late. Lee immediately reappointed Joseph Johnston in command of the remnants of the Army of Tennessee, but Johnston's force never was strong enough to offer any substantial defense as Sherman inched his way north to combine his forces with Grant at Petersburg.

The Final Campaigns

For the Confederacy, Lee's last chance lay in somehow escaping Grant's grasp at Petersburg, then uniting his forces with Johnston's in North Carolina, defeating Sherman, and finally turning on Grant. First, Lee directed one final assault on the Union lines to his front on March 25, 1865, at Fort Stedman. The attack was a disaster. Lee lost 5,000 men he could not afford to lose. A week later, on April 1, Grant finally outflanked Lee's line at Five Forks and delivered the Confederates a major blow. The next day, Grant ordered a general offensive along the entire line. The line that Lee had held since mid-June simply collapsed. Lee informed Davis he could no longer defend Richmond, and Davis evacuated Richmond the same day. While Lee fled west, President Lincoln visited the Confederate capital on April 3. He was immediately surrounded by hundreds, if not thousands, of freed slaves. Hailed as the Great Emancipator, Lincoln was visibly moved by the adulation. He ordered Grant to press Lee, and Grant did exactly that. The end came a week later. Cut off and surrounded by numerically superior forces, Lee surrendered the Army of Northern Virginia to Grant at Appomattox Courthouse on April 9, 1865. Other Confederate armies quickly followed suit. The Civil War was over, but the conflict had yet to claim its final victim. On April 14 President Lincoln was assassinated by John Wilkes Booth in Ford's Theater. Booth was a well-known Southern sympathizer who hoped to avenge the South's defeat. Carried across the street to a local boardinghouse, Lincoln died the following day. As for Jefferson Davis, he was captured by Union cavalry outside Irwinville, Georgia on May 10. With his capture, the Confederate government ceased to exist.

The Final Reckoning

By any standard, the Civil War had been a bloodbath. With the loss of 620,000 Americans, the conflict was, and still remains, the bloodiest war in American history. As tragic as was the cost in human lives, the Civil War ended slavery and preserved the Union. Additionally, the Civil War altered the conduct of warfare by introducing the widespread use of railroads, the telegraph, observation balloons, and industrial mobilization. The increased lethality of rifles and longer-range artillery had made massed infantry assaults obsolete, but armies learned this lesson sparingly until high casualties forced doctrinal changes in tactics and strategy. While the Franco–Prussian War of 1870–1871 made a greater impact than the American Civil War on the armies of foreign nations, no one could deny that naval warfare was unalterably changed by the introduction of ironclad warships off Hampton Roads in March 1862. The marriage between naval planners and industrialists resulted in the construction of the huge battle fleets that dominated naval warfare for the next century.

On the domestic front, the Civil War produced important political, social, and economic changes in American society. Four years of war spawned the industrial revolution that made the United States the most powerful industrial state in the world by the turn of the century. Fed by the increasing number of immigrants to man American factories, industrialization began an economic trend in which the majority of the working class moved from rural areas to urban centers. Politically, the war killed the concept of secession forever and cemented the fabric of a new nation. No longer was there talk of a union of sovereign states; now the United States was a single entity. Lincoln's vision of a democratic nation based on human equality, albeit delayed, became the American vision. And it would be left to posterity to ensure that this vision would continue to characterize the American republic.

Notes

1. As quoted in Geoffrey C. Ward with Ric Burns and Ken Burns, *The Civil War: An Illustrated History* (New York: Alfred A. Knopf, 1990), xvi.

2. Both quotations appear in Dumas Malone, *Jefferson and His Time: The Sage of Monticello* (Boston: Little, Brown, 1981), 328.

3. Samuel E. Morison, *The Oxford History of the American People* (New York: Oxford University Press, 1965), 572.

4. Ibid., 572–573.

5. All quoted material is from James McPherson, *Battle Cry of Freedom* (New York: Oxford University Press, 1988), 88–90.

6. For the complete text of Lincoln's "House Divided" speech during the Lincoln–Douglas debates, see David S. Heidler and Jeanne T. Heidler eds., *Encyclopedia of the American Civil War* (New York: W. W. Norton, 2000), 2187–2190.

7. William Davis, *"A Government of Our Own": The Making of the Confederacy* (New York: Free Press, 1994), 3.

8. As quoted in Michael Perman, ed., *Major Problems in the Civil War and Reconstruction* (Lexington, MA: D.C. Heath, 1991), 134.

9. For the details of Lincoln's address, see David Donald, *Lincoln* (London: Jonathan Cape, 1995), 282–284.

10. McPherson, *Battle Cry of Freedom*, 638.

11. Ulysses S. Grant, *Personal Memoirs* (New York: Modern Library, 1999), 375.

12. Thomas J. Goss, *The War Within the Union High Command* (Lawrence: University Press of Kansas, 2003), 173.

13. For Sherman's precise orders, see William T. Sherman, *Memoirs of General William T. Sherman,* vol. 2 (New York: Da Capo Press, 1984), 26–27.

14. Geoffrey Perret, *Ulysses S. Grant* (New York: Random House, 1997), 318.

15. Quoted in Russell F. Weigley, *A Great Civil War* (Bloomington: Indiana University Press, 2002), 389.

CHAPTER 2

THE MYTH OF SOUTHERN MARTIAL SUPREMACY

In assessing the military prowess of the Northern and Southern armies at the beginning of the Civil War, most contemporary observers believed that the Confederacy enjoyed a marked superiority over its Union adversary. According to numerous accounts, the Southern soldiers were far more accustomed to outdoor life than the urbanized Northerners, and the South processed a social organization better suited for creating an efficient fighting force. For any society or army to be successful in battle, however, highly trained and skilled officers are needed. How good were the Confederate commanders? Noted historian Samuel Eliot Morison claims that the secession of Virginia gave the Confederacy many of the ablest officers of the U.S. Army; no new nation had ever had commanders such as Robert E. Lee, Joseph and Albert Sidney Johnston, Ambrose Powell, Daniel Harvey Hill, and Thomas J. "Stonewall" Jackson at its birth.[1] Nowhere was this superiority more evident than during the First Battle of Bull Run/Manassas, where the combined forces of Confederate Generals Joseph E. Johnston and Pierre G. T. Beauregard defeated Major General Irwin McDowell in the war's first major battle. The Confederate victory not only produced a spirit of euphoria across the South, but it also seemingly confirmed the conviction of the Confederacy's invincibility. This Southern martial superiority remained particularly apparent in the Eastern Theater, where Lee, Jackson, James Longstreet, and J.E.B. Stuart led the Army of Northern Virginia to a series of remarkable victories between the summer of 1862 and 1863. In the West, Confederate victories were scarce, but by the second summer of the war, Southern armies were on the move, invading both Kentucky and Maryland in the hope of securing international recognition for the Confederacy. A closer examination, however, reveals that with a few notable exceptions, Southern commanders were mediocre at best in adapting to battlefield conditions, and certainly no more tactically proficient than their Union counterparts.

Southern Advantages

Despite its numerical inferiority and the absence of a regular force, the South possessed several advantages that presaged military success. Two elements in particular gave the South an initial advantage in the war's first year: first, Union General-in-Chief Winfield Scott decided to keep the Regular Army on the plains to fight the Native American tribes, thus denying the new federal army a corps of experienced officers; second, the South's military schools produced a number of officers who formed the nucleus of trained leaders.[2] Both Lincoln and Davis called for volunteers to fight the war, and both chief executives relied heavily on graduates of the U.S. Military Academy to command the newly raised armies in the field. By the late summer of 1861, 313 officers had resigned from the army to fight for the Confederacy. The West Point classes of May and June 1861 not only indicate the sharp divisions within the country as a whole, but also give some indication of the talent that the North lost when Southern cadets resigned to fight for their native states. The May class of 1861 originally contained fifty members, of whom thirty-eight fought for the Union and eleven for the Confederacy (there was also one deserter). Six of the eleven future Confederates officers managed to graduate before they resigned, while five others resigned as soon as they received word that their states seceded from the Union. The June class of 1861, of which George Armstrong Custer was a member, listed fifty-seven members. Of these cadets, thirty-one became Union officers and twenty-six joined the Confederacy. Of the twenty-six Confederates, only three graduated before resigning their commissions.[3] As the war exacted its deadly toll on the West Point classes, 16 percent of the class of May 1861 died during the struggle; 25 percent of the June class succumbed to battle and disease. In terms of losses incurred during the war, the U.S. Military Academy's two classes of 1861 were representative of previous graduating classes.

The South also drew upon its various state military colleges to find men qualified to lead its armies. Of the eight so-called military colleges in the United States in 1861, seven were in the slave states. The two most famous institutions were the Virginia Military Institute in Lexington,

Virginia, and The Citadel in Charleston, South Carolina. Graduates of any college could petition their respective governors for commissions in the volunteer regiments, but state governors naturally turned to graduates who had undergone some degree of military training in their past. One-third of the field officers (in the grades of major through colonel) of Virginia regiments in 1861 were VMI graduates. Of the 1,902 men who had attended VMI since it opened in 1839, 1,781 fought for the South.[4]

These figures alone can be misleading when placed in the overall context of total numbers who served. Twenty Virginians were on the active list of the Regular Army in 1861 at the grade of field or general officer. Only nine of the twenty cast their fortunes with the South. Virginians in the U.S. Army also included sixty-four officers in the grade of lieutenant or captain; of these, forty-seven fought for the Confederacy and thirteen retired officers joined the Southern armies. The net result of these totals was that if every Virginia graduate from West Point and VMI, and every native veteran officer of the Mexican War joined the Confederacy, they would have supplied trained officers for the equivalent of only fourteen regiments. When Virginia seceded on April 17, 1861, its militia roster carried 187 regiments of infantry and five regiments each of artillery and cavalry.[5] Where the alumni of the South's military colleges made their greatest contribution was in the rapid improvement of the troops in drill and in discipline. Here the South enjoyed a distinct advantage over the Union Army because the militia system throughout the South was preparing for war long before the attack on Fort Sumter in April 1861. Thus the Confederate army at First Bull Run/Manassas had been in training several months longer than its opponents.

There was an additional source of senior officers with whom both Presidents Davis and Lincoln had to contend: the political generals. In this category the balance sheet was about equal. Political generals were more often than not incompetent commanders who sacrificed countless soldiers on the altar of their personal ambitions. Political generals were politicians in uniform or men made general officers and given important commands for political reasons, as demonstrated by the immense level of political pressure exerted on both presidents.[6] In the Confederacy, Davis routinely appointed officers to mollify powerful state governors, many of whom had undermined Davis's position as commander in chief and president of the Confederacy. Such was the case when he appointed Kentucky's George B. Crittenden and Tennessee's Gideon J. Pillow to senior command.

Crittenden proceeded immediately to lose most of eastern Tennessee, partially due to the fact that he was intoxicated during a battle, and Pillow deserted his post on the evening before Fort Donelson surrendered to U. S. Grant. Grant fared equally poorly with John McClernand, a political friend of Lincoln, an officer whom Grant considered both "unmanageable and incompetent."[7]

President Davis and His Friends

If the South enjoyed an advantage over the North with respect to leadership, it seemed that Jefferson Davis was far more qualified than Abraham Lincoln to serve as constitutional commander-in-chief. Unlike President Lincoln, whose military service was confined to a few weeks as a militia officer during the Black Hawk War in the 1830s, Davis was a West Point graduate and a former secretary of war. As such he was intimately familiar with many of the officers who resigned their commissions to fight for the Confederacy. Davis's background, however, proved to be a two-edged sword. Though Davis knew a great many U.S. Army officers, his most glaring weakness was that the closer his personal association with the officer in question, the less reliable was his judgment.[8] For example, Davis steadfastly supported old military and political cronies like Albert Sidney Johnston, Samuel Cooper, and Leonidas Polk. Davis, however, considered his familiarity with the officer corps a strength rather than a weakness. While at West Point, Davis was a cadet in the class behind Robert E. Lee and Joseph E. Johnston, both destined to command the principal Confederate army in the Virginia Theater. Other schoolmates of Davis at West Point included Albert S. Johnston and Leonidas Polk, whom Davis soon appointed to command the Southern armies in the Mississippi River Valley in 1861. While serving in the War Department, Davis also made the acquaintance of Samuel Cooper, a bureaucrat who enjoyed a reputation as an administrative genius. With the exception of Polk, Davis nominated each of these officers for promotion to full general on the last day of August 1861. The Confederate Congress immediately confirmed the president's nominees in September 1861, in the order they had been proposed: Cooper, Albert S. Johnston, Lee, Joseph E. Johnston, and Beauregard.

As the war progressed, only Lee met Davis's expectations. Of the first five full generals of the Confederacy, Beauregard was the first to fall from the president's favor. The hero of Fort Sumter, Beauregard held command at First Manassas until Joe Johnston arrived on the field and assumed command of the Confederate forces. Both Beauregard and Johnston later claimed credit for the victory, but Beauregard wrote an impolite report of the engagement in which he criticized the overall Confederate strategy, an indirect attack on Davis's management of the war. Both Beauregard and Johnston possessed oversized egos, and it was no secret that one would have to go. Davis soon dispatched Beauregard to the West, where he immediately proceeded to mishandle the Southern army at Shiloh after Sidney Johnston fell mortally wounded. Beauregard then failed to halt the Union advance into northern Mississippi as the Union army captured Corinth and a vital rail center. In the ensuing months, Davis and Beauregard remained at loggerheads over strategy, reinforcements, and supplies. Davis never forgave him for the loss of northern Mississippi and soon replaced Beauregard with Braxton Bragg, an old friend from the Mexican War. Though he continued to hold several important posts due to his elevated rank, Beauregard never again held a major field command.

Next to go was Albert S. Johnston, whom Davis always considered to be the first soldier of the Confederacy. When war began, Johnston was a rising star in the U.S. Army. Brevetted a brigadier general for his subjugation of the Mormons in the late 1850s, Johnston was one of the most distinguished soldiers in active service. Davis had monitored his career closely. When a colonelcy opened for one of the two new cavalry regiments on the Texas border, Davis ensured that Johnston received the coveted assignment. When Fort Sumter surrendered on April 14, 1861, Johnston was making his way east from California, where he was commanding the Department of the West. Arriving in Richmond in early September, Johnston found that he held a full general's rank, second only to Samuel Cooper. He should not have been surprised, for Davis's affection for Johnston bordered on idolatry. Sidney Johnston was, said Davis, "the only man he felt able to lean upon with entire confidence," believing that his "consistency of action and conduct and his equanimity were different from any other man he ever saw."[9] Davis immediately sent him to the West to salvage the deteriorating situation. Johnston performed satisfactorily, though not brilliantly. He concentrated Confederate forces, but was unable to halt U. S. Grant's drive into western Tennessee. Grant broke Johnston's northern defensive line in February 1862 by capturing Forts Henry and Donelson. Johnston then planned a counterattack and advanced on Grant's army at Shiloh/Pittsburg Landing in early April. Foolishly leaving the tactical dispositions to Beauregard, who was serving as his second in command, Johnston commenced his attack on April 6. On the first day of the battle, he was struck in the leg and bled to death. What the future would have held for Sidney Johnston is anyone's guess, but Davis lost the officer in whom he had the greatest confidence in the first pitched battle between the western armies.

While Sidney Johnston sought to reverse Union victories along the Mississippi River Valley, Joseph E. Johnston was commanding the Confederate army in Virginia. Already on Davis's bad side for a letter in which he complained about his seniority vis-à-vis the other full generals of the Confederacy, Joe Johnston often let his ego get the better of him. As far as Davis was concerned, however, Johnston's chief problem was his reluctance to fight. In the span between the Battle of First Bull Run/Manassas and the onset of the Peninsula Campaign, Johnston had not engaged the enemy in battle. Only when Union Major General George B. McClellan transferred the Army of the Potomac to the Virginia peninsula between the York and James Rivers in early 1862 did Johnston move to engage the enemy. Following a brief engagement around Williamsburg, Virginia, in the first week of May 1862, Johnston again retreated before McClellan until he reached the outer limits of Richmond. There, with no place to withdraw, he finally attacked the enemy. The battle was badly managed, and the most significant result of the engagement was that Johnston was severely wounded and replaced by Lee. It proved to be Davis's most inspired selection of the war. By the time Johnston recovered, Lee had driven McClellan from Richmond and won several victories. With no reason to return Johnston to command in the East, Davis now dispatched him to the West. There Joseph Johnston validated the president's lack of confidence in his abilities and proceeded to mismanage the relief of the garrison at Vicksburg in July 1863. With no suitable alternative to replace the commander of the Army of Tennessee after the Battle of Chattanooga, Davis again turned to Johnston, who once again displayed a lack of aggressiveness in resisting William T. Sherman's advance on Atlanta from May to July 1864. This time Davis had had enough, and the president relieved Johnston of his command in July after the loss of all northwest Georgia.

Unlike Beauregard and the two Johnstons, Samuel Cooper never held a field command. The ranking officer in Confederate service, he held the same positions that he had held in the old army, that of adjutant general and inspector general. Friendship alone explains why Davis nominated Cooper for such an elevated rank. As adjutant to the president, Cooper was a staff officer whose principal function was to make recommendations to Davis. In this position, he served the president unfailingly and never questioned his authority or his strategic direction of the war. Davis leaned on Cooper to handle the administrative burden of the War Department: "The Adjutant and Inspector General in our service is not a Bureau officer, but holds the commission of General in the C.S. Army. He is by assignment the Chief of Staff of the whole army."[10] Senior officer or not, Cooper was ill-suited for that post. Davis remembered Cooper from President Franklin Pierce's administration, where Davis served as secretary of war and Cooper served as his dutiful subordinate. Friendship could go only so far, and Davis soon discovered that Cooper's talents were more suited for administration of a peacetime army than an army at war. To compensate for Cooper's obvious inadequacies, Davis appointed Lee as his principal military adviser in the spring of 1862.

The third-ranking officer in Confederate service was Robert E. Lee, whom Union General-in-Chief Winfield Scott labeled "the greatest military genius" in America. At the beginning of the war, Davis and Lee were not particularly close. Lee certainly did not garner the admiration Davis reserved for Sidney Johnston. A graduate of the Military Academy in 1829, Lee had earned the admiration of Scott in the Mexican War by routinely finding routes around the Mexican army that Scott exploited with characteristic vigor. While on leave at Arlington in October 1859, Lee led a company of U.S. Marines who captured John Brown. In the immediate aftermath of Fort Sumter, Lee was offered command of all the Union armies, but he respectfully declined when Virginia left the Union. Offering his services to Virginia, Lee became the state's commanding general, and upon the assimilation of Virginia's forces into the Confederate national army, he acquired a commensurate rank. His first field command, however, had ended in complete disaster. Davis at once transferred Lee into present-day West Virginia to reverse a tide of Union victories, but even Lee could not repair the damage. His reputation tarnished, Lee then supervised the coastal defenses of South Carolina and Georgia before returning to Richmond to serve as Davis's military adviser. When Joe Johnston was wounded in late May 1862, Lee assumed command of the Confederate army outside Richmond. He rechristened it the Army of Northern Virginia and within a month raised the siege of Richmond. He then drove another Union army from Virginia in the Second Battle of Bull Run/ Manassas in August, and invaded the North in September. Lee suffered an operational reverse at Sharpsburg, and then defeated the Union Army of the Potomac at Fredericksburg and Chancellorsville. One year after his victory outside Richmond, Lee's army was in southern Pennsylvania, where it met its destiny at Gettysburg. As a tactician Lee was the war's most outstanding commander, and the fact that he held overwhelming Union forces at bay for two years after Gettysburg is indicative of his military genius. Lee and Davis emerged as one of the most effective high-command collaborations of the Civil War.[11]

Davis would nominate, and the Confederate Congress would approve, three other officers for promotion to full general as the war progressed: Braxton Bragg, E. Kirby Smith, and John Bell Hood. Of the three, Smith was the most successful and received command of the Trans-Mississippi Department in the spring of 1863. Relegated to a theater of tertiary importance, he performed adequately and did not surrender until late May 1865, nearly two months after Lee capitulated at Appomattox. As for Braxton Bragg, he commanded the Army of Tennessee from the summer of 1862 until the fall of Chattanooga in November 1863. In the interim, Bragg botched the invasion of Kentucky, lost the Battle of Stones River/Murfreesboro, won an exceedingly costly battle at Chickamauga in September 1863, and was then routed at Chattanooga by Grant. In the process, his irascible character and faulty troop dispositions had so alienated his subordinate commanders that the senior officers of the Army of Tennessee were on the verge of mutiny on several occasions. Upon being relieved, Bragg, ever Davis's friend, went to Richmond, where he advised the president for the duration of the war.

Like Bragg, John Bell Hood failed to command effectively the Army of Tennessee. A brilliant division commander in Lee's army, Hood served as a corps commander in the West after Chickamauga and succeeded Johnston in command of the army in July 1864. In appointing Hood commander of the army, Davis seriously considered the advice of Bragg, who warned him that "Hood was neither a genius nor a great general, but simply better than anyone else available."[12] This was one instance when Bragg's assessment was correct. In command of the Army of Tennessee for less than six months, Hood sacrificed the cream of his army in a series of attacks that resulted in the loss of Atlanta, a major defeat at Franklin, and the total destruction of his army at Nashville in December 1864. Hood was a classic case of an officer rising above his level of competence. No army commander on the Confederate side performed as poorly as John Bell Hood. His resignation in January 1865 came too late to save the lives of thousands of Confederate soldiers.

The Confederate Army of Tennessee

Nor was the South overly fortunate in the selection of senior commanders in its western army. Since Sidney Johnston was still in California when the war commenced in Charleston Harbor, Davis selected Leonidas Polk, a West Point graduate who had befriended Cadet Davis and had resigned his commission immediately upon graduation to pursue theological studies, to command the all-important Western Department until Johnston arrived to take permanent command. Polk's selection was an unmitigated disaster for the Confederacy. Why Davis selected Polk defies understanding since his military experience was negligible. Polk arrived on July 12, 1861, to command a Confederate district that extended from the Appalachian Mountains to the west bank of the Tennessee River. Once on station, he immediately clashed with his subcommander and then inexplicably violated Kentucky's neutrality by seizing Columbus, Kentucky. This action jeopardized Sidney Johnston's own defensive scheme when the latter arrived in theater by early autumn. Polk remained with the Army of Tennessee until he fell at Pine Mountain in the Atlanta campaign of 1864. In the interim he was known mainly as a malcontent who repeatedly conspired with his colleagues against army commanders Generals Bragg and Johnston. Such insubordination was totally unprofessional, and would not have been tolerated had not Polk enjoyed such a close relationship with the Confederate president.

Between 1861 and 1864 the Army of Tennessee was also plagued by serious logistical problems and dysfunctional command teams. Unlike the Army of Northern Virginia, which Lee commanded for the better part of three years, the turnover in army command in the West seriously detracted from the Army of Tennessee's effectiveness. While two of its commanders, Bragg and Joseph Johnston, complained that Davis remained fixated on the Virginia theater of operations, and Lee's army in particular, for allocation of supplies and reinforcements, in truth the senior command of the

Army of Tennessee was its own worst enemy. To counter the emerging military generalship of such extraordinary Union commanders as Grant and Sherman, the South fielded corps commanders Polk, William Hardee, and John C. Breckinridge, to name but a few. Each of these routinely argued with his officers, senior and subordinate alike. The command problems were exacerbated by the refusal of the army commander, namely Bragg, to consider proposals submitted by his principal subordinates. By the end of 1862, command of the Army of Tennessee was beset with nearly insurmountable problems, not the least of which were a weak command structure, poor liaison with Richmond, and the burden of defending a region far beyond the capabilities of a single army.[13]

Conclusion

With respect to battlefield leadership at the junior ranks, the South's two principal armies, the Army of Northern Virginia and the Army of Tennessee, fielded officers at a commensurate level to those of the North. In the war's first year, the rank and file of both armies elected their company-grade officers (officers in the grade of lieutenant and captain). It took until October 1862 before the Confederate Congress authorized examining boards to select qualified officers, four months after the Union Congress had established a similar program.[14] What hampered the Confederates in the West was the exact problem that hindered the Union Army of the Potomac in the East: repeated changes in command that often mirrored infighting among the army's senior command.[15] In the Army of Northern Virginia, Lee managed to maintain a higher degree of stability that allowed the promotion of skilled officers at a more rapid pace. It was not until battlefield casualties devastated the ranks of the officer corps that Lee encountered significant problems in identifying worthy officers for accelerated commands.

The Confederacy enjoyed superior martial superiority only in the initial engagements. Battlefield attrition exacted a horrific toll on senior commanders on both sides. For the Confederacy, casualties among division and corps commanders reached catastrophic proportions as the war progressed. At the army level, Albert Sidney Johnston died at Shiloh, too early to determine if he would have been the Western Theater equivalent of Lee. Joseph E. Johnston was wounded and forced to relinquish command of the Army of Virginia in May 1862. At the corps level, Stonewall

Jackson, Leonidas Polk, A. P. Hill, and J.E.B. Stuart were killed in action. Richard Ewell and James Longstreet suffered debilitating wounds. At the division and brigade levels, those commands led by colonels and brigadier generals, casualties were so numerous that it is impossible to list them here.

Two battles, however, illustrate the extent of battlefield injuries and deaths. At Gettysburg, casualties among Lee's forty-six divisional and brigade infantry commanders numbered nineteen, roughly 40 percent. Losses at the field-grade level, majors through colonels, were equally severe. All told, of 171 infantry regiments, 78 suffered command casualties.[16] The Confederate Army of Tennessee suffered a similar fate at Franklin, Tennessee, in November 1864, when an ill-advised attack produced 7,000 casualties, including a dozen Confederate generals, six of whom were killed. No nation could endure losses among general officers at this rate, and the Confederacy was no exception.

In the final analysis, both Union and Confederate armies possessed a small number of extraordinarily competent commanders who routinely succeeded in every engagement. Despite the mythology, no fixed advantage was enjoyed by the Confederacy. Davis and his principal army commanders encountered the same problems as their Northern adversaries in identifying skilled practitioners of the military art over the course of the conflict. At the senior level of command, only Lee and Jackson emerged as true military geniuses, and their efforts were more than offset by the advent of Ulysses S. Grant, William T. Sherman, George Thomas, and Philip Sheridan. While this Union quartet fought in the West, Lee and the Army of Northern Virginia compiled a string of successes in the East against a series of mediocre commanders that included John Pope, George McClellan, Ambrose Burnside, and Joseph Hooker. Key to Lee's victories was the superb command team of the army's two senior corps commanders, James Longstreet and Stonewall Jackson. Even before these corps were officially authorized by the Confederate Congress in late 1862, Lee had for all intents and purposes created these organizations by assigning Longstreet and Jackson to command the two wings of the Army of Northern Virginia in the battles around Second Manassas and Antietam/Sharpsburg. Under Lee's able tutelage, Longstreet and Jackson flourished, but only Jackson excelled in independent command, highlighted by his exceptional performance in the Shenandoah Valley campaign of March through June 1862. When Longstreet commanded an independent operation at Knoxville in the autumn of 1863, he met defeat at the hands of Ambrose Burnside, who had been Lee's victim at Fredericksburg the preceding December. By 1864, with Jackson gone, Lee no longer possessed the offensive capability to threaten the Union capital or to destroy the Northern Army of the Potomac. Casualties among the army's leaders had reduced the effectiveness of the Army of Northern Virginia. That it survived and waged war successfully against vastly superior numbers for another year is a testament to the genius of its commander.

Lee himself, both as military adviser to President Davis and as commander of the Army of Northern Virginia, recognized the problems surrounding the promotion of skilled officers to assume positions of increased responsibility. From 1861 to 1863, the Southern army underwent three principal reorganizations. When the army was initially organized in 1861, there seemed to be an abundance of qualified officers to fill the ranks of command. As commander of the Army of Virginia in the autumn of 1861, Joseph E. Johnston announced he had sufficient officers for brigade and higher commands. Lee was less optimistic. In the first full-scale reorganization after the Seven Days' Campaign outside Richmond, Lee removed inexperienced and tactically inept commanders. He did so again after his first invasion of the North in the fall of 1862. Battlefield casualties, coupled with tactical incompetence, soon reduced the officer ranks of Lee's army to such a degree that Lee experienced significant problems in identifying officers to promote to command division-level units. After Jackson died following Lee's greatest victory at Chancellorsville in May 1863, Lee was forced to promote two officers, A. P. Hill and Richard Ewell, to corps-level command. Both were far more proficient division-level commanders than corps commanders, and both failed miserably in the ensuing Gettysburg campaign. Gettysburg also left the Army of Northern Virginia depleted at the major, colonel, and brigadier general levels. A recent study of command within Lee's army indicates that where "capable officers rise fast, their death or invalidism may mean that less competent men will succeed them . . . sustaining qualified officers in the face of heavy casualties then may depend less on training and combat experience than on the size of the population."[17] This was certainly the case in the Army of Northern Virginia, as well as the Confederate armies in the Western Theater, where a shrinking manpower pool reduced the number of eligible officers. In fact, "After the second year of hostilities, in an army [of Northern Virginia] of nine infantry divisions, roughly 150 regiments, two officers only, John B.

Gordon and William Mahone, added materially to the vigor of the high command" of Lee's army.[18]

When the Confederacy finally collapsed in April 1865, there were few familiar faces among the senior commanders who had marched off to war in 1861. Generals Robert E. Lee and Joseph Johnston still commanded the South's two principal armies, but surviving officers at junior ranks had emerged over the course of the conflict to command the South's brigades and divisions. Attrition had exacted an exceedingly high toll. Take, for example, the initial five full generals of the Confederacy: Albert Sidney Johnston was dead; Beauregard was disgraced; Joseph Johnston had been relieved, albeit subsequently reinstated; and Cooper remained administratively competent, but strategically inept. Only Lee had exceeded Davis's expectations. Two other full generals, Braxton Bragg and John Bell Hood, had resigned after they had needlessly sacrificed their armies in a series of military disasters. For the South to have demonstrated military superiority against the North, it needed a dozen commanders the caliber of Robert E. Lee. To his eternal misfortune, President Jefferson Davis found only one, as he confided to his brother Joseph, and therein lies the fallacy of the myth of Southern martial superiority.[19]

Notes

1. Samuel E. Morison, *The Oxford History of the American People* (New York: Oxford University Press, 1965), 619.

2. James McPherson, *Battle Cry of Freedom* (New York: Oxford University Press, 1988), 327–328.

3. Mary Elizabeth Sergent, An *Unremaining Glory (Being A Supplement to They Lie Forgotten)* (Middletown, NY: Prior King Press, 1997), 7.

4. All figures from McPherson, *Battle Cry of Freedom*, 328.

5. Douglas S. Freeman, *Lee's Lieutenants,* vol.1 (New York: Scribner's, 1942), xxii–xxiii, 701.

6. This criterion is best explored by Thomas Goss, *The War Within the Union High Command* (Lawrence: University Press of Kansas, 2003), xvii.

7. Geoffrey Perret, *Ulysses S. Grant: Soldier and President* (New York: Macmillan, 1997), 241.

8. Steven E. Woodworth, *Jefferson Davis and His Generals* (Lawrence: University Press of Kansas, 1990), 33.

9. William C. Davis, *Jefferson Davis: The Man and His Hour* (New York: HarperCollins, 1991), 360–361.

10. Ibid., 23.

11. Steven E. Woodworth, *Davis and Lee at War* (Lawrence: University Press of Kansas, 1995), 329.

12. U.S. War Department, *Official Records of the War of the Rebellion*, vol. 1, pt. 2 (Washington, DC: Government Printing Office, 1880), 712–714. See also Davis, *Jefferson Davis,* 561.

13. Thomas Connelly, *Army of the Heartland: The Army of Tennessee, 1861–1862* (Baton Rouge: Louisiana State University Press, 1967), 280.

14. McPherson, *Battle Cry of Freedom*, 327.

15. For a breakdown in the Army of Tennessee, see Thomas Connelly, *Autumn of Glory: The Army of Tennessee, 1862–1865* (Baton Rouge: Louisiana University Press, 1971), 535.

16. Stephen W. Sears, *Gettysburg* (Boston: Houghton Mifflin, 2003), 498–499.

17. These quotations and figures are taken verbatim from Freeman's *Lee's Lieutenants,* vol. 1, xxvi–xxvii.

18. Ibid.

19. As quoted in Davis, *Jefferson Davis,* 699.

CHAPTER 3

THE TRANSFORMATION OF ABRAHAM LINCOLN

Just as the Civil War heralded the transition of the United States of America from a union of seemingly sovereign states to a single national entity, so, too, did it mark the transition of Abraham Lincoln from a unionist to a nationalist. In the process Lincoln also transformed himself into an ardent abolitionist. The transformation was not happenstance; once he decided upon a course of action, Lincoln moved with a firmness of purpose from which no one could deter him until the issue was resolved. Said Mary Lincoln, "[Lincoln] was a terribly firm man when he set his foot down—none of us—no man no woman could rule him after he had made up his mind."[1] Lincoln seldom accepted public credit for the direction of the war to which he dedicated his presidency, claiming merely that he was sailing on a river of destiny, over which he exercised scant control: "In telling this tale [of my transformation to an emancipationist], I attempt no compliment to my own sagacity. I claim not to have controlled events, but confess plainly that events have controlled me."[2] The president thus moved slowly, but deliberately, in redefining his concept of American democracy and nationalism between 1861 and 1865. How and why he so transformed himself is the subject of this chapter.

There was little to presage Lincoln's impact on a divided country when he assumed the presidency on March 4, 1861. Indeed, even Edward Everett, who was destined to join the president on the podium at Gettysburg on November 19, 1863, said prior to the inauguration in 1861 that Lincoln was "evidently a person of very inferior cast of character, wholly unequal to the crisis."[3] Everett would later champion the president's cause, but considerable skepticism prevailed when Lincoln arrived in the federal capital in February 1861. Those who questioned the president-elect's sagacity and determination would soon discover that Lincoln's purpose was to fulfill the presidential oath "to preserve, protect, and defend the Constitution of the United States."

Lincoln's Speeches

To best understand Lincoln's commitment to unionism and democracy, one only need examine his major addresses and speeches. He readily confessed that he had always been anti-slavery, but as a legalist, he felt any president could do nothing where slavery already existed. Still, he realized the inherent dangers posed by the peculiar institution of involuntary servitude. On the Illinois prairie and in countless towns where he debated Stephen A Douglas in 1858, Lincoln spoke only of the preservation of the Union. "A house divided against itself cannot stand," he warned. "I believe this government cannot endure permanently half slave and half free, I do not expect the *Union* to be dissolved; I do not expect the house to fall; but I do expect it will cease to be divided."[4]

Defeated in his bid to oust Senator Douglas, Lincoln found himself a highly requested speaker on the traveling circuit. A year after he made a series of widely publicized speeches throughout Ohio in 1859, a transcript of his debates with Douglas appeared in print. Over the winter, Lincoln broadened his political base by accepting an invitation from the Young Men's Central Republican Union of New York City to deliver a series of addresses in which he could expound upon his political views. In particular, those who invited Lincoln requested that he elaborate upon his "House Divided" speech. The timing could not have been better, for in the previous October, John Brown had led an unsuccessful raid to "arm the Negro." Brown's capture by Colonel Robert E. Lee and his subsequent execution on December 2, 1859, not only inflamed the South and greatly increased sectional strife a year before the 1860 presidential election, but they also reverberated throughout the North. How Lincoln would respond to the sectional crisis would either make or break his political fortunes. Speaking in front of a capacity crowd at New York's Cooper Union on February 27, Lincoln used historical analysis to illustrate that twenty-one of the thirty-nine signers of the U.S. Constitution had expressly concurred that the federal government had the power to control the extension of slavery in the territories. Lincoln had vigorously supported this interpretation in his senatorial debates with Douglas. Next he stressed that the Republican Party was the party of the true moderates on the issue of slavery, not the fire-eaters of the South, who had become increasingly radicalized. Indeed, Lincoln urged that the Republican Party "must let [the South] alone" and "wrong as we think slavery is, we can yet afford to let it alone where it is, because that much is due to necessity arising from the actual presence in the nation." But could the Republican Party, "while it has the votes, allow slavery to spread into the national territories and overrun us here in the free states?" Lincoln's answer was a resounding "No!" What, then, needed to be done? Lincoln urged his followers "to persist in excluding slavery from the national territories, confining it to the states where it already existed." He then summarized: "Let us have faith that right makes might, and in that faith, let us, to the end, dare to do our duty as we understand it."[5]

The Cooper Union speech was the opening volley in Lincoln's bid for the Republican Party's presidential nomination, although he would have denied that he was that interested in the national office. Over the course of the next few weeks, he toured New England. Despite Lincoln's increasing popularity, his nomination as the Republican Party candidate was due more to his ability to carry Illinois and Indiana in the upcoming election than to his fame. Indeed, New York Senator William Seward, Lincoln's future secretary of state, was fully expected to capture the party's nomination. Fate intervened, however, and the nomination fell to Lincoln when the party convention met in Chicago in May. In November, Abraham Lincoln was elected sixteenth president of the United States.

As Lincoln prepared to deliver his inaugural address, the county had disintegrated. Seven states of the Lower South had already seceded from the Union and formed the Confederate States of America. All federal property in the South, except Fort Sumter in Charleston Harbor and Fort Pickens, now lay in Confederate hands. Unlike his predecessor, Lincoln was determined to make a stand. When he gave his initial presidential address at noon, March 4, 1861, his stance was unequivocal: the Union would be preserved, by force if necessary. In the president's view the Union predated the Constitution, which was written in part to "form a more perfect Union." If the destruction of the Union by one or by a number of states were lawfully possible, "the Union is LESS perfect than before the Constitution, having lost the vital element of perpetuity." To Lincoln, then, "the Union is unbroken; and to the extent of my ability I shall take care, as the Constitution itself expressly enjoins upon me, that the laws of the Union be faithfully executed in all the States." The die was thus cast. To preserve the Union, Lincoln was willing to accept civil war if it should be thrust upon him. The U.S. government would not make the first move; that option resided with the South. "In your hands, my dissatisfied fellow countrymen, and not in mine, is the momentous issue of civil war. The government will not assail you. You can have no conflict without being yourselves the aggressors. You have no oath registered in heaven to destroy the government, while I shall have the most solemn one to 'preserve, protect and defend it.'"[6]

Lincoln had drawn a line in the sand from which he would not retreat. He had his answer on April 12, 1861, when Confederate forces fired upon Fort Sumter. The Civil War had begun. Lincoln immediately called for 75,000 volunteers to put down the rebellion and imposed a naval blockade on Southern ports. Throughout May and June he concentrated on the preservation of the Union and defining the nature of the war, and avoided any discussion of slavery. Once Congress convened for a special session on July 4, Lincoln reviewed the outbreak of hostilities and clarified why he had accepted war. In his mind the war was nothing more than a domestic insurrection, not a conflict between sovereign states, which would legitimize secession and demonstrate to the world that the federal Union was not perpetual. In defining the war, Lincoln informed the legislative branch that he intended to exercise his constitutional prerogatives as commander-in-chief to wage the war with little interference from either Congress or the Supreme Court. "It was with the deepest regret that the Executive found the duty of employing the war-power, in defense of the government, forced upon him." These measures, though extra-legal, were forced upon him by popular demand and public necessity; Lincoln trusted that Congress would ratify them. And Congress did just that in a series of bills that became effective retroactively.

Lincoln next addressed the nature of the war. "This," said the president, "is essentially a People's contest. On the side of the Union, it is a struggle for maintaining in the world, that form, and substance of government, whose leading object is, to elevate the condition of men." And "Our popular government has often been called an experiment. . . . Two points in it, our people have already settled—the successful establishing, and the successful administering of it. One still remains—its successful maintenance against a formidable internal attempt to overthrow it. . . . This issue embraces more than the fate of these United States. It presents to the whole family of man, the question, whether a constitutional republic, or a democracy . . . can or cannot, maintain its territorial integrity, against its own domestic foes."[7] Thus the war was not only for the preservation of the Union but also for the preservation of democracy.

The Road Toward Emancipation

By the summer of 1862, the war had entered its second year and Lincoln, despite military reverses in Virginia, felt comfortable enough to address the thorny issue of emancipation. Pressured by abolitionist groups and notables such as Frederick Douglass and newspaper editor Horace Greeley, Lincoln felt it was time to move toward the liberation of the slaves. He and the Radical Republican Congress had already taken the initial steps. On April 16, 1862, Congress abolished slavery in the District of Columbia, and in mid-July passed a second bill authorizing the confiscation of Confederate property, including slaves. Captured slaves were now declared prisoners of war and were set free. The president signed the Second Confiscation Act with reservations. Next Lincoln moved forward with his personal agenda. Congress, he reasoned, lacked the power to abolish slavery within the United States. Consequently, Lincoln informed several members of his cabinet on July 13 that he "had about come to the conclusion that we must free the slaves or be ourselves subdued."[8] He first met with the governors of the border states and urged them to accept emancipation, but was stiffly rebuffed. In Lincoln's mind the question was not if the slaves were to be freed, but when and under what circumstances. Lincoln had twice previously halted attempts at emancipation. On April 13, 1862, General David Hunter had issued a proclamation abolishing slavery in his Department of the South, consisting of South Carolina, Georgia, and Florida. Lincoln promptly rescinded the order and chastised the general as quickly as he had countermanded Major General John C. Frémont, who had issued a similar edict in Missouri on August 30, 1861. Any such emancipation proclamation was the responsibility of the chief executive alone. Now, on July 22, 1862, the president summoned his cabinet and informed them that he had made "a covenant with God," and as commander-in-chief of the army and the navy and "as fit and necessary military measure," he would on January 1, 1863, declare "all persons held as slaves within any state . . . wherein the people whereof shall then be in rebellion against the United States, shall be then, thenceforward, and forever free."[9] It was a historic occasion, but not all the cabinet members realized they were witnessing history. Before he would issue a final proclamation, Lincoln decided to wait for a Union victory in the Eastern Theater.

Lincoln next moved to prepare the Northern people for emancipation. The vast majority of Northern soldiers had volunteered to preserve the Union, not to liberate the slaves. Unsure of their reaction, Lincoln pursued a cautious policy. As pressure to abolish slavery increased, he remained convinced that any action must support the preservation of the Union. How to balance emancipation with the expressed war aim of preserving the Union remained a delicate political question. Horace Greeley gave Lincoln the opening he needed. On August 19, 1862, Greeley wrote to the president that "millions of your countrymen require of you a frank, declared, unqualified, ungrudging execution of the laws of the land." Lincoln responded three days later in an open letter to the editor. "As to the policy I 'seem to be pursuing' as you say, I have not meant to leave any one in doubt. I would save the Union. I would save it the shortest way under the Constitution," Lincoln informed Greeley. "My paramount object in this struggle is to save the Union, and is not either to save or to destroy slavery. If I could save the Union without freeing any slave I would do it; and if I could save it by freeing all the slaves, I would do it; and if I could save it by freeing some and leaving others alone I would also do that. What I do about slavery, and the colored race, I do because I believe it helps to save the Union; and what I forbear, I forbear because I do not believe it would help to save the Union."[10] No clearer expression of presidential decision-making exists.

The letter was already written when the draft emancipation proclamation was sitting on the president's desk, and Lincoln patiently waited for his victory. The victory came on September 17, when Major General George B. McClellan battled Lee to a tactical draw at Sharpsburg, Maryland. Five days later, Lincoln issued the preliminary emancipation proclamation, announcing to his cabinet and to the American public that as of January 1, 1863, all slaves in those states still opposing the Union "shall be then, thenceforward, and forever free." When he announced his decision to the cabinet, he informed them that he was not seeking their consent or advice, but that he would appreciate any suggestions that they might have with respect to wording and style. The proclamation was his and his alone. As Lincoln informed the cabinet, "I made a solemn vow before God that if General Lee was driven back from Pennsylvania, I would crown the result by the declaration of freedom to the slaves."[11] The Emancipation Proclamation was a war measure designed to weaken the Confederacy, pure and simple. And it did just that. Not only did the document weaken the Southern economy, but it also halted any halfhearted attempts by Great Britain and France to afford diplomatic recognition to the Confederacy. By this move, Lincoln had transformed the war from merely preserving a political institution to a moral crusade for human equality.

Lincoln had gauged the nation's reaction accurately. Had he issued the proclamation six months earlier, the country would not have been prepared for it. Now, with Washington no longer threatened by Lee's army, a spirit of euphoria, albeit brief, gripped the North. "All I can say now is that I believe the Proclamation has knocked the bottom out of slavery, though at no time have I expected any sudden results from it," Lincoln told guests in the White House. To Northern Democrats whom he knew would oppose the document, he appeared a reluctant emancipationist. The president informed a Unionist Democrat from his home state of Illinois, "I have issued the emancipation proclamation, and I can not retract it." Once the proclamation took effect, he reminded his critics, "I struggled nearly a year and a half to get along without touching the 'institution,' and when finally I conditionally determined to touch it, I gave a hundred days fair notice of my purpose. . . . They [Southern states still in rebellion] chose to disregard it, and I made the peremptory proclamation on what appeared to me to be a military necessity. And being made, it must stand."[12]

As predicted, Lincoln's preliminary proclamation had the desired effect. Mary Chesnut, the Richmond diarist, noted, "Three hundred of Mr. Walter Blake's negroes have gone to the Yankees." Southern leaders despised Lincoln's unilateral proclamation and immediately railed against what they termed a treacherous act. To Jefferson Davis, the proclamation confirmed the reasons why the Southern states were forced to secede. The proclamation, exclaimed the Confederate president, was "the most execrable measure recorded in the history of guilty man." Lincoln's supporters, quite naturally, held an opposing view and hailed the proclamation as long overdue and "a gigantic stride in the paths of Christian and civilized progress." As Lincoln hoped, across the Atlantic the proclamation undercut the South's attempt to secure foreign recognition. "[The American civil war] is destined to be a turning point, for good or evil, of the course of human affairs," said John Stuart Mill. Mill continued, "The triumph of the Confederacy would be a victory of the powers of evil." Charles Francis Adams, the American ambassador to the Court of St. James, cabled the president that the Emancipation Proclamation had the desired effect in Great Britain, for it "annihilate[d] all agitation for recognition." American voters were not so sure, and indicated their disapproval by reducing the Republican Party majority in both houses of Congress during the autumn elections. As for Lincoln, he believed that the Emancipation Proclamation was the supreme act of his presidency. "If my name ever goes into history," he said, "it was for this act."[13]

The issuance of the Emancipation Proclamation did not end the president's desire to eliminate slavery. Important questions still needed to be answered. Should black regiments be raised in support of Union armies? What of the slaves in the border states? Which branch of government had the constitutional authority to abolish the institution of slavery? Lincoln's success depended on the Northern armies in the field. Midsummer 1863 produced some of those victories, the two most notable being Gettysburg in southern Pennsylvania and Vicksburg, the last major Confederate bastion on the Mississippi River. The year 1863 also witnessed the raising and formation of the first black infantry regiments with white officers. From 1863 to 1865, 186,017 African Americans, nearly all Southern, served in the Union Army and Navy.[14] In spite of the tremendous progress that the president had made in advancing the civil rights of all Americans, there were still doubters as to Lincoln's intent and the speed with which he had moved. Others opposed the president's policy of enlisting former slaves and freedmen as soldiers. On April 4, 1864, Lincoln, now confident of victory, decided to put the matter to rest once and for all. He wrote a long letter to Albert G. Hodges, editor of the *Frankfort* (Kentucky) *Commonwealth*, explaining his personal journey toward emancipation from his inaugural promise not to interfere with slavery to where it was now. Again Lincoln made the distinction between Union and nation and clarified his position that he had always been anti-slavery, for if "slavery is not wrong, nothing is wrong."[15] The president then explained that his oath to protect, preserve, and defend the Constitution had imposed upon him "the duty of preserving, by every indispensable means, that government—that nation—of which that constitution was the organic law." Repeatedly Lincoln mentioned the "nation" and cited the 1860 Union only in the context of the "Union side" and a "Union man." In a larger context, the president confessed that he had been "driven to the alternative of either surrendering the Union, and with it, the Constitution, or of laying strong hand upon the colored element. I chose the latter. In choosing it, I hoped for greater gain than loss." When he decided to act, it had been due to "indispensable necessity."[16]

Lincoln delivered the death blow to slavery as the war dramatically wound to a close. The elections of 1864 had returned the requisite majority of Republicans to both houses of Congress for the passage of a constitutional amendment outlawing involuntary servitude. With a three-fourths majority, Lincoln now possessed the necessary votes to pass the Thirteenth Amendment, prohibiting forever the existence of slavery. Though the newly elected legislators would not take office until March, Lincoln felt comfortable enough to ask Democratic Party incumbents to unite with Republicans in a spirit of bipartisanship and pass the amendment before the term of the current Congress expired on March 4. After incessant lobbying by the president, on January 31, 1865, the House of Representatives passed the Thirteenth Amendment with two votes to spare. Most Northern state legislatures immediately ratified the amendment, the exception being those states whose electoral votes had been cast for McClellan in the preceding November election. So, too, did the reconstructed state legislatures of Louisiana, Arkansas, and Tennessee. Lincoln would not survive to witness the required number of states approve the amendment, but the outcome was never in doubt. He had long ago decided that ratification of the amendment would be required for the remaining Southern states to be fully incorporated into the new federal union. Any reconstruction plan, the president's or otherwise, would insist on Southern compliance. The president's victory over slavery, the issue that had precipitated civil war, was now complete.

From Unionist to Nationalist

There was, however, still work that needed to be done, not the least of which was preparing the stage for reconstruction of a nation torn by four years of civil strife. As Lincoln took the necessary steps to end the institution of slavery, he also directed his efforts to creating a new America.

In the process, he evolved into an ardent nationalist. After two years of war, Lincoln realized that the Union as it existed in 1860 was gone forever. The Emancipation Proclamation alone bore witness to that, for the Southern states would never voluntarily rejoin the Union unless forced by the advance of federal armies. As he would later state in his second inaugural address, "Neither party expected for the war, the magnitude, or the duration, which it has already attained." The old Union had been torn asunder. Now, fully confident that the North would eventually prevail, Lincoln envisioned a new state that would rise from the ashes of civil war. That entity would be based on representative government whose solidarity and existence would never again be threatened from within. The national entity that a prescient Lincoln foresaw encompassed all Americans, regardless of origin, race, or religious belief. This nation was founded on the remnants of the old Union, but tempered by war and the sacrifice of thousands of men who had paid the ultimate price for the preservation of the Union and the emancipation of the slaves. Lincoln's new *nation* found its most eloquent expression in the Gettysburg Address and Lincoln's second inaugural address.

The Gettysburg Address

Four months after General Meade and the Army of the Potomac won a decisive victory over Lee in the hills south of Gettysburg, Pennsylvania, and forced the Confederate army to return to Virginia, Lincoln received an invitation from Gettysburg native David Wills, the chairman of the committee responsible for the ceremonies dedicating a national military cemetery on the site of the battle, to offer a few appropriate remarks "to set apart these grounds to their sacred use." As president, Lincoln received hundreds of invitations to deliver speeches and to make personal appearances in support of worthy enterprises. As commander-in-chief, he politely refused the vast majority of such offers, but this one arrived in the wake of dramatic Northern victories at Gettysburg and Vicksburg, and an improved situation at Chattanooga. Lincoln accepted this specific invitation not only to fulfill its expressed purpose, but also to seize the moment to explain to the American people the significance of the Civil War and to remind them that the road ahead would be bloody and costly, but that in the end, the victory would be worth the cost.

Contrary to popular belief, the president did not hastily pen the address on the back of an envelope while he was aboard a train to

Gettysburg. Although he put the finishing touches on the speech the evening he arrived in the small Pennsylvania community, he had thought long and hard about the contents of the remarks he was to deliver on November 19. The resulting speech was perhaps the greatest oration in American history. Never once did Lincoln speak of the old Union; but now he used the word "nation" not once but five times. And what of this nation? Returning to his pre-presidential days, in which he had argued so persuasively with Stephen Douglas, Lincoln suggested that the nation predated the Constitution in that it rested on a principle originally articulated in 1776—that the *nation* was "conceived in liberty and dedicated to the proposition that all men were created equal." Lincoln next reminded the assembly who gathered at the cemetery that the United States was engaged in a great civil war, "testing whether that *nation* or any *nation*" could endure. After a brief tribute to those who had fallen in battle, came the crux of the president's message: the country must be dedicated to the unfinished work that lay ahead. The cost would continue to be extraordinarily high, but the nation must "highly resolve that these dead shall not have died in vain" and that "the *nation* shall, under God, have a new birth of freedom." Then followed the clincher: all Americans must unite to ensure "that government of the people, by the people, for the people, shall not perish from the earth."[17] This, then, was a war not only for the preservation of the government and the emancipation of the slaves, but also for the preservation of democracy as a whole. In only 272 words, Lincoln had broadened the war, in Lincoln biographer David Donald's opinion, from "union to equality and nation."[18]

The Second Inaugural Address

Continuing this theme in his second inaugural address, delivered on March 4, 1865, Lincoln reflected on four years of conflict and the tremendous changes that the country had witnessed since 1861, noting that when his initial address was being delivered, the North was devoted to "saving the Union without war, insurgent agents were in the city seeking to destroy it without war—seeking to dissolve the Union." War came only when "one of them [the Confederacy] would make war rather than let the *nation* survive; and the other [the North] would accept war rather than let it perish." He mentioned as well the role of slavery in causing the current conflict. "All knew," stated Lincoln, "that this interest was, somehow, the cause of the war. To strengthen, perpetuate, and extend this interest was the object for which the insurgents would rend the Union, even by war." Now, with victory in sight, Lincoln called upon a soon-to-be-united America to "bind up the nation's wounds" and for the people of the country to accept "a just and a lasting peace among themselves, and with all nations." Invoking almighty God, Lincoln now called for a time of healing; now was the time to put aside the calamity of war.

On reflection, Lincoln's second inaugural address may have been the most important inaugural address in the nation's history to that point. The president certainly thought so. Speaking to Thurlow Weed, Lincoln confessed, "I expect the latter to wear as well—perhaps better than anything I have produced."[19] Lincoln's purpose had been to extend the olive branch to the defeated South and to guide a unified nation toward "a just and lasting peace." Only sparingly did the president use the word "Union,"—and when he did, he referred to the events of 1861—for that entity no longer existed in Lincoln's mind.[20] No longer concerned about the antebellum union that no longer existed, the president focused on the birth of a united nation. In that sense, he intended his second inaugural address to be a beginning, not an ending to the tragic war that had beset the United States.

How, then, do we assess Lincoln as a unionist, an abolitionist, and a nationalist? He held the highest office at a critical time in our history, and by timely action he had achieved timeless results. When he assumed the presidency, he presided over a union of semi-independent states, eleven of which firmly believed that the federal union was a convenience and that the bonds could be severed by unilateral action by any state in the union. One-eighth of the population of the United States was enslaved in 1861. Four years later, the nation was united again and involuntary servitude was no more. How had it happened? Not by chance, not by the natural evolution of things, but by the dedicated efforts of one man who envisioned himself as an instrument of God. Douglas S. Freeman, who wrote the Pulitzer Prize biographies of George Washington and Robert E. Lee, stated categorically that the key to Lincoln's greatness was his self-mastery of mind and spirit. Freeman found three expressions of this self-mastery: Lincoln's extraordinary grasp of both political and military issues, his fixity of purpose, and the president's absence of malice in dealing with the South.[21] Through four years of catastrophic civil war, he had guided his nation to a rebirth of freedom and confirmed that the nation's basic values were established on the equality of all men and a firm belief in democratic principles. For Abraham Lincoln, the nation's journey as well as his personal journey was complete.

Notes

1. Quoted in David Herbert Donald, *"We Are Lincoln Men": Abraham Lincoln and His Friends* (New York: Simon and Schuster, 2003), 212.

2. Letter from Abraham Lincoln to Albert G. Hodges, April 4, 1864, as quoted in David Herbert Donald, *Lincoln* (New York: Simon and Schuster, 1995), 15.

3. Quoted in Carl Sandburg, *Abraham Lincoln: The War Years*, vol. 2 (New York: Harcourt, Brace, 1939), 453.

4. See Lincoln's "House Divided" speech in the Primary Documents section of this book. It is also in David S. Heidler and Jeanne T. Heidler, eds., *Encyclopedia of the American Civil War* (New York: W. W. Norton, 2000), 2187–2190.

5. See Carl Sandburg, *Abraham Lincoln: The Prairie Years*, vol. 2 (New York: Harcourt, Brace, 1926), 211–214. See also Donald, *Lincoln*, 239.

6. For complete text of Lincoln's inaugural address, see Heidler and Heidler, *Encyclopedia of the American Civil War*, 2287–2291.

7. Quoted in James McPherson, *Battle Cry of Freedom* (New York: Oxford University Press, 1988), 309.

8. Ibid., 504.

9. For a discussion of the cabinet's reaction to Lincoln's announcement, see William Klingaman, *Abraham Lincoln and the Road to Emancipation* (New York: Viking, 2001), 155–158.

10. Lincoln's reply to Greeley is included in Heidler and Heidler, *Encyclopedia of the American Civil War*, 2429. Excerpts from Lincoln's letter are in McPherson, *Battle Cry of Freedom*, 510, and Donald, *Lincoln*, 368.

11. Quoted in Klingaman, *Abraham Lincoln and the Road to Emancipation*, 187.

12. Ibid. All Lincoln's statements are quoted in Klingaman, 238–239.

13. All quotes in this paragraph are from Geoffrey C. Ward, with Ric Burns and Ken Burns, *The Civil War: An Illustrated History* (New York: Alfred A. Knopf, 1990), 166–167, except the quotation from Charles F. Adams, which is from McPherson, *Battle Cry of Freedom*, 567.

14. Shelby Foote, *The Civil War: A Narrative*, vol. 1 (New York: Random House, 1958), 60.

15. The complete text of Lincoln's letter to Hodges is in Ronald C. White Jr., *Lincoln's Greatest Speech: The Second Inaugural* (New York: Simon and Schuster, 2002), 206–207.

16. Ibid.

17. Lincoln's Gettysburg Address appears in the Primary Documents section of this book.

18. In Donald, *Lincoln*, 466, the author uses the phrase "from Union to Equality and Union" to convey the same theme.

19. Quoted in White, *Lincoln's Greatest Speech*, 197.

20. The best analysis of Lincoln's second inaugural address is White's *Lincoln's Greatest Speech*.

21. Stuart W. Smith, ed., *Douglas Southall Freeman on Leadership* (Shippensburg, PA: White Mane, 1993), 41–43.

CHAPTER 4

COULD THE SOUTH HAVE WON THE CIVIL WAR?

In retrospect, historians and writers have examined the defeat of the Confederacy and have pondered if the South could ever have achieved independence against the overwhelming manpower superiority and economic resources of the industrial North. On the surface, the numerical odds seemed to have been so stacked against the South with respect to population, industrial output, and military resources that the Confederacy was doomed to fail. For Southern historians attempting to explain the Confederacy's defeat, this explanation has become a cottage industry. General Robert E. Lee unwittingly started it all when in his farewell address to the Army of Northern Virginia, he attributed his army's defeat to the North's "overwhelming numbers and resources."[1] But could the South have won the war under difference circumstances? The North's numerical superiority across the entire spectrum of conflict certainly contributed to its victory, but to claim that the North's preponderance of military and economic might was the principal factor in its victory does not necessarily bear up under the microscope of history.

History is replete with examples of nations with fewer resources defeating superior forces. The most common comparison of the South's prospects for victory is with that of the United States' chances for independence during the American Revolution. At the time the Second Continental Congress declared American independence in July 1776, the fledging nation faced odds every bit as daunting as those the Confederacy faced in 1861. Great Britain possessed the world's largest navy, the best-trained army, the most efficient economy, and a stable government built on sound financial resources. Yet five years later, the United States achieved its independence. There the comparison tends to break down, however, because American independence resulted in part from strong financial and military assistance from France and other European states. Moreover, England was thousands of miles from America's shores, while the North bordered the Confederacy. This proved a two-edged sword, though, for just as the North could invade the South, so could the Confederacy invade the North, something the Continental Army and Navy could never do in 1776–1781. Returning to 1861, then, the odds against the South were formidable, but not impossible to overcome. By no means was the Confederacy's defeat inevitable.

How, then, might the South have won the war? In recent decades authors have produced a mass of literature on contingency history, what Civil War historian James McPherson describes as "the recognition that at numerous critical points during the war things might have gone altogether differently."[2] Much of this history began with the war's centennial celebration in 1961, but historical fiction has lost none of its strength and persistence. From McKinlay Kantor's *If the South Had Won the Civil War* to Newt Gingrich's *Gettysburg: A Novel of the Civil War*, the action usually revolves around a Confederate victory at Gettysburg in July 1863. Defeating General Meade on Cemetery Ridge, Lee then marches to Washington, D.C., captures Lincoln in the White House, and forces the Union to grant the Confederate States of America its independence. Such historical fiction leads one to reconsider the South's strategic options and ponder at which points during the war the Confederacy might have pursued a different course to achieve its independence. In fact the South almost won, for at several points during the conflict, Union morale faltered and Great Britain and France seriously considered diplomatic recognition. How, then, could the South have won the war?

Southern Strategy

Any analysis of the course of the war must begin with a discussion of the military and diplomatic strategy employed by Jefferson Davis and the Confederacy. Drawing parallels to the American Revolution, Davis certainly recognized that without external assistance, the Confederacy faced a difficult task in confronting a United States whose resources clearly overshadowed those of the South in virtually every category. Foreign assistance could offset the North's numerical advantages, but no European nation would recognize the Confederacy unless the South demonstrated its ability to achieve a military victory, just as the United States did in 1777 when British General John Burgoyne surrendered his army to Horatio Gates at Saratoga. That American victory became the catalyst for the subsequent Franco–American Treaty of Amity and Commerce in February 1778. To achieve recognition, Davis dispatched two agents, James Mason of Virginia and John Slidell of Louisiana, to London and Paris in September 1861. They sought to secure European aid in those areas where the Confederacy was most weak: naval power, financial assistance, and foreign trade. When their ship was halted by a U.S. naval vessel on November 8, the agents were arrested and subsequently released to avoid a major diplomatic crisis. Mason and Slidell reached their respective foreign capitals, but soon found that the British and French were reluctant to extend recognition until Southern military prospects improved. And when Southern military prospects did improve, they did so only temporarily, and Lincoln countered Confederate military success by issuing the Emancipation Proclamation, which elevated the war to a moral crusade for human equality. No European power would risk alienation in the court of global public opinion by recognizing a state that advocated slavery. So much for foreign recognition to improve the Confederacy's chances for success.

What, then, of the South's strategy? Was the strategic defensive the proper strategy to employ against an adversary bent on its destruction? Could any defensive strategy succeed if the enemy was bound and determined to continue aggression, regardless of cost? A nation can win battles with poor tactics, but it is well-nigh impossible to win a war with a poor strategy. Strategically, Jefferson Davis decided early on that the South would pursue a defensive war even though a defensive strategy enhanced the inherent advantages of the North. "All we want is to be left alone," he told Congress on April 29, 1861. As president, he desired peace "at any sacrifice, save that of honor and independence." It is not surprising, then, the South would "meet"—not wage—the war now launched by Lincoln.[3] Thus the South would not assail the North, but await the Northern onslaught wherever and whenever it might strike.

The question soon confronting Davis was what territory to defend. In a confederacy of sovereign states, each state was important and no state governor seemed willing to risk the loss of any territory to the federal government. Nor would the governors relinquish command of their sons to a national government in Richmond unless Davis was determined to defend the Confederacy's entire northern border. Davis had too few troops to accomplish this task, but he considered that he had few available options. There is an adage within military circles that states "he who would defend everything, defends nothing," because the attacker can marshal a preponderance of forces in selecting the precise place and time to attack. And that is precisely what happened as several Union armies advanced down the Mississippi River Valley and into eastern Tennessee. To counter these attacks, Davis positioned his troops along the most likely avenues of approach into the heart of the Confederacy. Under the leadership of Robert E. Lee, the Confederates achieved a high degree of martial success in Virginia until the final year of the war; in the West, Davis's legions were generally unsuccessful in halting the combined naval and military forces of a series of Union commanders, the most prominent of whom were Ulysses S. Grant and William T. Sherman. As the war progressed, it became evident by 1863 that the South had lost the war in the West long before Lee was overwhelmed in Virginia in 1864.

What, then, would have been a more productive strategy? Any variation of the strategic defensive would be detrimental to the Confederacy's interest as long as Lincoln was intent on waging aggressive war. Lee might defeat Union general after Union general, as he did for two years, but as long as Lincoln was willing to send another army toward Richmond a few months later, attrition would eventually deplete Lee's resources until, in the end, the Northern army prevailed. The alternative route to Confederate strategic success would have been a more offensively minded strategy that would have taken advantage of early battlefield success. Such a strategy would undoubtedly have produced better results for the South, particularly during the first two years of the war, when the Confederacy possessed the appropriate resources to optimize its tactical success. An offensive strategy, however, was not without its critics. Lee's penchant for assuming the tactical and strategic offensive resulted in a disproportionate number of Confederate casualties. One prominent military historian goes so far as to state that Lee was too Napoleonic, in that "his passion for the strategy of annihilation and the climactic, decisive battle as its expression, destroyed in the end not the enemy armies, but the Army of Northern Virginia."[4] Lee, of course, would disagree. With its limited resources, the South could not wage a war of attrition against the superior North; and with the American president repeatedly dispatching armies to crush the Confederate army and secure the Southern capital, Southern casualties mounted at a rate which the Confederacy could not sustain. Only tactical victories on Northern soil would achieve strategic results and deter the North from prosecuting offensive war.

Nowhere was this more evident than in the immediate aftermath of the First Battle of Manassas/Bull Run on July 21, 1861. The first major battle of the Civil War ended in the rout of the Union army commanded by Major General Irwin McDowell with over 3,000 casualties. President Davis initially ordered a pursuit of the defeated army, but Confederate Generals Beauregard and Johnston begged off, citing fatigue and confusion. Thomas J. Jackson, whose stand on Henry House Hill earned him the sobriquet "Stonewall," also urged an immediate pursuit. "Give me ten thousand men and I will take Washington tomorrow," Jackson cried.[5] But there would be no pursuit. The Southern leadership failed to exploit their victory, in part because of the inadequacy of the Confederate logistical system to support a spirited pursuit after First Manassas. Regardless of the reason for the inaction, the South forfeited a splendid opportunity to destroy an entire enemy army and to march on its seat of government. Such possibilities seldom occur in modern warfare. If the truth be told, the Confederate army was as disorganized by its victory as the North was by its defeat. Still, the federal capital briefly lay within reach of the Confederate army, and never again would the South come as close to capturing Washington as on the evening of July 21, 1861.

In later years the Confederate president and his two senior commanders blamed each other for the failure to follow and crush the defeated Federals, but hindsight is always nonproductive. In reality, both Northern and Southern politicians and generals anticipated a short war in 1861. Davis, Johnston, and Beauregard were so enthralled with their victory that they felt that the war had been won after the initial engagement. Nearly 1,500 Union soldiers had been captured, as well as scores of artillery pieces and ammunition wagons. Surely the North would be willing to let "its warring sisters go." What the Confederate senior leadership failed to consider was the single-mindedness of Lincoln, who viewed First Manassas as little more than a temporary setback. Within days the president appointed Major General George B. McClellan to command the remnants of McDowell's defeated army and then directed him to prepare the army around Washington for a new campaign.

The Turning Point

The second period during which Confederate fortunes might have altered the outcome of the war occurred in the summer of 1862, when the South mounted two major counteroffensives into Kentucky and Maryland and a minor offensive against Corinth, Mississippi. Never was more at stake. Union advances were stalled along the border of the Confederacy, and Great Britain was seriously contemplating recognition of the South. Eager to announce the Emancipation Proclamation, Lincoln nonetheless shelved the document in late July, waiting for a major victory in the field. Moreover, Union morale sagged with each Confederate victory. If the South could win a significant victory on Northern soil, independence was at hand. Regrettably, Davis failed to coordinate the two principal invasions, though both hoped to achieve similar results: foreign recognition of the Confederacy and the allegiance of two critical border states. Late summer 1862 found both Braxton Bragg in east Tennessee and Robert E. Lee in northern Virginia poised to carry the war north. While Lee confronted John Pope near the old battlefield of Manassas/Bull Run, Confederate forces in Tennessee marched northward in an attempt to sever Union supply lines and reach the Ohio River. As Bragg told his veterans, "The enemy is before you and your banners are free. It is for you to decide whether our brothers and sisters of Tennessee and Kentucky shall remain bondmen and bondwomen of the Abolition tyrant or be restored to the freedom inherited from their fathers."[6] What the Army of Tennessee encountered as they proceeded north was the same ambivalence that Lee's Army of Northern Virginia met as it moved into Maryland. Neither Kentuckians nor Marylanders were predisposed to welcome an invading army, regardless of its origin.

In the West, the Southern invasion of Kentucky was a two-pronged affair, one column led by General Braxton Bragg, who commanded the Confederate forces in the vicinity of Chattanooga, and the other commanded by Major General E. Kirby Smith, a transplant from the Army of Northern Virginia, who now commanded the Department of East Tennessee. Rather than unite the two Confederate armies under a single commander, Davis anticipated that they would voluntarily cooperate in their joint endeavor. It was a critical mistake; neither commander could put aside his personal prejudices and ego. The invasion began well enough with Smith annihilating a Federal column near Richmond, Kentucky, just short of Lexington. He then seized Lexington and patiently waited for Bragg to join him. Bragg moved north from Chattanooga on a parallel course with Union General Don Carlos Buell. By late September the initial elements of the two Confederate armies were united. Buell, too, received reinforcements, and during the first week of October, the armies were on a collision course. They need not have been, for Bragg was already considering a withdrawal due to his disappointment that Kentuckians had not rallied to his cause. Before he could move, the opposing armies accidentally ran into each other at Perryville, Kentucky, on October 8. The resulting battle was a confused engagement with the Southerners having the numerical advantage earlier in the day, but the North assembling numerically superior forces as the battle continued into midafternoon. Though he incurred fewer casualties, 3,396 to 4,211 Union losses, Bragg lost his nerve and withdrew back into Tennessee.[7] A more aggressive commander, like Lee, would have seized the advantage and subjected the opposing army to an attack on its flank, but Bragg was no Lee. Refusing to subject his force to the type of climactic battle that Lee sought, Bragg withdrew southward. Never again would Confederate forces threaten Kentucky. That state, birthplace of both Lincoln and Davis, remained solidly in Union hands for the remainder of the war.

In the East, Confederate fortunes waned as rapidly as they did in Kentucky. Here, however, the stakes were higher, for Lee had a record of success. In command of the Army of Northern Virginia for only three months, Lee had performed miracles in Virginia. By any standards his achievements that summer were remarkable. Assigned command of the army when McClellan was within sight of the spires of Richmond, Lee had raised the siege in late June, then immediately moved north, where he crushed a second Union army near Manassas Junction on August 30. Without pausing to rest his tired army, Lee convinced President Davis to allow him to cross the Potomac and threaten Pennsylvania and Baltimore. At this stage in the war, Lee lacked the resources to attack Washington, D.C., which had been considerably strengthened by a series of fortifications and a garrison whose size exceeded Lee's entire army. Crossing the Potomac to the tune of "Maryland, My Maryland," the Army of Northern Virginia met a lukewarm populace. Then fate intervened. Having divided his army into five separate groups, Lee expected McClellan to hesitate until he consolidated his army. Outside Frederick, Maryland, three Union troops discovered a copy of Lee's orders which outlined the location of his dispersed forces. If he moved rapidly, McClellan could destroy Lee's army in detail. He failed to do so, and September 16 found the majority of Lee's army defending a line astride Antietam Creek outside Sharpsburg, Maryland. McClellan attacked the following day, and in the bloodiest single day in American history, Lee battled him to a standstill. With victory in his grasp, McClellan hesitated and refused to renew the assault, even though he had an entire corps in reserve. With no reserves, Lee could not have withstood a determined assault. Overly cautious and unwilling to risk losing a battle that had already cost him 13,000 casualties, McClellan did nothing. To make matters worse, he then allowed Lee to escape to Virginia. Why McClellan failed to attack when he outnumbered his adversary over two to one remains one of the great mysteries of the Civil War. With one blow he could have destroyed the principal Confederate army and ended the war. Because he failed to deliver the decisive blow, the war continued for two and a half years. Within two months, McClellan was gone, fired by a distraught president who could not get him to engage the enemy.

In retrospect, the summer and early fall of 1862 proved to be the high-water mark of the Confederacy. Never again would the South possess the resources to launch simultaneous invasions east and west of the Appalachian Mountains. And if the Confederate counteroffensives were the South's supreme moment, Antietam, not Gettysburg a year later, was the decisive campaign of the war. Lee certainly realized the significance of the 1862 invasion, which explains in part why the Confederate commander risked his army that was woefully overmatched by McClellan's Army of the Potomac. To achieve absolute victory, both tactically and strategically, he was willing to risk absolute defeat.[8] General James Longstreet, who commanded the center of Lee's line, also understood how decisive the battle had been. Twenty years after the war, he wrote, "At Sharpsburg was sprung the keystone of the arch upon which the Confederate cause rested."[9] Though Lee would try another invasion the following summer, never was the Confederacy as close to ultimate victory as it was that September day. To gain the victory that would ensure Southern independence, Lee put his faith in the Army of Northern Virginia and dared McClellan to stop him. The Army of the Potomac, not its commander, rose to the challenge, but "Little Mac" focused too much on winning the battle rather than on winning the war. Lee lived to fight another day, but time was clearly running out for Confederate dreams of independence.

The Summer of 1863

The next time the South had an opportunity for military success, and probably the final time, was the summer of 1863. By the third summer of the war, Lincoln had effectively mobilized the North's expanding economy. Time was clearly acting against the Confederacy. If the South were to prevail, it must be now. Sagging Union morale also dictated a bold stroke by Confederate arms. In the West the Confederates still held Vicksburg, and Grant seemed no closer to capturing the garrison there than he had been on three previous attempts. In Virginia, Lincoln and the North despaired when Lee crushed "Fighting Joe" Hooker's army at Chancellorsville in early May. "My God, my God, what will the country say?" asked Lincoln when he heard the news of yet another Union disaster at the hands of Lee. With growing dissent on the home front and increasing unrest in the cities over the high cost of war, Lincoln feared "the fire in the rear" that threatened his administration's prosecution of the war. Exacerbating the problem was the Enrollment Act of March 3, 1863, Congress's attempt to spur enlistment to offset the casualties incurred during two years of war. Frustration over the first wartime draft in American history would eventually lead to riots in New York City in July, weeks after the Federal army halted Lee's divisions at Gettysburg. In proposing his second Northern invasion, Lee reasoned that another victory over the Army of the Potomac, this time in Pennsylvania, was the most viable course of action available to the Confederacy. There were alternatives, however. Some proposed that Lee detach elements from his army and send them to the West, in the hope that they might raise the siege of Vicksburg. Others proposed that Lee be transferred to the Mississippi Theater and take command of the Confederacy's western armies. A quick victory outside Harrisburg or Baltimore, however, might deliver such a psychological blow to Northern morale that the Peace Democrats would gain political ascendancy and force the Lincoln administration into a negotiated settlement. In considering all available alternatives, Lee, a Virginian, chose the East, and on June 3, 1863, the lead elements of the Army of Northern Virginia started the trek north.

Neither Lee nor George Gordon Meade, newly appointed commander of the Army of the Potomac, ever intended to fight at Gettysburg, though both generals were searching for a climactic battle, Lee viewing battle as the surest means to destroy an enemy army, and Meade searching for an opportunity to drive the invaders back to Virginia soil. That the two armies collided at Gettysburg was mere happenstance. In selecting Gettysburg as the battleground, Lee had the battle he sought, but this time his options were quite limited. He won the first round when superior Confederate numbers forced Union troops through Gettysburg to a series of hills south of town on July 1. Now engaged in a severe battle, Lee attacked relentlessly the following day. Casualties were horrendous, but Meade held his ground. On July 3, with few reserves available and suffering from severe logistical shortages in Northern territory, Lee ordered a massive assault against the center of the Union line on Cemetery Ridge. Commanded by James Longstreet, but spearheaded by Major General George Pickett's all-Virginian division, the charge was doomed to fail. And fail it did, at a cost of nearly half the attacking force. As Pickett's survivors straggled back to their jumping-off point on Seminary Ridge, Lee realized that he had not only lost the battle, but that in all probability he had lost the war. He had suffered 28,000 casualties to Meade's 23,000 losses, but his army was irrevocably shattered in terms of losses among senior officers and junior commanders. Never again would the Army of Northern Virginia possess the capability of conducting sustained offensive operations. For all intents and purposes, Lee would remain on the defensive. On July 4, Independence Day, while Confederate General John C. Pemberton surrendered the garrison of Vicksburg to Grant, Lee prepared his army for the retreat back to Virginia. Like McClellan before him, Meade foolishly permitted him to withdraw the army to Southern soil. Another opportunity to destroy Lee had floundered on the back of a Union commander too cautious to strike a beaten adversary.

With nearly 70,000 killed, wounded, and missing at the twin disasters of Gettysburg and Vicksburg, the Confederacy had sustained a mortal blow. Criticism of the Davis administration increased exponentially with each Union victory. There was a brief respite in the West in mid-September when General Braxton Bragg achieved a great, albeit costly, victory at Chickamauga. Lincoln then appointed Grant commanding general of all his western armies. Joining the Union army at Chattanooga in late October, Grant immediately made provisions for a concentrated attack. By late November he was ready, and in but a few days of fighting, he raised the siege of Chattanooga and routed Bragg's army. The door was now open to the heart of the Confederacy. No nation could sustain the losses of Gettysburg, Vicksburg, and Chattanooga within a six-month period, and the Confederacy was no exception. The year 1863 would long be remembered as a bitter time for Southern arms. The residents of Vicksburg refused to celebrate Independence Day, the day their garrison surrendered, well into the twentieth century. Confederate military victory was now a forlorn hope. That the Confederacy survived eighteen more months of war was a tribute to the military genius of its foremost military commander, Robert E. Lee.

The Presidential Election of 1864

The final opportunity for the South to win its independence occurred in late 1864 as the presidential election loomed, but this time the Confederacy had little power to affect the outcome. Lincoln had been nominated for a second term by the Republican Party, but he realized his political fortunes were inexorably tied to the progress of Union armies in the field. And in mid-1864 the Federal armies were making little progress. In Virginia, Grant, now general-in-chief of all the Northern armies, was locked in a stalemate with Lee in the trenches of Petersburg, following the bloodiest campaign of the war, in which he had sustained 55,000 casualties. Casualties flowed into the nation's capital at a rate of 2,000 a day for the month since Grant had initiated his campaign against Lee. All Washington's cemeteries were filled, so Congress confiscated Robert E. Lee's home across the Potomac River at Arlington and used its grounds for a national military cemetery. Despite his losses, Grant remained undeterred and promised to fight it out on the Virginia line if it took all summer. Not only would it take all summer, but the fall and winter, and into the following spring. Under siege at Petersburg, Lee was still dangerous, but even he knew that it was only a matter of time before Grant could amass superior numbers and force a decision. Grant's inactivity was matched by William T. Sherman's slow advance toward Atlanta. While Grant lay stalemated at Petersburg, the North's principal Western army, under command of Sherman, inched its way along a 100-mile trek from Chattanooga to Atlanta. By late August, Sherman was still outside Georgia's future capital, but the Northern press was calling for action to offset the tremendous loss of life that Confederate arms had inflicted on the North since the commencement of the campaigns in early May.

As Lincoln awaited word of a Union victory to give momentum for his reelection, his spirits dampened. Opposing him was George McClellan, whom the Democrats had nominated as a war hero and a peace candidate amid cries that the war was an abject failure. Prone to periods of self-doubt and deep reflection, Lincoln fully expected he would lose the November election, and so he prepared to return home to Springfield, Illinois. Not only did he face growing opposition from the Peace Democrats, but he also encountered increasing turmoil within the ranks of his own party. By 1864, Radical Republicans had clearly drawn the line in the sand against the president's lenient policy toward reconstruction of the rebellious states. On August 23, one week before the Democratic Party convention convened in Chicago, Lincoln asked his cabinet to endorse a memorandum that stated in part, "It seems exceeding probable that this Administration will not be reelected. Then it will be my duty to so cooperate with the President-elect as to save the Union between the election and the inauguration."[10]

Lincoln need not have worried. To his rescue sailed Admiral David G. Farragut, conqueror of New Orleans in April 1862. At the end of the first week in August, Farragut sailed his fleet into Mobile Bay, Alabama, and closed the last port on the Gulf Coast. Then the army had its turn in the person of "Uncle Billy" Sherman. Following a week of costly battles in which Sherman inflicted twice as many casualties as his own troops suffered on General John B. Hood's Army of Tennessee, Hood abandoned Atlanta, and the city capitulated to Sherman on September 2. Church bells rang throughout the North, and for the first time all summer, Lincoln was buoyed by news from the front. In the ensuing election, he crushed McClellan in the Electoral College, though New Jersey, Delaware, and Kentucky were won by the Democrats. Of the popular votes, Lincoln accrued 2,203,831 votes to McClellan's 1,797,019, testament to the increasing dissatisfaction with Lincoln's management of the war.[11] For President Lincoln the election was vindication of his efforts to bring the war to a speedy conclusion. And with his victory the last hope for Southern independence vanished. Lincoln would prosecute the war to its finale.

In Retrospect

War would continue for six more months, but Lincoln's election ensured the president would stay the course. Could the outcome have been different? It is difficult to say, but clearly other outcomes were possible if different decisions had been made at critical points during the conflict.

After First Manassas/Bull Run, both sides misjudged the nature of the war, and neither fully comprehended that a short war was not likely because the war aims of North and South were diametrically opposed and no compromise was possible. Lincoln could not preserve the Union if the Confederacy was independent, and the South could not have persevered if the North remained strong. This misunderstanding of the nature of the conflict helps explain why the South failed to follow up its initial victory on the battlefield. The strategic situation west of the Appalachian Mountains presents a different problem. As stated earlier in this chapter, the South lost the war in the West long before Lee surrendered at Appomattox. Any discussion of contingency history must take into account that though the war was lost in the Western Theater, it could not have been won in the Mississippi River Valley without a similar victory in Virginia. Here Lee had been correct. The South might lose the war in the West, but it could only win the war in the East. Though twentieth-century critics would assail him for his penchant to constantly attack the Army of the Potomac, Lee believed that decisive battle was the most efficient means to destroy the enemy's army. Only with the destruction of the enemy army and the accompanying degradation of Northern morale could he march on Washington and force a decision in the South's favor. Lee's inability to convert tactical success into strategic triumph floundered on a variety of factors, what Prussian theorist Karl von Clausewitz would call "the fog of war." Still, Lee persisted because he understood that time was running out for the South. This course of action found its best expression in Lee's ill-fated invasions of Maryland in 1862 and Pennsylvania in 1863. Victories on the North's own soil could have proven to be the catalyst in undermining public support for Lincoln's administration.

Confederate resources and military talent were spread too thin across the spectrum of conflict to counter an aggressive enemy with vastly superior resources. It took Lincoln close to two years to mobilize the North's vast reserves of manpower and the region's industrial capability. For the Confederacy to take its place among the world's sovereign nations, Davis and his generals stood their best chance to secure their independence during the first two years of the war. By 1863 the North's military resources were probably too powerful, even if Lee had defeated Meade at Gettysburg. Unless he totally destroyed the Army of the Potomac in the process—an unlikely prospect, considering the disparity in forces—he did not possess sufficient strength to capture the federal capital. A year earlier was a different story, but then a copy of the lost order inexplicably found its way into McClellan's hands. Had it not, Lee's success in Maryland would have been greatly enhanced. Thus September 17, 1862, not July 3, 1863, was the true turning point of the war. Along the banks of the Antietam, not on the ridges south of Gettysburg, lay the real high-water mark of the Confederacy.

Notes

1. Lee's farewell order is in the Primary Documents section of this book.

2. James McPherson, *Battle Cry of Freedom* (New York: Oxford University Press, 1988), 858. McPherson identifies four periods when the South might have reversed the tide of the war: the summer of 1862, when the Confederates launched two counteroffensives into Maryland and Kentucky; the fall of 1862, when Union victories at Perryville and Antietam threw back the South's offensives; the summer of 1863, when Gettysburg, Vicksburg, and Chattanooga turned the tide of war irrevocably in the North's favor; and the summer of 1864, when excessive Northern casualties threatened Lincoln's bid for reelection.

3. Shelby Foote, *The Civil War: A Narrative,* vol. 1 (New York: Random House, 1958), 55.

4. Russell Weigley, *The American Way of War* (New York: Macmillan, 1973), 127.

5. Quoted in James I. Robertson, Jr., *Stonewall Jackson: The Man, the Soldier, the Legend* (New York: Macmillan, 1997), 269.

6. Quoted in Foote, *The Civil War,* 584.

7. Casualty figures from Russell Weigley, *A Great Civil War* (Bloomington: Indiana University Press, 2000), 159.

8. Bruce Catton posits this thesis in *Terrible Swift Sword* (New York: Doubleday, 1963), 452.

9. Quoted in James McPherson, *Crossroads of Freedom: Antietam* (New York: Oxford University Press, 2002), 156.

10. Allan Nevins, *The War for the Union: The Organized War to Victory 1864–1865* (New York: Scribner's, 1971), 92–93.

11. Vote totals are from Foote, *The Civil War: A Narrative,* vol. 3 (New York: Random House, 1974), 625.

CHAPTER 5

ANATOMY OF DEFEAT:
WHY LEE LOST THE
BATTLE OF GETTYSBURG

More books have been written on the Civil War than on any other war in American history, and more books have been written on the Battle of Gettysburg than on any other battle in that war. Gettysburg was the greatest battle ever fought on the North American continent. The battle marked the apogee of Lee's second invasion of the North, and it was the South's last major offensive into Union territory. At no time in the war were Confederate hopes raised as high as they were in the summer of 1863, when the Army of Northern Virginia crossed the Potomac River and set its sights on the Northern cities of Harrisburg, Baltimore, and Washington, D.C. If Lee could win a major victory on Union soil and then exploit that victory, the war might be over. Such were the stakes when two armies collided west of Gettysburg, Pennsylvania, during the first three days in July 1863. Over the course of the battle 165,000 men engaged in a death struggle that determined the course of the Civil War. When it was over, nearly 51,000 of these soldiers were killed, wounded, or missing. Of the total 11,000 were killed or mortally wounded; another 29,000 were wounded and survived, often to fight in subsequent campaigns. To put the casualties in perspective, losses at Gettysburg were ten times the number of American casualties on D-Day, June 6, 1944.[1] To many historians Gettysburg was the "high-water mark of the Confederacy." To others Gettysburg was an unnecessary battle that resulted from one man's penchant with offensive warfare, an obsession that bled the South white in terms of manpower and resources. What was evident even to contemporary observers was that Gettysburg represented not only a turning point of the war but also an irreversible decline in the fortunes of Lee's Army of Northern Virginia. Never again would the South enter a battle so contemptuous of its enemy, and never again would Lee so intimidate his adversary as he had on numerous battlefields prior to the campaign of Gettysburg. This chapter explains why Robert E. Lee lost the most crucial battle and determines the factors that contributed so mightily to the Confederate defeat.

Opening the Campaign

In early June 1863, Lee assembled his army for his most ambitious campaign of the war. In other theaters, Southern fortunes collapsed under the repeated hammering of Union armies and navies. In the Mississippi River Valley, U. S. Grant laid siege to Vicksburg, the last Confederate city of any significance along the South's principal internal waterway. The U.S. Navy had seized virtually all Confederate ports and had blockaded the entire coastline from Brownsville, Texas, to the Potomac River. Only in Virginia had the South experienced martial success. In May 1863 Lee and Stonewall Jackson had defeated the Army of the Potomac at Chancellorsville. With his strategic options narrowing and with a desire to maintain the momentum of his recent victory, Lee proposed to invade the North a second time in as many years, in the hope that a victory on Northern soil would compel Lincoln to acknowledge Southern independence and to negotiate an end to the war. In developing his plan, Lee realized he could not stay in Virginia and simply wait for Lincoln to send another army to capture Richmond. His men were hungry, the surrounding countryside offered little forage for his horses, and he was convinced that the Army of Northern Virginia possessed an élan that would lead it to victory. Thus he would take the war to Pennsylvania, where ample supplies existed and where he hoped "to turn back the tide of war that is now pressing South."[2]

President Jefferson Davis acquiesced in Lee's plan and reinforced him with as many troops as he could spare. As Lee gathered his army around Culpeper Courthouse, Virginia, his forces were flush with victory and confident of their success in the ensuing campaign. Numbering 75,000, the Army of Northern Virginia was the largest host that Lee had commanded since his first campaign against George B. McClellan at the gates of Richmond in June 1862. To command such a sizable force, Lee needed experienced commanders but,regrettably, few were available. Commanding the 1st Corps was James Longstreet, Lee's second in command and the

officer whom Lee referred to as "my old war horse." The 2nd Corps was
now under Richard S. Ewell, who had served as Jackson's second in com-
mand in the Valley Campaign the preceding year. The 3rd Corps now
belonged to Ambrose Powell Hill, a superb division commander who, like
Ewell, had never exercised corps-level command. The Army of Northern
Virginia, then, consisted of three infantry corps, commanded by Longstreet,
Ewell, and Hill, and a separate cavalry corps under the incomparable leader
J.E.B. Stuart. Missing from Lee's command structure was Stonewall
Jackson, who had succumbed to pneumonia resulting from wounds incurred at Chancellorsville. To compensate for the loss of his most aggres-
sive subordinate, Lee had been forced to divide Jackson's old corps into
two smaller corps, now commanded by Ewell and Hill.

Opposing Lee was Major General "Fighting Joe" Hooker, commanding the Army of the Potomac. The Northern army was a polyglot force who
had lost faith in its leadership, but not in themselves. The Army of the
Potomac was divided into seven infantry corps and a cavalry corps. Its best
corps commanders were John Reynolds, Winfield Scott Hancock, and
George Gordon Meade, all veterans of numerous campaigns against Lee
and his army. In total the Northern force numbered nearly 90,000 soldiers.
Such was how matters stood when the lead elements of Lee's army slipped
across the Potomac River into Maryland on June 15.

As the Army of Northern Virginia advanced into Pennsylvania,
Hooker's army dallied. Never satisfied with the command relationship
between the War Department and his headquarters, Hooker moved slowly,
always keeping his army between Lee's force and the federal capital. By
late June, Lee's forward elements were in the vicinity of Harrisburg. Hill
and Longstreet were farther west, near Chambersburg, Pennsylvania. Traveling in dispersed formations in order to facilitate the logistical support
of his army, Lee intended to concentrate before falling upon Hooker's force.
Unfortunately, Lee did not know the location of the Army of the Potomac,
nor did he realize that Hooker was no longer in command. On June 28,
Lincoln relieved Hooker of command and appointed George Gordon
Meade in his stead. Meade, a Pennsylvanian who had commanded the
army's 5th Corps, did not desire army-level command. Lincoln had originally offered command to John Reynolds, but Reynolds politely declined.
Lincoln and Secretary of War Edwin Stanton next turned to Meade. Meade
accepted command only after being ordered to do so. Lee's ignorance of
these events was the result of the absence of Jeb Stuart, whose principal

mission was to keep Lee informed of the Army of the Potomac's northward advance. Leaving only a small force to accompany Lee, Stuart took the remainder of his cavalry on a raid deep into enemy territory. When Hooker and then Meade pursued Lee, they inadvertently positioned their force between Stuart and Lee. Now Lee was moving blind, with no idea that the Army of the Potomac was close by. When a spy informed Longstreet that the Union army was only a day's march away, Lee immediately notified his corps commanders to concentrate the army in the vicinity of Chambersburg and Gettysburg, a crossroads town that stood at the juncture of seven roads that reached toward Harrisburg, York, Baltimore, and Taneytown, Maryland. On June 30, Union cavalry under command of Brigadier General John Buford occupied Gettysburg and manned the ridges west of town, where they reported the advance of A. P. Hill's corps. The ensuing battle was a phased engagement that neither commander intended to fight; yet it was a battle that neither commander intended to avoid.

The First Day: July 1, 1863

Contrary to popular belief, the Battle of Gettysburg did not begin with a clash over shoes. Any shoes that had been stored in Gettysburg would have been confiscated days earlier when Ewell's corps had moved through the town enroute to Harrisburg. In every sense, however, the battle began as a meeting engagement, a military term used to describe a situation where neither army knew the precise location of the other. As Lee prepared to concentrate his army west of Gettysburg, he cautioned his officers to avoid a general engagement until the concentration was complete. Hill's men desired to explore Gettysburg and requested permission to do so. Hill and Lee approved their request, provided that they not become decisively engaged. As Hill's lead divisions approached Gettysburg, they ran smack into Buford's cavalrymen strung out along McPherson's Ridge, astride a Lutheran seminary one mile west of town. Buford sought to delay the Confederates until Reynolds and Meade brought the remainder of the army from the south. Located in Cashtown, seven miles west of Gettysburg, was Hill's headquarters. When riders brought back word that his infantry was heavily engaged with Buford's cavalry, he did nothing, and let the battle get out of hand. More Confederate divisions joined the fight, spilling over the flanks of the exposed Northerners. Reynolds finally arrived on the scene around 9 A.M. with his 1st Corps and was promptly killed by a Southern sharpshooter. Another Union corps joined the fight and defended a series of hills north of town.

Lee, irate that a battle had commenced without his approval, ordered Hill to break off the engagement. Just then Ewell's 2nd Corps arrived from the north, and Lee sensed an opportunity. If, with the superior numbers he now possessed, he could crush the two Union corps, the numerical odds would be about even. He thus ordered Hill and Ewell to continue the attack, and by midafternoon Lee's men had driven the Northerners through the town. Victory seemed to be in his grasp, but Union corps were arriving on the battlefield at a faster rate than Lee could reinforce. Under Winfield Scott Hancock's cool direction, the Army of the Potomac occupied a series of hills and ridges south of Gettysburg. The key to the Union line was Cemetery Hill, sitting on the north of the defensive positions. Whoever held it could command the surrounding countryside.

Now it was Ewell's turn to fail to demonstrate initiative. Ecstatic that his army had crushed two Union corps, Lee ordered Ewell to take Cemetery Hill "if practicable." In such a situation, Stonewall Jackson would have instantly attacked. His replacement Ewell hesitated, citing the fatigue of his men and the uncertainty of the situation. Thus Ewell lost a splendid opportunity to capture what proved to be the most decisive terrain on the battlefield. Hancock fortified the hill and defeated a halfhearted Confederate attack. By midnight Meade had arrived on the field with the bulk of the Union army, and both sides prepared for the next day's fighting. By any standard, the first day of the battle had been a Confederate victory. Two Union corps, Reynolds's 1st and Howard's 11th, had been routed and driven through Gettysburg. Union casualties had been heavy: nearly 9,500, to the Confederates' 6,500. The initiative belonged solidly in Lee's corner, and he intended to use it. "If Meade is on those hills tomorrow, I intend to attack him," Lee told Longstreet. Longstreet argued against such a move and suggested that Lee pull back the army, find suitable terrain, and wait until Meade attacked him. Lee listened patiently, but rejected his advice.

The Second Day: July 2, 1863

If July 1 was an improvised battle, July 2 was more orchestrated. Still unsure of the exact Union strength because Stuart had not yet arrived, Lee planned a double envelopment. Ewell was to renew his attack against the northern portion of the Union line on Culp's Hill and Cemetery Hill, while Longstreet simultaneously delivered the main attack on the Confederate right against two round-topped hills, suitably named Big Round Top and Little Round Top. Here again the absence of Stuart impeded the Confederate attack, for unbeknownst to Lee, the entire Union army had arrived on the field. Nor was Little Round Top unoccupied, although the defending force was woefully inadequate. Longstreet wasted two hours getting his men in attack formation, and it was not until late afternoon that he struck. In his path stood Major General Daniel Sickles's 3rd Corps. Dissatisfied with the position Meade had assigned him on the southern end of Cemetery Ridge and Little Round Top, Sickles moved to a more exposed position that placed him directly in the path of Longstreet's attack. Longstreet hit Sickles hard and decimated his corps in two hours of savage fighting. Longstreet then swung around the Union left flank, leaving the Peach Orchard, the Wheatfield, and the Devil's Den littered with Union and Confederate dead. Key leaders were struck down, including John Bell Hood, Longstreet's finest division commander, and William Barksdale, one of his most talented brigade commanders.

By 5:30 the Confederate tide surged toward Little Round Top, now occupied by a Union brigade of 2500 men. One of the Union regimental commanders was Joshua Lawrence Chamberlain, commanding the 20th Maine. Prior to the war he had been a professor of rhetoric at Maine's Bowdoin College. Chamberlain's orders were to hold Little Round Top at "all hazards." He did just that, thwarting several Confederate attacks and earning the Medal of Honor in the process. At times the combat was so intense that Chamberlain remembered "at times I saw around me more of the enemy than my own men; gaps opening, swallowing, closing again; squads of stalwart men who had cut their way through us, disappearing as if translated."[3] Heavily outnumbered and without ammunition, Chamberlain ordered his men to fix bayonets and attack the enemy. By early evening the battle on Little Round Top was over. Union casualties were heavy, but the ground was held. For all his efforts, Longstreet's attack had failed. His corps suffered nearly 8,000 casualties, "the finest day's fighting my corps had ever seen," he told Lee. Fine day or not, the attack had failed to carry the heights. On the other end of the Confederate line, Ewell finally attacked, hours behind schedule, and like Longstreet his attack failed, although his men seized the forward positions at the base of Culp's Hill.

Day two of the fighting had hardly produced the results Lee desired, but he was not entirely dissatisfied. After his initial success on July 1, Lee had hoped to drive Meade from the high ground He had expended an extraordinary amount of capital for little apparent gain. Still, he had stretched the Union line and destroyed a third Union corps. Moreover, Confederate infantry had actually reached the summit of Cemetery Ridge before a determined Union counterattack had plugged the gap. One more push might be all that was needed. Again Longstreet urged Lee to abandon the field and to maneuver the army between Meade and Washington, to force Meade to be the aggressor. Again Lee refused. Gettysburg was to be the decisive battlefield. Any withdrawal would demoralize the army, and Lee was unwilling to surrender the initiative that he had seized at such a high human cost. As he gazed over the battlefield, he realized that Meade was now stronger than he had been in the morning, and Lee was definitely weaker. Yet Lee still had one card to play, for George Pickett's all-Virginia division from Longstreet's corps had finally reached the field and taken position behind the center of Lee's line on Seminary Ridge. Tomorrow, Lee intended to make one last attempt to defeat the Army of the Potomac. In considering his options, Robert E. Lee set the stage for the most famous infantry charge in American history.

The Third Day: July 3, 1863

To any modern observer of the Gettysburg battlefield, Lee's attack across nearly a mile of open ground seems sheer lunacy. One ponders what was going on in his head for him to order 12,000 men to advance across open fields in the face of Union artillery and infantry fire. Longstreet, his most valued subordinate, told Lee in no uncertain terms that 15,000 men could not take the Union position on Cemetery Ridge. Yet Lee persisted, because he believed he had few alternatives. His original plan was to attack both flanks of the Union line as he had done the preceding day, if for no reason other than that those attacks, particularly Longstreet's, had almost succeeded. Two things prevented him from replicating that attack on July 3. In Ewell's front, the Union army attacked and threw back the Confederate forces that had captured the slopes of Culp's Hill. And in the south, Longstreet informed his commander that his corps "was fought out." Two of his divisions, McLaw's and Hood's, had sustained horrific casualties and were now incapable of sustained offensive operations. Consequently, Lee turned to Pickett, his only reserve, to be the centerpiece of an attack against the Union center.

In preparing for battle, Lee followed a time-proven principle that had resulted in repeated success the preceding year. He would bring the army to battle, create the conditions for success, then leave the execution of the battle to his corps commanders. Even during the intense struggle on July 2, the Confederate commander "only sent one message and only received one report," according to the British observer Arthur Fremantle.[4] Such an attitude made Lee appear removed from the conduct of the battle, but the formula had succeeded against McClellan, Pope, Burnside, and Hooker. The critical difference at Gettysburg was the absence of Jackson, who in tandem with the hard-hitting Longstreet had produced victories at Richmond, Second Manassas, Fredericksburg, and Chancellorsville. With complete confidence in the morale and strength of his men, Lee prepared to assault the Union center. Unfortunately for him, Meade saw it coming, telling the commander on Cemetery Ridge on the evening of July 2, "If Lee attacks tomorrow, it will be on your front."[5]

What, then, did Lee do to ensure the success of his assault? First, he gathered all available troops for the attack, Pickett's division and two divisions from Hill's corps, who had not seen action since the first day of the battle. The total approached 12,000 officers and men. Next, he directed Stuart to launch a simultaneous attack against the rear of the Union line. Stuart's attack was subsequently intercepted by Union cavalrymen under the command of David Gregg and George A. Custer and played no important part in the battle. Then, he placed Longstreet, his most seasoned commander, in charge of the assault. Finally, he allocated nearly 175 artillery guns to support the attack. As commander on the ground, Longstreet was directed to initiate the attack when he deemed appropriate.

At approximately 1 P.M. on July 3, Longstreet's guns erupted across the entire front. Union artillery answered the Confederate cannonade, producing the largest artillery duel ever heard on the North American continent. After two hours of bombardment, Union commanders slackened their fire, determined to conserve ammunition for the inevitable infantry assault. At approximately three o'clock, Pickett approached

Longstreet and requested permission to initiate the attack. Longstreet, convinced the assault would fail, was unable to give the order verbally. He merely nodded his assent, and Pickett's men commenced the attack. "Up, men, and to your posts! Don't forget today that you are from Old Virginia," he summoned his troops.[6] To Pickett's left were Pettigrew's and Trimble's divisions from Hill's corps.

As the Confederate attack advanced toward Hancock's corps on Cemetery Ridge, the assaulting force immediately came under intense artillery fire. Behind a stone wall on Cemetery Ridge, one Union soldier observed "a rising tide of armed men rolling towards us in steel crested billows." Another remarked, "It was a Glorious Sight to see, Rebels though they were." The Rebels marched as "though upon Parade, and were confident of carrying all before them."[7] The Confederates reached the Emmitsburg Pike, only 150 yards in front of the Union line, when the Union force stood and delivered a devastating volley into their ranks. Still the Southern tide surged forward, but in vain. Of the entire force, scarcely a few hundred reached the crest of Cemetery Ridge, and these immediately became casualties. "Pickett's Charge" was over almost as fast as it began. Of the 12,000 men who had initiated the attack, nearly 6,500 had fallen. As the survivors streamed back toward Seminary Ridge, Lee rode forward to console his defeated troops. "It is all my fault," he said repeatedly. There was little time to commiserate. Both Lee and Longstreet prepared for a counterattack that never came. Meade was content to win the battle and be the first Union commander to best Lee in a major engagement.

The Tally Sheet

On Saturday, July 4, the nation's eighty-seventh anniversary of independence, the Army of Northern Virginia and the Army of the Potomac licked their collective wounds. A heavy rain cleansed the battlefield where nearly a third of the combatants had fallen. For reasons that Lincoln never understood, Meade failed to deliver the coup de grâce to Lee's battered army, and his dilatory pursuit allowed Lee to escape into Virginia ten days later. The primary reasons Meade did not attack Lee lay in the disruption of his own command structure and the losses the Army of the Potomac had sustained. According to the official records, Union casualties over the three days numbered 23,049, including 3,155 killed, 14,529 wounded, and 5,365 missing or captured.[8] The exact number of Confederate casualties is unknown, but what is known is that the number of casualties made even the most hardened veteran shudder. Depending on which source you consult, Lee's losses were anywhere between 23,000 and 28,000. Lee's foremost biographer, Douglas S. Freeman, computed Confederate losses at 2,592 killed, 12,709 wounded, and 5,150 missing or captured. This seems exceedingly low, given the nature of the battle, but when the toll of prisoners and an additional 5000 casualties are added to take into account the march north to Gettysburg and the retreat to Virginia, Lee lost at least 28,000 men in the month that he remained north of the Potomac. To make matters worse, many of Lee's wounded were either captured by pursuing Union soldiers or died of wounds. Moreover, the campaign had taken a severe toll on the Confederate high command. Six general officers had been killed or mortally wounded, three had been captured, and eight had been wounded. The Army of Northern Virginia had entered Pennsylvania with fifty-two officers above the rank of colonel; nearly one-third became casualties. The killed and wounded included every brigade commander in Pickett's division, as well as William Barksdale, Dorsey Pender, Johnston Pettigrew, and Paul Semmes, all of whom had performed brilliantly in the army's history.[9] All the field-grade officers in Pickett's 5,000-man division were casualties except one. The most seriously wounded of the Confederate high command were cavalryman Wade Hampton and division commander John Bell Hood, who one day would command the Army of Tennessee. Both would eventually recover from their wounds, but like so many others, they would not return to the army for several months. Small wonder that Lee praised God when the army finally reached Virginia on July 13 and 14.

The recent battle also took a personal toll on Lee. Though he would claim the campaign achieved some of its objectives—namely, relieving the Virginia countryside from the ravages of war, albeit temporarily—Lee had failed utterly to defeat the Union army. Moreover, the great number of casualties among battle captains proved an irreversible loss to the Army of Northern Virginia. On August 8, Lee wrote a pensive letter to Davis and tendered his resignation. "I cannot even accomplish what I myself desire," he told the president. Perhaps Davis ought to appoint a younger man who had the physical stamina necessary to see the battlefield and to exercise effective command. Davis would have none of it, responding three days later and informing Lee that "to ask me to substitute you by some one in my judgment more fit to command, or would possess more of the confidence of the army, or of the reflecting men of the country, is to demand an impossibility."[10] Lee remained in command. Fortunately, Meade did not initiate another sustained campaign against Lee during the remainder of the season that lasted until late October. By the time Grant assumed command of all Union armies and launched the Overland Campaign in May 1864, Lee and his army had had time to recover, but never again were they capable of conducting the swift offensive campaigns that had given the army its character.

Assessment

Any postmortem of the Confederate disaster at the Battle of Gettysburg must begin with Lee himself. He had staked everything on a campaign to destroy the Union army, and he clearly lost the bet. The three-day battle was undoubtedly the Southern commander's worst-fought engagement of the entire war. Only once before had he commanded an army as large as he did at Gettysburg—that was against McClellan on the peninsula before Richmond the previous year—and there, too,he had expended countless thousands of lives in a series of relentless attacks against an enemy defending well-fortified positions. In both cases Lee sacrificed a huge proportion of his army, nearly 25 percent against McClellan, and closer to 35 percent against Meade. The Confederacy could not sustain such casualties and prosecute the war. Shelby Foote, the renowned Southern historian, said Gettysburg was the price the South paid for having Robert E. Lee.[11] He was correct, because Lee took chances on that field that he would not have taken on other battlefields because he realized that time was working against the Confederacy, and that unless he drove Meade from those ridges, the battle, as well as the war, was lost. Thus he attacked for three consecutive days, even though his chances of success on July 3 were slim. With the exception of July 1, Lee was clearly outgeneraled by Meade. In an army that prided itself on rapid execution and maneuverability, the Army of Northern Virginia slipped back a year, and for that Lee must bear the lion's share of responsibility. With a new team of corps commanders on board, he never adjusted his leadership style to take into account that Ewell and Hill were new to their jobs and required more intense supervision than had Longstreet and Stonewall Jackson in previous campaigns. When Ewell and Hill made catastrophic errors in judgment on the first day of the battle, Lee did not take a decisive role in redirecting their efforts. Consequently, he forfeited the tactical advantage he possessed on July 1, when the Army of Northern Virginia clearly outnumbered the Army of the Potomac that was arriving only piecemeal at the battlefield. Lee then allowed Meade adequate time to establish highly defensible fortifications on the ridges and hills south of the town. Instead of the firm hand that guided his army in previous campaigns, at Gettysburg, Lee allowed his new commanders too much discretion and then restricted the latitude of his most trusted subordinate, James Longstreet. All in all, it was a dismal performance in contrast to his tactical brilliance at Chancellorsville in early May.

The second component of the Confederate defeat lay with Lee's major subordinate commanders. Each of the corps-level commanders failed his chief in turn. Jeb Stuart, commanding the cavalry corps, proved the most disappointing. Still bristling at having been surprised at Brandy Station in early June, Stuart sought to regain his prestige by conducting a raid deep into enemy country. In so doing, he neglected his primary responsibility of providing Lee with intelligence on the movement and the disposition of the enemy army. In essence, Lee moved into Pennsylvania blind to the enemy's intentions and the actual disposition of Union forces. When the two armies stumbled into contact west of Gettysburg, Lee initiated the engagement totally oblivious to the strength of the enemy. Here Stuart must accept a huge portion of the blame, though Lee, who had additional cavalry at his disposal, must bear his share of the responsibility. When Stuart finally arrived in the early evening of July 2, the battle had really been decided, and all that remained was a desperate move that resulted in Pickett's ill-advised attack on July 3. Like Stuart, corps commanders A. P. Hill and Richard Ewell failed miserably in the campaign. Hill effectively lost control of his divisions on July 1 when Lee held the numerical advantage over the Union forces. Instead of carefully orchestrating the developing battle, Hill did nothing and allowed his division commanders to fight the battle on their own terms. Consequently, the Confederates incurred excessive casualties against a numerically inferior force. Only the timely arrival of Ewell's corps on the enemy's exposed flank permitted the Confederates to reap a tactical success. On days two and three of the battle, Hill again did nothing of consequence, although two of his divisions participated in the final assault against the Union line on Cemetery Ridge on July 3. What is instructive about what history has come to call Pickett's

Charge is that two of the three divisions that participated in the attack were from Hill's corps, but Hill was not entrusted to command them. With respect to Ewell, the commander of the 2nd Corps of the Army of Northern Virginia performed brilliantly in the opening stages of the Gettysburg Campaign, and then faltered badly on the afternoon of July 1. Having routed an entire corps of the Army of the Potomac and driven the enemy army through the town, Ewell uncharacteristically hesitated and failed to dislodge the enemy from Cemetery Hill, which both he and Hancock recognized as decisive terrain. Whether he could have taken and held this critical piece of terrain remains highly debatable, but Ewell did not even try. Thus he missed a golden opportunity that comes only once in any battle. Had he dislodged the enemy, Meade would have been unable to occupy the most defensible terrain in the area, and he would have been forced either to attack Lee or to find more suitable terrain on which to prepare his defenses. Finally, Longstreet, Lee's old "war horse," performed lethargically during the last two days of the battle. Adamantly opposed to pursuing an offensive tactical battle, he dallied too long in his attack against the Union left on July 2, and his delay permitted Meade sufficient time to concentrate his forces to meet the Confederate onslaught. When he finally attacked, Longstreet struck as hard as he ever did, but in battle, time is an element that frequently cannot be regained. When Lee directed Longstreet to command the grand assault against Meade's center the following day, the I Corps commander seemed removed from the execution of the battle, not even able to give the verbal order to initiate the attack.

There is a final factor contributing to Lee's defeat, one that is constantly overlooked, and that is Meade's and the Army of the Potomac's superior performance during the battle. If the South lost Gettysburg, Meade and his army definitely won it. In command only four days when the battle began, Meade made the proper decisions throughout the climactic battle. He directed Major General John Reynolds, his best corps commander, to take charge of three corps of the army and to develop the battle before he committed the remainder of the Army of the Potomac. When Reynolds was killed, Meade sent Winfield Scott Hancock to supervise the battle and to determine if Gettysburg was the right place to engage Lee. When Hancock responded in the affirmative, Meade brought the army to Gettysburg and personally supervised its disposition. In contrast to Lee, who dealt with his corps commanders separately, Meade hosted several councils of war that ensured that each major Union commander clearly understood Meade's intent. When Dan Sickles disobeyed orders and moved his corps forward, thus opening the Union army for a potential envelopment, Meade personally moved forward to order Sickles return to the original line. Longstreet's attack on July 2 prevented Sickles from returning, but Meade then directed reinforcements forward to strengthen Sickles's exposed line and repositioned his own forces to points on the field where Confederate attacks endangered the Union line. More important, Meade was able to decipher Lee's intentions, as is evinced by his anticipation of the location of the Confederate attack on July 3. Meade's only error in the campaign was not following up his tactical success and permitting Lee's army to escape to Virginia. In the final analysis, Meade was content to win the battle, and consequently he forfeited a splendid opportunity to win the war. But for a commander in charge of an army for less than a week, Meade's performance at Gettysburg was spectacular to say the least.

When all was said and done, the South never recovered from losing Gettysburg. Was it worth the cost for the Confederacy to invade the North? In retrospect it was not, but to Robert E. Lee in 1863, Gettysburg was worth the attempt. Perhaps the South's greatest opportunity to win the Civil War occurred in the fall of 1862, when foreign recognition of the Confederacy was a distinct possibility, but the summer of 1863 was the last feasible opportunity to reverse the tide of Union victories in the West and to secure Southern independence. Lee staked all in invading the North a second time, and he rolled the dice at Gettysburg in a final attempt to destroy the Army of the Potomac and to force a negotiated settlement of the war. That he failed was the result of failures in the Confederate high command and the transformation of the Army of the Potomac into a disciplined fighting force under a new commander who rose to the occasion and fought his finest campaign of the Civil War.

Notes

1. James McPherson, *Hallowed Ground: A Walk at Gettysburg* (New York: Crown, 2003), 21.

2. Lee, quoted in Stephen W. Sears, *Gettysburg* (Boston: Houghton Mifflin, 2003), 16.

3. See Chamberlain's report of the battle in the Primary Documents section of this book.

4. Freemantle, quoted in Noah Andre Trudeau, *Gettysburg: A Testing of Courage* (New York: HarperCollins, 2002), 411.

5. Sears, *Gettysburg*, 345.

6. Pickett, quoted in Geoffrey C. Ward, Ric Burns, and Ken Burns, *The Civil War: An Illustrated History* (New York: Alfred A. Knopf, 1990), 228.

7. Quoted in Jeffry D. Wert, *Gettysburg: Day Three* (New York: Simon and Schuster, 2001), 194–195.

8. *Official Records of the War of the Rebellion*, vol. 27, pt. 1, 187.

9. For a list of casualties in Lee's army and the price of Gettysburg, see Douglas S. Freeman, *Lee's Lieutenants*, vol. 3 (New York: Scribner's, 1944), 190–205.

10. Quoted in David S. Heidler and Jeanne T. Heidler, eds., *Encyclopedia of the American Civil War* (New York: W.W. Norton, 2000), 2358.

11. Ward, Burns, and Burns, *The Civil War: An Illustrated History*, 268.

CHAPTER 6

CONSEQUENCES OF CIVIL WAR:
A CONTEMPORARY PERSPECTIVE

In his Pulitzer Prize-winning account of the Civil War, James McPherson notes that arguments about the "consequences of the Civil War will continue as long as there are historians to wield the pen—which is, perhaps even for this bloody conflict, mightier than the sword."[1] Was the war inevitable? Here, again, there is little consensus other than a general agreement that neither side was willing to compromise on the principles that each held dear. As a result, North or South had to yield principles that it deemed dearer than life before the war could be brought to an end. That the conflict lasted four excruciating years is testament to the strength of their convictions. Other historians and the veterans themselves pondered the meaning of four years of sacrifice and bloodletting that seemed to know no bounds. Sam Watkins, a Confederate veteran in the Army of Tennessee, nostalgically reflected on his own experience: "Were these things real? . . . Did I see the flag of my country, that I had followed so long, furled to be no more unfurled forever? Surely they are but the vagaries of mine own imagination."[2] As the war receded in their memories, veterans reunited with old friends and adversaries, for no other purpose, said Joshua Lawrence Chamberlain, the hero of Little Round Top, than that they were loath "to think we shall see them no more together—these men, these horses, these colors afield." Chamberlain would later announce, "I have had great & deep experiences—& my life has gone into the history of the days that are past."[3]

By 1959 the veterans had all passed on, joining their comrades in eternal bliss. Now was the historians' turn to use their craft and put the war into perspective. Writing on the centennial of the conflict, Bruce Catton ended his magnificent trilogy by simply stating, "Something had been won; but it was nothing more, and at the same time nothing less, than a chance to make a new approach toward a goal that had to be reached if the war and the nation that had endured it had final meaning." He continued, "The ship [of state] was moving through Lincoln's dream, toward a dark indefinite shore, it had a long way to go. . . . All that was certain was that the voyage was under way."[4] It seemed a fitting epitaph, for the Civil War had paved the way for a resurgent and a reunited America on the verge of international greatness.

Historians' Retrospective

Some historians, among them James McPherson and Shelby Foote, view the Civil War not only as the defining event in the history of the republic, but also as a transitional phase that foreshadowed a larger role in the international arena. From the war sprang the great flood that caused "the stream of American history to surge into a new channel and transferred the burden of exceptionalism from North to South."[5] Foote, the dean of Southern historians, posits that the war defined us as a nation and that any understanding of the United States in modern times can be gained only by examining the enormous catastrophe of the preceding century. Many historians look to the past and ponder the reasons why the South was defeated. In *King Cotton Diplomacy*, Frank Owsley viewed the Confederate demise as the result of the political doctrine of states' rights. Bell Wiley attributed Union victory to the North's economic superiority over the South's agrarian and provincial society that remained "bound by its old ways and concepts." David Herbert Donald, Pulitzer Prize winner for his biography of Lincoln, concluded that the "Confederacy destroyed itself through an excess of democracy among its statesmen and soldiers."[6] Another category of historians focuses on the war's outcome and its promise for posterity. Allan Nevins gazes into the future and opines that the general sense of Americans in 1865 was that they stood at the close of one era and the beginning of another, a sense which gave millions a new hopefulness and a firmer belief in the national destiny. With regional aspirations behind them, the population of the postwar United States believed that "the country had swiftly and unexpectedly, but undeniably, become one of the principal world powers, with a new set of responsibilities, challenges, and opportunities."[7] Regardless of which school you believe, there is little doubt that the American Civil War altered forever the character of the American people and the role of government in daily life. A resident of the United States in 1860 would scarcely recognize the nation that emerged in 1865. As a *New York Times* editorial viewed it in October 1867, "The contest touches everything and leaves nothing as it found it. . . . It leaves us a different people in everything."[8]

The War's Cost

The most obvious price of the conflict was manifested in the loss of human life. The Civil War was by far the most destructive war in American history. In monetary terms, the war cost an estimated $20 billion, eleven times total governmental expenditures from Presidents George Washington to James Buchanan. The cost in human life was even greater. In the 1860 census white males between the ages of fifteen and forty numbered 1,140,000 in the South and 4,070,000 in the North.[9] During the war the Northern population increased dramatically due to immigration, despite the loss of 360,222 dead, including 110,100 battle deaths. The official Union casualties from disease included 29,336 from typhoid, 15,570 from other "fevers," 44,558 from dysentery, and 26,468 from pulmonary diseases, mainly tuberculosis. With the wounded added to the fatalities, total Union casualties totaled 642,427 killed and wounded. In round figures, then, 2 million Union soldiers and sailors were reduced by roughly 25 percent. Typical of the Northern commitment was the state of Iowa, where half the men of military age filled forty-six regiments in the Union Army. Between 1861 and 1865, 12,553 Iowans died: 3,540 on the battlefield, 515 in prison camps, and 8,498 from disease. An additional 8,500 went home with serious wounds.[10]

Southern casualties were proportionately in excess of those of the North. The Southern white male population decreased roughly 25 percent over the course of the war, a figure based on 258,000 deaths in battle and from disease and an additional 200,000 wounded. During the Civil War, roughly 750,000 Confederates entered military service; they incurred casualties in excess of 50 percent killed and wounded. Not surprisingly, the population disparity between North and South in 1865 was far greater than in 1860. The combined casualties during the American Civil War were at least 1,094,453 dead or wounded, more than any war in American history, including World War II, and more than all this nation's wars combined until the very end of the Vietnam War.[11] Overall fatalities were greater in proportion to population that those of Great Britain and France in World War I. When all was said and done, the nearly 76 full-scale battles, 301 engagements, and 6,337 skirmishes and sieges had produced one terrible bloodletting. What made the losses even worse was the fact that they were inflicted by fellow Americans, testimony that civil wars are the most destructive of all wars and the repercussions are often felt for generations by citizens trying to cope with how their country had sunk to such depths of despair and savagery.

And the men who survived would wear their scars for the remainder of their lives. In Mississippi, for example, one-fifth of the state budget in 1866 was allocated for artificial limbs, so great was the number of injuries inflicted on Mississippi's populace in the nation's most tragic conflict. Had it been worth the cost? As president, Lincoln lamented the sacrifice, but he unequivocally would have answered that question in the affirmative because the nation that emerged, witnessed a rebirth of freedom. Two great evils, slavery and secession, were forever laid to rest, never to resurface. The war had seen to that. The nation changed in other ways as well.[12]

"The United States Is . . ."

No event in American history so transformed the republic as the American Civil War. Among those accustomed to the country in 1860, few would recognize the entity that emerged from the war. Socially, politically, and economically, the United States of 1865 was a new nation. George Ticknor, a prominent author and critic, contended that the war had left "a great gulf between what happened before it in our century and what has happened since, or what is likely to happen hereafter. It does not seem to me as if I were living in the country in which I was born."[13] Former Confederate Sam Watkins, who served from day one to the disbanding of the Army of Tennessee, concurred: "America has no north, no south, no east, no west . . . the sun rises over the hills and sets over the mountains, the compass just points up and down, and we can laugh now at the absurd notion of there being a north and a south . . . . We are one and undivided."[14]

Perhaps the most radical change as a result of the war was the replacement of a fragmented society by a unified national state. Prior to 1861 the common vernacular taught in schools was "The United States are"; after 1865 the accepted usage both at home and abroad was "The United States is." The change was more than a question of semantics. Returning veterans generally accepted, some more readily than others, a renewed sense of nationhood. Whereas prior to the opening guns the vast majority of Americans never traveled more than fifty miles from where they were born and raised, the war's conclusion saw them no longer content to remain at home. Grant viewed the conflict as generating "a spirit of independence and enterprise" that compelled a youth to cut loose from his old surroundings. The soldiers who returned from the battlefields "were no longer satisfied with the farm, the store, or the work-shop of the villages."[15] They wanted larger fields in which to pursue their individual goals. Moreover, they now knew that there was a country beyond the borders of their native states because they had seen it. They had sailed down the nation's rivers, climbed the hills of the Blue Ridge Mountains, journeyed along the country's back roads and trails, and traveled by rail or foot as supply lines were constructed to support the armies in the field. Take, for example, an average soldier in one of the Union's western armies. He might have enlisted in Michigan, traveled to the state's capital by foot, jumped on a railroad car to a mobilization camp, then moved to a debarkation point on the Ohio River, sailed down the Mississippi to Vicksburg, then marched to Chattanooga, Tennessee, before joining Sherman in his campaign against Atlanta and later marching through Georgia to Savannah. Reaching the coast, Billie Yank then headed northward through both Carolinas, before ending the war on Pennsylvania Avenue in Washington, D.C., for the grand review of the Armies of the Republic in May 1865.

With the war over, he would have returned home and either taken up his antebellum career or gazed westward, where new economic opportunities awaited him. Such was the case with one of the principal characters in the cinematic production *How the West Was Won*. A Confederate soldier would have experienced a similar journey. When Johnny Reb returned home, however, his home would have most likely been destroyed and his land desolated by four years of conflict. He, too, might have proceeded westward, where the Homestead Act of 1862 offered fertile land and the opportunity to build a new home as well as to begin a new life.

The Economic Transformation of America

Economically the United States was transformed at a faster and more complete rate than at any other time in its history.[16] In the South, the economic plight was deplorable, far worse than that of central Europe in 1918 and 1945. Where Northern armies marched, there was little remaining of economic value. There was a lack of currency and capital following the war, and the conflict had rendered much of the land temporarily unsuitable for farming. In the states that formed the Confederacy, $10 billion in property had been destroyed; two-fifths of the livestock had been killed; and every sizable city east of the Mississippi River had either been occupied during the war or garrisoned during the period of reconstruction that followed the capitulation of Southern armies. Small wonder that during the winter of 1865 there was starvation at unprecedented levels. Until federal capital flowed to the South during Reconstruction, few banks were solvent. The immediate postwar period produced additional changes as well. As the white race in the South reluctantly accepted the transition from slave to free labor, the region's rural economy did not entirely disappear; indeed, the majority of freed slaves later worked the same fields as sharecroppers, but the large plantations virtually disappeared from the American scene. In his classic *Origins of the New South*, historian C. Vann Woodward argues that the South's planter class was replaced by a new middle class of bankers, merchants, and industrialists. Others disagree, and posit that the planter class retained much of its land, but altered its political priorities to take advantage of the changing economic realities.

Another visible change was the rise of interior cities and railroads across the once predominantly agricultural South. The emphasis on railroad construction, of course, was not restricted to the old South; rather, it reflected a national phenomenon most visibly represented by railroad entrepreneur Cornelius Vanderbilt. Normal trade was immediately restored between the regions that had waged war for four years, but the disparity of economic wealth between the two regions was greater in 1900 than it had been in 1860. Whereas in 1860, 17.2 percent of national industrial production and 11.5 percent of national industrial capital came from the South, by 1904 the respective figures had declined to 15.3 percent and 11 percent. Moreover, per capita income two decades following the war in the South was only a third of the national average.[17] Despite some innovations and adaptations, the South remained firmly rooted in its past several decades after the war. By the onset of the twentieth century, however, the steel and rail industries had made monumental strides into the heart of old Dixie. More important, the war acted as a catalyst that jump-started the Industrial Revolution, which in turn would propel the United States to world prominence a century later. Beginning in 1877, the year that witnessed the end of Reconstruction with the withdrawal of federal troops from the South, American exports exceeded imports.

Why the economic transformation? Among many factors were the amalgamation of six powerful forces: the explosive expansion of communications; the discovery of new treasures of natural resources throughout the American West; the increasing confidence of foreign governments and investors in the permanence of American political and economic institutions; the accumulation of capital ready to be poured into the New World; the U.S. demand for labor; and the irresistible progress of urbanization in both North and South. Presiding over this "New America" was what E. L. Godkin termed "the shrewdest and most indomitable speculators the world had ever seen."[18]

The Expanded Role of Government

Few would argue that the role of the federal government in the people's daily lives was not fundamentally altered as a result of the war. Aside from an occasional public address by local and state politicians running for national office, few Americans had any contact with the national government other than the post office. To wage modern war successfully, however, a strong central government is necessary, for only a national entity can accumulate sufficient resources to wage war on a national scale. Such had been the inherent contradiction in the Confederacy, which prided itself on states' rights but soon discovered that a government weak at its core could hardly muster sufficient amounts of men and matériel to combat a strong and determined enemy backed by a stable political system of self-rule. The Civil War was hardly an exception.

Between 1861 and 1865, and certainly in the immediate postwar period, the central government greatly expanded its clout and its influence. Over the course of the conflict both sides had resorted to a national draft, and the U.S. 37th Congress was the most active legislative body in memory. While Lincoln directed the Union armies in the field, Congress passed the Homestead Act of 1862, which opened the American West to settlement by giving each tenant 160 acres of arable land for cultivation. The legislative body also enacted a truly national currency—the "greenbacks"—and a national banking system. To finance the war, Congress passed a national income tax that was temporarily suspended after the war, but was later reinstituted by a constitutional amendment fifty years later. The 37th Congress also passed the Morrill Act on July 2, 1862, granting public lands to the states for the establishment of institutions of higher education in "agricultural and the mechanic arts." Congress next approved a new Department of Agriculture and passed the Pacific Railroad Act, which granted public lands and monetary support for the construction of the transcontinental railroad that was completed on May 10, 1869, six years after the initial tracks were laid. This latter act united America "west and east as much as Lee's surrender united this nation north and south." According to historian Stephen E. Ambrose, next to winning the Civil War and the abolition of slavery, "the construction of the first transcontinental railroad from Omaha, Nebraska to Sacramento, California was the greatest achievement of the American people in the nineteenth century."[19] Not until the completion of the Panama Canal in 1914 was it rivaled as an engineering feat. That the Lincoln government oversaw each of these developments in the midst of fighting a major conflict staggers the imagination.

Social and Cultural Changes

At Gettysburg, Lincoln envisioned a nation based on a new birth of freedom for all Americans, black and white. The liberation and the enfranchisement of the Negro were the most visible social changes resulting from the war. Again the federal government remained in the forefront of this transformation by passing the Thirteenth, Fourteenth, and Fifteenth Amendments to the U.S. Constitution, then creating the Freedmen's Bureau on March 3, 1865. As the first government program designed to coordinate the various departments implementing social welfare, the Freedmen's Bureau dispensed rations, and relief for those uprooted by the war. Nor was the bureau's support confined to African Americans. Of 21 million rations distributed between 1865 and 1867, 5.5 million were issued to white people.[20] Under control of the War Department, the bureau was also empowered to distribute up to forty acres of "abandoned" and confiscated land to the individual freedmen. Ownership could be obtained after three years of rental, with an option to buy with "such title that the United States can convey."[21]

Enfranchisement of the black race was another matter. Although granted by the Fifteenth Amendment, no preparation for voting occurred in the states comprising the old Confederacy. And with the states legally empowered to regulate the voting process, the Southern states moved rapidly to limit the franchise by the institution of a series of "black codes" in 1865–1866 that either established impediments to black suffrage or restricted economic opportunities by forbidding blacks to engage in any occupation other than domestic service or agriculture, unless they paid excessive licensing fees. The net result was the same: although legally free with full rights of citizenship and enfranchisement, the freedman enjoyed far fewer rights than his white counterpart.

Congress moved to correct the political and economic abuses in the occupied South by passing a series of Reconstruction Acts in 1867–1868, but again the victors failed to prepare the freedmen for expanded political rights. The terms of the Reconstruction Acts were so severe that when federal troops were eventually withdrawn from the South in the wake of the 1876 presidential election, white Southerners reinstituted white rule with a vengeance that rivaled the worst cases of despotic government. Secret societies were formed—the Ku Klux Klan and the Knights of the White Camellia, to name only two—specifically designed to intimidate the black race and to ensure white supremacy for generations. Not until the civil rights' movement of the 1950s and the 1960s did black Americans achieve the political rights that had been guaranteed on paper a century earlier.

Changes also occurred in the conduct of warfare as hundreds of military observers accompanied the armies in the field. In national myth, the American Civil War was "the first modern war." European officers were not so sure, citing the technological advances that occurred in the Franco–Prussian War of 1870–1871. In both conflicts the adversaries made wide use of railroads, telegraphs, observation balloons, and earthworks. The Prussians exceeded the Americans, however, in the utilization of a general staff that prepared orders, oversaw their implementation, and conducted operational planning for subsequent campaigns. The Americans, in turn, produced significant improvements in naval warfare. The Civil War introduced the first battle between ironclad ships, an engagement that immediately made all the world's navies obsolete. Outside Charleston Harbor, a Confederate submarine sank a Union warship, the first such instance in maritime warfare. These innovations, coupled with rapid improvements in naval gunnery, were readily copied by European and Asian navies.

Epilogue

And so it was over—four years of horrendous slaughter on a scale unprecedented in American history. European governments were astonished that the former Confederacy accepted the outcome of the war so rapidly. No senior Confederate leader—not Davis, not Lee, nor any other army-level commander—seriously advocated continuing the struggle by guerrilla warfare. One prominent historian opined that Confederate nationalism died so abruptly and so completely because it was "never a true nationalism, that the fatal split in the Confederate psyche prevented the national spirit from ever flowering fully enough to nourish a resolve that would have persevered in the contest after all the romance was gone."[22]

As horrible as was the carnage, the Civil War was a necessary step in the evolution of the democratic system of government. Without war, it is impossible to envision that slavery would have been eradicated by peaceful means. Lincoln had been correct in his assessment at the war's beginning when he addressed Congress and stated that the great test of this democracy was its perseverance against a determined effort to overthrow it from within. That American democracy and its corresponding system of government had survived the war was testament enough not only that democracy would survive well into the future, but also that it would flourish. Grant, too, expressed hope for a better future when he alluded to the war's aftermath and said that despite the evils of the recent conflict, "wars are not always evils unmixed with some good."[23] The decades immediately following the war, with the tremendous strides in economic growth and the expansion of human rights, demonstrated just how thoroughly the country had refined itself following four years of death and destruction.

As the war faded into memory, the Civil War generation celebrated the triumph of democracy and fondly recalled the days when, in the words of jurist Oliver Wendell Holmes Jr., they "shared the incommunicable experience of war. We have felt, we still feel, the passion of life to its top. . . . In our youths, our hearts were touched by fire."[24] The spirit of the Old South would continue, now etched in memory as "The Lost Cause," but even ex-Confederates possessed an overwhelming sense that the United States had closed a chapter on its past and now stood on the threshold of a new era that held unlimited potential for future growth. Tragically, Abraham Lincoln, who had done so much to ensure this dream and who paid the ultimate price to guide the nation toward that threshold, would not see the fulfillment of his dream. He would have undoubtedly concurred with his principal general, Grant, who concluded his reminiscences by expressing his belief "that we are on the eve of a new era, when there is to be great harmony between the Federal and Confederate. I cannot stay to be a living witness to the correctness of this prophecy; but I feel it within me that it is to be so."[25] And so it would be, but that is the subject of a subsequent volume in this series.

Notes

1. James McPherson, *Battle Cry of Freedom* (New York: Oxford University Press, 1988), 859.

2. Quoted in Geoffrey C. Ward, with Ric Burns and Ken Burns, *The Civil War: An Illustrated History* (New York: Alfred A. Knopf, 1990), 417.

3. Alice Rains Trulock, *In the Hands of Providence* (Chapel Hill: University of North Carolina Press, 1992), 366.

4. Bruce Catton, *Never Call Retreat* (New York: Doubleday, 1965), 469.

5. McPherson, *Battle Cry of Freedom*, 861–862.

6. Owsley's, Wiley's, and Donald's observations are quoted in Charles P. Roland, *An American Iliad* (New York: McGraw Hill, 1991), 257.

7. Allan Nevins, *The War for the Union: The Organized War to Victory 1864–1865* (New York: Scribner's, 1959), 404.

8. Quoted in Ward, Burns, and Burns, *The Civil War: An Illustrated History*, 400.

9. Shelby Foote, *The Civil War: A Narrative*, vol. 1 (New York: Random House, 1958), 60.

10. Iowa casualties are from Ward, Burns, and Burns, *The Civil War: An Illustrated History*, 404.

11. Casualty figures are from Russell Weigley, *A Great Civil War* (Bloomington: Indiana University Press, 2000), 451; Samuel Eliot Morison, *The Oxford History of the American People* (New York: Oxford University Press, 1965), 624; and Foote, *The Civil War: A Narrative*, vol. 3 (New York: Random House, 1974), 1040.

12. In McPherson, *Battle Cry of Freedom*, 859–862, the author selects four factors beyond the destruction of slavery and secession as fundamental changes

that occurred as a result of the Civil War: the transition of the United States to a singular noun, the change in the federal balance of political power from South to North, the permanent change in the direction of American development, and the destruction of the Southern vision of America.

13. Ticknor, quoted in McPherson, *Battle Cry of Freedom*, 861.

14. Watkins, quoted in Ward, Burns, and Burns, *The Civil War: An Illustrated History*, 404.

15. U. S. Grant, *Personal Memoirs* (New York: Modern Library, 1999), 616.

16. See Michael Perman, ed., *Major Problems in the Civil War and Reconstruction* (Lexington, MA: D.C. Heath, 1991), 579–597, for conflicting interpretations by economists Morton Keller and Gavin Wright on postwar changes in the economic role of the federal government and in the Southern economy.

17. Wolfgang Schivelbusch, *The Culture of Defeat* (New York: Metropolitan Books, 2003), 84.

18. Nevins lists these six forces as the basis for America's leap forward as an industrial giant in *The War for the Union: The Organized War to Victory 1864–1865*, 394.

19. Stephen Ambrose, *Nothing Like It in the World* (New York: Simon and Schuster, 2000), 17.

20. Figures quoted in Morison, *The Oxford History of the American People*, 711.

21. McPherson, *Battle Cry of Freedom*, 842.

22. Weigley, *A Great Civil War*, 456.

23. Grant, *Personal Memoirs*, 616.

24. Holmes quoted in Ward et al., *The Civil War: An Illustrated History*, 394.

25. Grant, *Personal Memoirs*, 616–617.

BIOGRAPHIES:
THE PERSONALITIES BEHIND
THE WAR

Clara Barton (1821–1912)

Clara Barton was a Northern relief worker who later founded the American Red Cross. Nicknamed the Army of the Potomac's "angel of the battlefield," she ministered to the sick and wounded through four years of war and earned international renown for her relief efforts in the United States and Europe.

Born in Massachusetts in 1821, Clarissa Harlowe Barton was the youngest of five children of Stephen and Sarah Barton. A schoolteacher by trade, she secured an appointment as a U.S. Patent Office copyist in Washington, D.C., in 1854. Still working in the Patent Office at the start of the war, Barton began a one-woman crusade and founded an agency to collect and provide tobacco, brandy, and other comforts to Massachusetts troops when they entered the federal capital following Lincoln's call for volunteers. Appalled by the casualties of First Manasses/Bull Run, Barton decided that the exigencies of war required greater humanitarian efforts. Within a year, she found herself ministering to the wounded during the savage battles of Virginia and Maryland in the summer and winter of 1862. Inspired by her example, other female nurses joined Barton, and soon their presence on the battlefield became a source of pride and comfort for the Army of the Potomac. Later Barton's friendship with several influential Northern congressmen resulted in increasing pressure to reform the medical practices that marked battlefield surgery.

Not used to having women play such a leading role in humanitarian relief, the U.S. Sanitary Commission set up numerous obstacles to hinder Barton's relief efforts. The year 1864 found Barton with Benjamin Butler's Army of the James. In that capacity, she set up a mobile field hospital to minister to the Union wounded. Her claim that Butler had appointed her superintendent of nursing is dubious at best, but in no way detracts from the goodwill that she brought to the suffering. During the final year of the war, Barton worked closely with federal authorities to establish a bureau of missing soldiers. Her efforts were later rewarded by the creation of the U.S. Burial Bureau, though Barton failed to receive the coveted directorship of the bureau that she helped create.

Following the Civil War, Barton remained popular on the lecture circuit, then traveled abroad and ministered to the wounded of the Franco–Prussian War of 1870–1871. After the war, the German emperor, Kaiser Wilhelm I, awarded Barton the Iron Cross in recognition of her services. Returning to the United States, she capitalized on her fame and her affiliation with the International Red Cross to found the American Red Cross. Barton then served as its director for twenty-three years. A dedicated humanitarian to the end, she remained active in the women's suffrage movement and promoted disaster relief until her death in 1912, at the age of ninety-one.

Matthew B. Brady (1823–1896)

Matthew B. Brady was the Civil War's most famous photographer, and his studios in New York City and Washington, D.C., brought the images of war home to the American public.

Born in Warren County, New York, in 1823, Brady suffered from an undiagnosed eye ailment as a youth. Seeking a cure, he traveled to upstate New York, where he encountered several photographers who prompted his curiosity in daguerreotypes, a new form of photography. By 1844 he had opened his first studio and won several prominent awards. Now determined to photograph America's leading citizens, Brady established a studio in Washington, D.C., in 1849. By the time of the Civil War, his National Photographic Art Gallery on Pennsylvania Avenue contained photographs of Abraham Lincoln, Henry Clay, Daniel Webster, John C. Calhoun, Stephen Douglas, and virtually every American president since Zachary Taylor. His fame was at its peak when the Civil War erupted and presented Brady with an unparalleled opportunity for further renown.

Taking his camera to the battlefield, Brady and his team of photographers, which included Alexander Gardner, Timothy O'Sullivan, and James F. Gibson, photographed the grisly aftermath of Lee's first invasion of the North. When the exhibition titled "The Dead of Antietam" opened at his New York studio in late September 1862, a public outcry arose over the carnage of the battlefield. By now Brady was a household name and increasingly popular with Washington's leading politicians and generals. To sit for a Brady portrait became a badge of honor and distinction.

For the remainder of the war, Brady's team created a portfolio that numbered thousands of photographs and engravings. His photographs of Gettysburg and Grant's Virginia campaign of 1864 were particularly graphic. Unfortunately, the costs incurred by these battlefield visits and the increasing availability of reproductions detracted from the popularity of his private studios, and Brady was in severe financial straits by 1865. In an effort to recoup his fortunes, he closed his studios and filed for bankruptcy in 1872. Three years later, the U.S. Congress purchased the Brady collection for $25,000. Many of his original photographs are now in the National Archives.

Brady's later years were shadowed by ill health and poverty. Opening his last studio in Washington in 1890, Brady remained a visible symbol of a passing era. Always popular with the veterans of the Grand Army of the Republic, he lectured frequently on his wartime exploits. He died quietly in New York on January 16, 1896. His primary contributions lay in making the American Civil War the most photographed war to date and setting the professional standard for future wartime photography.

John Brown (1800–1859)

John Brown was a noted abolitionist who led the infamous raid on Harpers Ferry, Virginia (now West Virginia), on October 16, 1859. Vilified by the South as a "radical Satan" and honored by the North as a "crucified hero," Brown symbolized the growing sectional strife that divided the nation on the eve of the Civil War.

John Brown was born in Torrington, Connecticut, in 1800 and raised in Ohio. His father was a noted abolitionist and instilled in his son a deep commitment to religion and an abiding hatred of slavery. In 1820 Brown married Dianthe Lusk and later engaged in several failed business enterprises. Nearly bankrupt at age thirty-seven, he deepened his religious convictions and swore to dedicate his life to the abolition of slavery. Growing increasingly militant, Brown advocated the use of force to achieve his objective. The passage of the Kansas–Nebraska Act in 1854 presented him with the opportunity to put his thoughts and convictions into practice.

The year 1855 found Brown and his sons in "Bleeding Kansas," the very heart of the regional conflict. Brown joined the Potawatomi Rifles, an anti-slavery force dedicated to maintaining Kansas's free-soil status. Increasingly frustrated by the organized pro-slavery forces, Brown and his sons massacred five pro-slavery men at Pottawatomie Creek on May 25, 1856. His action sparked increased violence on the Kansas frontier. Southern border ruffians retaliated and killed one of Brown's sons at Osawatomie on August 30. Brown then vowed that he would die fighting for the abolition of slavery. For the next three years Brown lectured in support of his personal anti-slavery crusade, fought numerous skirmishes in Kansas, and built support for his plan to seize the federal arsenal at Harpers Ferry. Armed with firearms and pikes, the slaves would then rebel against their owners and foment a larger revolt across the South. On the evening of October 16, 1859, Brown, accompanied by several of his sons and a small detachment of abolitionists, crossed the border from Maryland, and seized the arsenal. Federal troops under the command of Robert E. Lee arrived the next day and stormed the engine house where Brown and his followers had taken refuge. Wounded in the ensuing battle, Brown was captured and immediately tried for murder, treason, and fomenting insurrection against the state of Virginia. Convicted and sentenced to death, Brown was hanged in Charlestown, Virginia, on December 2.

In death John Brown emerged as a martyr to Northern abolitionists, but to the South, he represented the increasing radicalization of the North. More than any single event, the raid on Harpers Ferry set the stage for the Civil War. Southerners were now convinced that continued union with their Northern brethren would result in the destruction of their civilization. Brown himself never wavered in his conviction that only violence would free the slaves. In so doing, he paid the ultimate price for his conviction, but not before setting off the chain of events that would erupt in full-fledged civil war in 1861.

Joshua L. Chamberlain (1828–1914)

Joshua Lawrence Chamberlain was a Union general and recipient of the Congressional Medal of Honor for his heroic defense of Little Round Top during the Battle of Gettysburg. During the assault on Petersburg in 1864, Chamberlain received a battlefield promotion to brigadier general, and later presided over the surrender ceremony at Appomattox Courthouse.

Chamberlain was born on September 8, 1828, outside Brewer, Maine. An industrious youth, he graduated from Bowdoin College and Bangor Theological Seminary, and joined the faculty of Bowdoin as a professor of rhetoric just prior to the Civil War. When war came, Chamberlain applied for and received a sabbatical to pursue an advanced degree. Rather than travel to Europe, he accepted a commission as lieutenant colonel in the Twentieth Maine Regiment. The regiment joined the Army of the Potomac on the eve of the Battle of Sharpsburg/Antietam, but neither Chamberlain nor the regiment participated in the battle. He saw his first combat at Fredericksburg on December 13, 1862. Spending the night on the battlefield amid the dead and dying, Chamberlain noted that "the living and the dead were alike to me." Illness prevented him from fighting in the army's next engagement, at Chancellorsville, but he received a promotion and command of the regiment on the eve of the Battle of Gettysburg.

During the height of the struggle to defend Little Round Top on July 2, 1863, Chamberlain again distinguished himself in combat and led a bayonet charge that prevented the Confederate capture of the vital hilltop. Years later, he received the Medal of Honor for his battlefield leadership. Chamberlain continued to command the regiment, and later a brigade, in the Army of the Potomac throughout Grant's 1864 Virginia Campaign. He suffered a debilitating wound in the Union attack on Petersburg, Virginia, on June 18, 1864. Cited for bravery during the assault, Chamberlain received a battlefield promotion to brigadier general. Local newspapers contained accounts of his demise, but Chamberlain miraculously recovered from his wounds in time to join the Army of the Potomac for the attack at Five Forks that enveloped Lee's defenses on April 1, 1865. Again General Ulysses S. Grant recognized his conspicuous gallantry and selected Chamberlain to receive the surrender of Lee's infantry divisions following Lee's surrender of the Army of Northern Virginia.

Following the war, Chamberlain, now one of Maine's most decorated war heroes, successfully ran for governor of the state in 1866 and was reelected for three consecutive terms. He then served as president of Bowdoin College from 1870 to 1883. In later years Chamberlain recounted his wartime experience in *The Passing of the Armies* and made a final visit to the hallowed ground of Gettysburg in May 1913. He died on February 24, 1914, from the effects of his wounds at Petersburg. Immortalized in Michael Shaara's *The Killer Angels* and movie mogul Ted Turner's *Gettysburg*,

Joshua L. Chamberlain remains Maine's most distinguished war veteran and a national hero.

Jefferson Davis (1808–1889)

Jefferson Davis served as U.S. senator from Mississippi and the Confederate States of America's only president.

Jefferson Davis was born in 1808, the son of a veteran of the Revolutionary War. Matriculating at West Point from Transylvania University in Lexington, Kentucky, he graduated in the U.S.M.A. class of 1828. During his time at West Point, he became familiar with Albert Sidney Johnston, Joseph E. Johnston, and Robert E. Lee, three cadets who would later play prominent roles in the fortunes of the Confederacy. Temporarily forsaking a military career for the political sphere, Davis served in the House of Representatives in 1845. In the Mexican War, he commanded the 1st Mississippi Rifles Regiment and gained national fame. By 1847, Davis was back in Washington, this time as a U.S. senator from Mississippi. Hitching his political fortunes to the Democratic Party, he served with distinction as secretary of war in the administration of President Franklin Pierce. Returning to the Senate in 1857, he became an ardent and vocal supporter of states' rights.

Upon Mississippi's secession from the Union on January 9, 1861, Davis resigned his Senate seat and returned to his plantation, Brierfield, outside Vicksburg. On February 9, 1861, he received word that the provisional Confederate Congress had elected him president of the Confederate States of America. Davis answered his new country's call, but felt himself unequal to the task. In the ensuing months, he developed the initial Confederate war strategy and appointed the first contingent of army commanders. As a wartime commander-in-chief, Davis was far inferior to Lincoln. His political and military appointees, with rare exceptions, proved inadequate. Of his principal military commanders, only Robert E. Lee met the challenge. Davis's unflinching support of inept Generals Braxton Bragg and Leonidas Polk defied logic. Moreover, Davis remained transfixed on the Virginia Theater of operations, thereby contributing immensely to the Confederate defeat in the Mississippi and Tennessee Valleys. Maintaining his reputation as an aloof aristocrat, he trusted few men outside his inner circle or his West Point classmates. Not surprisingly, by war's end, his critics numbered several Southern governors and his own vice president.

Upon the fall of Richmond on April 2, 1865, Davis fled the Confederate capital with the remnants of the Confederate government and headed west. Following his capture outside Irwinville, Georgia, on May 10, Davis was interred at Fortress Monroe, Virginia, for two years, then released on bond, but was never pardoned during his lifetime. In an effort to recoup his financial fortunes, he traveled extensively during the next two decades and then decided to write his memoirs. Published in two volumes in 1877, *The Rise and Fall of the Confederate Government* was an unabashed constitutional defense of the Lost Cause. Davis spent his remaining years in splendid isolation, participating in the twenty-fifth anniversary of the establishment of the Confederacy in Montgomery, Alabama, in 1886. Now the living symbol of the Confederacy, Jefferson Davis contacted bronchitis in the winter of 1889. The Confederacy's only president died in New Orleans on December 6, 1889. Remaining true to his convictions and to the righteousness of the Confederate cause, Davis never applied for a federal pardon.

Frederick Douglass (1817–1895)

Frederick Douglass was an African American orator and writer, and one of the most fervent abolitionists in the United States. A former slave and an early practitioner of nonviolence, Douglass advanced the cause of civil rights and was instrumental in the eventual emancipation of the slaves.

Born Frederick Augustus Washington Bailey on February 7, 1817, Douglass was the son of a slave and a white man, After twice running away from his owner, Douglass fled to Boston in 1838 and began a career dedicated to freeing the slaves. Within three years, he became popular on the lecture circuit, prompting abolitionist William Lloyd Garrison to enlist his support for the Massachusetts Anti-Slavery Society. In 1845 Douglass published his memoirs, titled *Narrative of the Life of Frederick Douglass.* Two years later, with some help from English patrons, he had raised enough money to purchase his freedom. The publication of his journal, the *North Star,* quickly followed. By the century's midpoint, Douglass was a leading spokesman for emancipation of the slaves, as well as for women's suffrage and temperance.

Prior to 1850, Douglass considered himself a pacifist, but the enactment of the Fugitive Slave Law as part of the Compromise of 1850 led him to advocate "forcible resistance" to the law. Although he proclaimed that "slave-holders . . . have no right to live," Douglass still balanced ends with means. He opposed John Brown's raid on Harpers Ferry in October 1859, on the grounds that an attack on a federal arsenal would inflame the South and be counterproductive. Douglas was correct—Brown's failed raid radicalized the sectional strife between North and South. Once the nation embarked on war, Douglass repeatedly petitioned the Republican Congress and the Lincoln administration to abolish slavery. He thought Lincoln moved too slowly at first, but he vigorously supported the Emancipation Proclamation. Now free to raise black regiments, Douglass helped recruit two Massachusetts regiments of black soldiers, contributing two sons in the process. In March 1865, he attended a highly publicized inaugural reception in the White House.

With the war over, Douglass continued to seek to advance civil rights and equality among the races. Over the course of the next three decades, he held several important federal posts, including marshal of the District of Columbia and assistant secretary of the Santo Domingo Commission. He served as minister-resident and consul general to Haiti from 1889 to 1891. Four years later, on February 20, 1895, Douglass died while attending a women's suffrage convention in the nation's capital. His life spanned a century of struggle for human equality in the United States. In his lifetime, Douglass proved a dedicated and effective reformer who left a lasting legacy for future generations to advance human rights.

David G. Farragut (1801–1870)

David G. Farragut was the victor in the Battles of New Orleans and Mobile Bay. The North's greatest naval hero, he became the first admiral of the U.S. Navy.

James (later David) Glasgow Farragut was born on July 5, 1801, at Campbell's Station, Tennessee. Appointed a midshipman in the U.S. Navy when he was only nine years old, Farragut served under his adoptive father, Commodore David Porter, during the War of 1812. He was cited for gallantry during the battle between Porter's *Essex* and two British ships, and assumed Porter's first name after the war. Between the War of 1812 and the Civil War, Farragut was stationed on routine maritime duty in the Mediterranean and the Gulf of Mexico. He served with great distinction as commander of a sloop of war, the *Saratoga*, during the Mexican War and at various Atlantic ports until the Civil War began.

Given command of the West Gulf Blockading Squadron despite his Southern sympathies, Farragut sailed his fleet past the Confederate forts St. Philip and Jackson, and captured New Orleans on April 25, 1862. New Orleans was not only the Confederacy's largest city but also its busiest port. Natchez and Baton Rouge quickly followed, and a significant part of Louisiana was soon in Union hands. Promoted to rear admiral, Farragut spent the remainder of 1862 in a futile attempt to destroy the defenses of Vicksburg. Vicksburg finally capitulated in July 1863 to Ulysses S. Grant, and the Mississippi River now flowed, in Lincoln's words, "unvexed to the sea."

The year 1864 found Farragut determined to capture the last Confederate ports on the Gulf of Mexico. Taking a flotilla of eighteen ships past three Confederate forts, he attacked the Mobile Bay defenses on August 5. When a mine sank his lead monitor, Farragut had himself strapped to the rigging of his flagship *Hartford* and proclaimed, "Damn the torpedoes, full speed ahead." After a sharp battle, the Confederates surrendered, and the bay was closed to Confederate blockade runners. Ill health forced Farragut to decline Secretary of Navy Gideon Welles's request to take command of the North Atlantic Squadron, and he returned to shore duty. In April 1865, Farragut was one of the first Federals to enter Richmond when the Confederate capital fell.

In recognition of a half-century of distinguished maritime service, Congress approved Farragut's promotion to full admiral on July 26, 1866. He returned briefly to sea as commander of the Mediterranean Squadron after the war, but years of extended service had taken a toll. Farragut died on active duty at Portsmouth, New Hampshire, on August 14, 1870. The greatest sailor of his generation, he bequeathed a legacy of heroism and combat leadership in the finest traditions of the U.S. Navy.

Ulysses S. Grant (1822–1885)

Ulysses Simpson Grant was commander of all Union armies in the West, general-in-chief of the United States Army (1864–1869), and eighteenth president of the United States. He once admitted, "I am more a farmer than a soldier," but over the course of the war, he led the Union to victory.

Born Hiram Ulysses Grant in Point Pleasant, Ohio, on April 27, 1822, Grant enrolled at West Point in 1839 in order to obtain a free education.

Graduating four years later, he had been a mediocre student, excelling only in horsemanship. During the Mexican War, Grant served under both Zachary Taylor and Winfield Scott and participated in most of the campaigns in northern and central Mexico. Cited twice for gallantry, at Molino del Rey and Chapultepec, he received a Regular Army promotion to first lieutenant. Following the war, Grant served on the American frontier until 1854, when he resigned his commission. An abject failure in every civilian business endeavor, he was a clerk in his father's leather-goods store when the Civil War erupted.

The Civil War rescued Grant from obscurity. Raising a company and later appointed colonel of the 21st Illinois Infantry Regiment, he was mustered into federal service in June 1861. Promoted brigadier general of volunteers, Grant won the North's first significant victories in the West by capturing Confederate strongholds Forts Henry and Donelson in February 1862. By demanding unconditional surrender of the Donelson garrison, he earned the nickname "Unconditional Surrender" Grant and became an instant military hero. Promoted to command the Army of Tennessee, Grant next defeated Albert S. Johnston's forces at Shiloh in April, but allegations of unpreparedness and excessive casualties led to his temporary relief from command.

Reappointed to command the Union effort to capture Vicksburg, Grant conducted one of the most masterful campaigns of the war. On July 4, 1863, Vicksburg fell to Grant, who was now the most seasoned and successful Union commander. Lincoln next rushed him to Chattanooga, where he raised the siege of that city and routed Braxton Bragg's Army of Tennessee in November 1863. Grant's military success led to his promotion to lieutenant general and appointment as general-in-chief of all Union armies in March 1864. Grant then directed the movement of all Union armies to crush the remaining armies of the Confederacy. He accompanied Major General George Meade's Army of the Potomac in the climatic Wilderness/Overland Campaign in Virginia, which pinned Lee's army in the trenches of Petersburg in June 1864. Grant finally broke Lee's lines the following April and accepted Lee's surrender at Appomattox Courthouse on April 9, 1865.

Following the war, Grant served temporarily as secretary of war and accepted the Republican nomination for president in 1868. His two terms were highlighted by the era of Reconstruction, political corruption, and failure. Returning to the business realm, Grant proved once again that he excelled only in war. Diagnosed with throat cancer, he wrote his memoirs to salvage his business fortunes. Grant died at Mount McGregor, New York, on July 23 1885, and lies buried in a national tomb in New York City.

By all accounts Ulysses S. Grant was one of the nation's premier soldiers. As a tactician, he was less successful than Lee, but as a strategist, he had few equals. He remains the U.S. Army's greatest soldier of his age.

Thomas J. (Stonewall) Jackson (1824–1863)

Lieutenant General Thomas J. Jackson earned the name "Stonewall" and served as Robert E. Lee's most trusted and audacious battlefield commander. At the time of his death in May 1863, Jackson had emerged as Lee's "right arm" and was commander of the Army of Northern Virginia's II Corps.

Jackson was born in Clarksburg, Virginia (now West Virginia), on January 21, 1824. Orphaned at an early age, he secured an appointment to West Point and graduated in 1846, ranking seventeenth of fifty-nine cadets. Jackson was commissioned in the artillery and served with distinction in Mexico under Winfield Scott, earning three brevet promotions for gallantry under fire. He resigned his commission in 1851 and joined the faculty of the Virginia Military Institute, where he taught artillery tactics and natural and experimental philosophy. A devout Presbyterian, Jackson was known more for his piety than for his pedagogical talents. In December 1859, he led a small contingent of VMI cadets to Charlestown to witness the public execution of abolitionist John Brown.

Upon Virginia's secession, Jackson offered his services to the Confederacy. Appointed colonel of infantry and commander of the garrison at Harpers Ferry, he was promoted to brigadier general on July 3, 1861. His stand at the First Battle of Manassas brought the South its first great victory and earned Jackson the sobriquet of "Stonewall." His greatest military campaign occurred the following year when, during the Valley Campaign, Jackson won five battles and defeated four Union commanders in rapid succession. Lee then called Jackson to Richmond, where he participated in Lee's Seven Days' battles that lifted the siege of the Confederate capital. Though his individual performance was not up to par during this campaign, Jackson was the South's greatest military hero.

The last year of Jackson's life confirmed that he was Lee's most valued commander. In July 1862 Lee dispatched Jackson to northern Virginia to halt the advance of a Union army under John Pope. Jackson defeated Pope's vanguard at Cedar Mountain, then held the line at Second Manassas, where James Longstreet's corps smashed the remainder of Pope's army. During Lee's first invasion of Maryland, Jackson captured Harpers Ferry and performed brilliantly at Sharpsburg/Antietam. His battlefield success won Jackson command of the army's 2nd Corps in mid-autumn and promotion to lieutenant general. When a Union army under the command of Ambrose E. Burnside advanced on Fredericksburg in December, Jackson defended the right of Lee's line and won his easiest victory of the war.

Jackson's last battle was Chancellorsville in May 1863. Outnumbered two to one, Lee divided his army and sent Jackson on a circuitous flanking march to envelop General Joe Hooker's right flank. Completing the march on May 2, Jackson fell on the unsuspecting Federals and crushed the Union right flank. Unfortunately he fell wounded from the fire of his own men when he was conducting a night reconnaissance of the front lines. Evacuated from the field, Jackson succumbed to pneumonia eight days later at Guiney Station, Virginia. After a public funeral service in Richmond, Jackson was buried in Lexington, Virginia.

Jackson's death proved the greatest calamity for the South. A military genius of unquestionable ability, Jackson had provided the offensive thrust of the Army of Northern Virginia and was the commander most feared by his opponents. His absence at the Battle of Gettysburg undoubtedly contributed to Lee's ultimate defeat.

Robert E. Lee (1807–1870)

General Robert E. Lee was the commander of the Confederate Army of Northern Virginia and later named general-in-chief of all national forces on February 6, 1865. He proved to be the South's ablest soldier and gave the Confederacy its only real opportunity for strategic success by his tactical acumen and strength of character.

Robert E. Lee was born at Stratford Hall, Virginia, on January 19, 1807. The third son and fifth child of Henry "Light Horse Harry" Lee and Ann Hill Carter Lee, he graduated from West Point, second in the class of 1829, and entered the Corps of Engineers. At West Point he was known as the "Marble Man," an accolade to his strength of character and the fact that he never received a single demerit during his years at the U.S. Military Academy. Lee first captured national attention within the ranks as a staff officer in General Winfield S. Scott's campaign to capture Mexico City during the Mexican War. Repeatedly cited for heroism, Lee emerged from the war as Scott's protégé, destined for senior command. From 1852 to 1855 he served as superintendent at West Point, and later served in south Texas. While on leave in Virginia, he led the detachment of U.S. Marines that captured John Brown at Harpers Ferry in October 1859.

When the Civil War began, Lee was offered command of the Union forces on April 18, but he declined when Virginia subsequently seceded from the Union. Upon resigning from the U.S. Army, Lee was immediately named commander of Virginia's forces and became a military adviser to Confederate President Jefferson Davis. Appointed the third-ranking general in the Confederate Army, he conducted an unsuccessful campaign to hold the western counties of Virginia in the fall of 1861 and later directed the coastal defenses of South Carolina, Georgia, and Florida. Returning to Richmond in the spring of 1862, Lee assumed command of the Confederate army defending the Southern capital on June 1, when General Joseph E. Johnston fell wounded. Lee rechristened the force the Army of Northern Virginia and led it with marked success for the remainder of the war.

Driving Union General George B. McClellan from the gates of Richmond in June 1862, Lee next defeated John Pope at Second Manassas and invaded Maryland in September. Halted at Sharpsburg, he retreated to Virginia and won two more victories: at Fredericksburg, against Ambrose Burnside, and at Chancellorsville, against "Fighting Joe" Hooker. In June 1863, Lee embarked on his second invasion of the North and was decisively defeated at Gettysburg on July 3. In the spring of 1864, Lee and Ulysses S. Grant became locked in a deadly struggle for the Confederacy's very existence. Now relegated to defensive tactics, Lee inflicted catastrophic casualties on the Union Army of the Potomac, but sheer numbers resulted in Lee's army being penned up in Petersburg, thirty miles south of Richmond. Grant finally broke Lee's lines on April 2, 1865. Retreating westward, Lee was forced to surrender at Appomattox Courthouse on April 9.

With the war over, Lee accepted the presidency of Washington College (later Washington and Lee University) in Lexington, Virginia. Under his direction, the college resumed its status as one of Virginia's premier institutions of higher learning. Having been elevated to the position of a Southern icon, Lee toured the South in the spring of 1870, before returning to Lexington for the commencement of the academic year. Stricken with a stroke in late September, Lee succumbed to the effects of heart disease on October 12, 1870.

The South's greatest general, Lee demonstrated his genius at both a tactical and an operational level of war. For three years he gave the Confederacy its greatest chance of survival, and his eventual defeat was due more to inferior resources and complete fatigue than to lack of military skill. Although his generalship has recently attracted its share of critics, Robert E. Lee remains a Southern hero and the very embodiment of the Lost Cause.

Abraham Lincoln (1809–1865)

Abraham Lincoln was sixteenth president of the United States. Indispensable to the Northern victory, he devised the political strategy and set the strategic war aims for the North. His death by an assassin's bullet at the conclusion of the war proved disastrous to the peaceful reconciliation between North and South.

Lincoln was born in a log cabin near Hodgenville, Kentucky, on February 12, 1809, the son of Thomas and Nancy Hanks Lincoln. Mostly self-educated, he moved first to Indiana and eventually settled in 1831 in New Salem, Illinois, where he worked at a variety jobs. Six years later, Lincoln arrived in Springfield, the state capital, where he opened a successful law practice. Within two decades he emerged as one of the state's leading attorneys and one of the nation's foremost lawyers in legal matters involving the railroads. In 1842, Lincoln married Mary Todd, and they purchased a home in Springfield two years later. Becoming increasingly interested in politics, Lincoln served several terms in the state legislature and was elected to the U.S. House of Representatives in 1846. His brief stint at the national level produced no significant legislation, save his introduction of the "Spot Resolutions," in which Lincoln, a Whig and an opponent of the Mexican War, demanded to know if the spot where blood was shed on the Texas border was really American soil. Following the war, Lincoln returned to Springfield and, in the decade ahead, joined the Republican Party and advocated excluding slavery in the territories acquired as a result of the war. In 1858, he unsuccessfully challenged Senator Stephen A. Douglas for the U.S. Senate. Their debates brought Lincoln national prominence, and in 1860 he emerged as the Republican candidate for president. His election in November 1860 resulted in the secession of the states of the Lower South.

As president, Lincoln avoided direct military confrontation with the South, but moved decisively once the Confederate States fired on Fort Sumter. Calling for an immediate blockade of Southern ports and for 75,000 volunteers to put down the insurrection, he then defined the nation's war aim of preserving the Union. Over the course of the next four years, Lincoln greatly expanded the powers of the presidency and made the key decisions in all matters regarding political and military strategy, as well as the appointment of military commanders. On January 1, 1863, Lincoln's Emancipation Proclamation, liberating all slaves in territories still in rebellion against the United States, went into effect. Eleven months later, while at Gettysburg on November 19, 1863, Lincoln delivered the Gettysburg Address, arguably the greatest speech in American history. As the war entered its third year, Lincoln finally found a general whose strategic vision matched his own. The civil–military team of Abraham Lincoln and Ulysses S. Grant brought the Union victory in April 1865. One week after Lee surrendered to Grant at Appomattox Courthouse, John Wilkes Booth fatally wounded the president at Ford's Theater on April 14, 1865. Lincoln died the following day.

Lincoln's assassination was the final chapter in a tragic war. Lincoln was an advocate of peaceful reconciliation of North and South, but his call for "malice toward none and charity for all" went largely unanswered during the period of Reconstruction. Martyred just after the country's greatest victories, he is universally recognized as one of the nation's greatest presidents and most effective wartime leaders.

George B. McClellan (1826–1885)

General George B. McClellan was commander of the Union Army of the Potomac and later the Democratic Party nominee for president of the United States in 1864. Beloved by his soldiers as "Little Mac," he organized the Army of the Potomac, but his cautious tactics ultimately led to his relief from command.

George Brinton McClellan was born in Philadelphia on December 3, 1826. A child prodigy, he entered college at age thirteen, then transferred to the U.S. Military Academy in 1842. Graduating number two in his class in 1846, McClellan served on the staff of General Winfield Scott in Mexico and earned two brevets for gallantry in action. Following the war, he held a variety of engineering assignments and participated in an official commission of American officers to observe the

Crimean War. Resigning his commission in 1857, McClellan was serving as president of several Midwestern railroads when the Civil War beckoned him to military greatness.

Commissioned a major general of volunteers by the governor of Ohio, McClellan earned an early victory against Confederate forces at Philippi, Virginia. Subsequent victories cleared western Virginia of Confederate forces, prompting Lincoln to summon McClellan to Washington on July 26 and give him command of the Union army following the disaster at First Manassas/Bull Run. McClellan's transformation of the army and his christening of the force as the Army of the Potomac were nothing short of miraculous. McClellan succeeded Winfield Scott as commander of all Union armies on November 1, but his tempestuous relationship with Lincoln and Secretary of War Edwin Stanton later restricted his authority to command of the Army of the Potomac.

Ordered by Lincoln to initiate military action against the Confederate army outside Washington, McClellan performed poorly in the Peninsula Campaign and was defeated by Robert E. Lee in the Seven Days' battles outside Richmond in June and July 1862. Temporarily removed from command for his failure to capture Richmond, he was again summoned to command the Union army on the eve of Lee's first invasion of the North. Although he captured Lee's orders outlining the plans for his dispersed army, McClellan failed to destroy Lee's army in detail, allowing Lee to consolidate his forces along Antietam Creek in Maryland. Lee and McClellan fought to a tactical draw at Sharpsburg/Antietam on September 17, 1862. Though his army outnumbered Lee nearly two to one, McClellan failed to destroy Lee's army. He did, however, drive Lee back to Virginia, thus ending the South's greatest opportunity to win the war and prompting Lincoln to issue a preliminary Emancipation Proclamation. Lincoln urged him to pursue Lee, but McClellan allowed his adversary to escape to Virginia. Frustrated at his general's inaction, Lincoln removed McClellan from command of the Army of the Potomac a second time, thus ending his military service.

Selected by the Democratic Party to oppose Lincoln in 1864, McClellan was soundly defeated, capturing only three states. He later was elected governor of New Jersey and published his memoirs, but never found the military and political glory he so earnestly sought. He died at the age of fifty-nine on October 29, 1885, in Orange, New Jersey.

George G. Meade (1815–1872)

Major General George Gordon Meade commanded the Union forces at the Battle of Gettysburg. The first Union commander to decisively defeat Robert E. Lee's Army of Northern Virginia, he served as commander of the Union Army of the Potomac for the remainder of the war.

George Meade was born in Cadiz, Spain, in 1815. After graduating from West Point in 1835, he served for slightly more than one year before resigning his commission to become an engineer in railroad construction. He returned to the army in 1843 as a topographical engineer and served on the staff of Zachary Taylor during the Mexican War. When the Civil War began, Meade was appointed brigadier general of volunteers by the governor of Pennsylvania. He participated in the Peninsula Campaign and was severely wounded at Glendale. He recovered to lead his brigade at Second Manassas/Bull Run and commanded the Pennsylvania Reserves at Sharpsburg. Meade then assumed temporary command of Joseph's Hooker's corps when Hooker was wounded, and continued in command of a division during the Battle of Fredericksburg on December 13, 1862. During that battle, Meade's was the only division to penetrate the Confederate defenses, but Southern reinforcements forced his men to withdraw. Now in command of a corps, Meade again performed well during the Battle of Chancellorsville and assumed command of the Army of the Potomac on June 28, 1863, as Robert E. Lee's forces approached Harrisburg, Pennsylvania. At Gettysburg, Meade defeated Lee's Army of Northern Virginia in a three-day battle and drove it back to Virginia. His lackluster pursuit and Lee's eventual escape, however, earned him the censure of the War Department. Meade offered to resign, but remained in command of the Army of the Potomac for the remainder of the war.

When Grant, the new Union commander, came east in March 1864, he briefly considered relieving Meade and placing one of his protégés in command. Grant retained Meade in command, though he severely curtailed his freedom of action by locating his own headquarters in the vicinity of Meade's command post. Meade performed well during Grant's Virginia campaign of 1864, but never met Grant's expectations. Relations between the two headquarters remained tepid at best, and Meade bristled under the tight reins of Grant and his officers. Following the collapse of Lee's defenses outside Petersburg, Virginia, in early April 1865, Meade pursued his old adversary and helped bring Lee to bay at Appomattox

Courthouse on April 9, 1865. Still unpopular in Grant's inner circle, Meade did not attend the surrender ceremony.

Meade's crowning glory occurred on May 23, 1865, when he led his victorious army in a grand review before adoring masses in Washington, D.C. Following the war, Meade commanded the Division of the Atlantic and, temporarily, the Third Military District. He dedicated much of his remaining years to defending his actions following the Gettysburg campaign. He died of pneumonia on November 6, 1872.

Winfield Scott (1786–1866)

General Winfield Scott served as commanding general of the U.S. Army from 1841 to 1861. A national military hero of the War of 1812 and the Mexican-American War of 1846–1848, he developed the initial Union strategy of the Civil War.

Winfield Scott was born in 1786 and graduated from the College of William and Mary. Joining the army in 1808, he was commissioned the youngest general in service, and won victories at Chippewa and Lundy's Lane during the War of 1812. Scott remained in the army after the war and was an early proponent of army professionalism. He wrote most of the early training manuals and fostered the development of branch-specific training schools for officers. In 1841 Scott received a promotion to commanding general of the U.S. Army. In that capacity he led the successful military expedition from Vera Cruz to capture Mexico City in the war with Mexico. So brilliant was his campaign that the Duke of Wellington once called him the world's "greatest living soldier." One of the key factors of his martial success was a staff that included engineers Robert E. Lee and George B. McClellan. Lee and McClellan were but two of the Civil War's future generals who earned their combat spurs in service under Winfield Scott. Scott ran unsuccessfully for president in 1852, against Franklin Pierce.

On the eve of the Civil War, Scott, now seventy-five years old, supported the appointment of Colonel Robert E. Lee as field commander of the Union Army, but Lee's subsequent resignation altered the military landscape. Scott then urged the president to take time to build a formidable army before launching a premature strike at the Confederate forces. Lincoln accepted Scott's strategy to subjugate the Confederacy by a maritime strategy, but rejected his plan to delay an advance toward Richmond. Scott's Anaconda Plan called for a naval blockade of the Confederate coast and the seizure of the Mississippi River to split the Confederacy in two. Under intense political pressure, Scott approved the Union advance toward Manassas Junction in July 1861. The Union defeat at the Battle of First Manasses/Bull Run greatly curtailed Scott's influence within the administration, and the subsequent appointment of Major General George B. McClellan as commander of the Army of the Potomac left the aging Scott a mere figurehead of a by-gone era. Having lost the president's confidence, Scott resigned his position and retired from the army he had served for five decades on October 31, 1861.

Saddled with ill health, Scott spent his remaining years in New York. He wrote his memoirs in 1864, but their publication failed to resurrect his former glory. Over the course of his stellar military career, he had served under fourteen presidents, thirteen of them as a general officer. Winfield Scott died at West Point, New York, on May 30, 1866, and is buried in the national military cemetery at the U.S. Military Academy.

Philip H. Sheridan (1831–1888)

Together with his two great mentors, Generals Ulysses S. Grant and William T. Sherman, "Little Phil" Sheridan formed the triumvirate of Union generals most responsible for the Confederate defeat in the Civil War. By war's end he was the Union's most renowned leader of cavalry and a first-rate army commander.

Philip H. Sheridan was born on March 6, 1831, in Albany, New York, the third of six children. Like Grant and Sherman, he spent his boyhood in Ohio. In 1848 he enrolled in the U.S. Military Academy at West Point and graduated five years later, in the middle of his class. Upon graduation Sheridan saw service on the Texas and Oregon frontiers. Still in service when the Civil War began, he served on General William Halleck's staff in the Western Theater, and later received command of a regiment of cavalry in July 1862. His most distinguished service prior to the Chattanooga campaign of 1864 was during the Battle of Stones River/Murfreesboro in December 1862, where Sheridan, now a division commander, saved the Union army from disaster. Attached to General William Rosecrans's Army of the Cumberland, Sheridan again performed brilliantly during the Battle of Chickamauga (September 19–20, 1863). During Grant's subsequent relief of Chattanooga in November, it was Sheridan who captured the enemy rifle pits at the foot of Missionary Ridge, then led his men to the crest, nearly capturing the enemy commander in his tent. Grant was so impressed with Sheridan that he ordered him east to Virginia when Grant assumed command of all Union armies on March 9, 1864. Against the advice of many politicians and generals, Grant appointed Sheridan commander of cavalry and unleashed him to raid Richmond. Sheridan failed to capture the Confederate capital, but he battled Jeb Stuart's cavalry at Yellow Tavern (May 11), killing Stuart in the process. Grant then appointed Sheridan to command Union forces in the Shenandoah Valley, where Sheridan cleared the valley of all Rebel forces and devastated the "breadbasket of the South." In the final campaign of the war, Sheridan routed the Confederate forces at Five Forks (April 1, 1865) and ruthlessly pursued Lee until the Confederate general surrendered on April 9.

The postwar period found Sheridan in command of the Fifth Military District of Texas and Louisiana during Reconstruction. Unpopular with the populace, he was transferred to the Department of Missouri, where his principal duties included war against the Plains Indians. Sheridan's adoption of total war against the Native Americans led many politicians to call for his relief from command, but Sheridan waged war in the only manner to which he had been accustomed. Promoted to lieutenant general in 1869, he succeeded Sherman as commanding general of the Union Army in 1883. In that capacity he supervised the subjugation of the Northern Plains Indians and the capture of Geronimo. Phil Sheridan died of a massive heart attack on August 5, 1888, shortly after receiving a promotion to full general. With Sheridan's passing the nation lost a valuable link to its past because Grant, Sherman, and Sheridan each had displayed the indomitable spirit and aggressive leadership that had preserved the Union in the Civil War.

William T. Sherman (1820–1891)

General William Tecumseh Sherman served as commander of the Union armies in the Western Theater. His march to the sea, from Atlanta to Savannah, in 1864 epitomized the transition to total war and gutted the Confederacy, forever making his name anathema in Georgia.

William T. Sherman was born in Lancaster, Ohio, on February 8, 1820. Named after the Shawnee war chief, young Sherman was raised in a foster family and eventually matriculated at West Point in 1836. Graduating sixth in his class, he joined the field artillery branch. He served conspicuously in the Seminole War in Florida. Unlike many of his West Point classmates, Sherman saw no military action in the Mexican War. In 1853, he resigned his commission and accepted a position in a St. Louis bank. At the time of Lincoln's election, Sherman was president of the Louisiana Military Seminary. Casting his fate with the Union, he arrived in Washington, D.C., in time to receive a commission as a colonel and to participate in the First Battle of Bull Run/Manassas. Sherman was transferred to Kentucky to serve on the staff of Robert Anderson, the defender of Fort Sumter, and succeeded Anderson in command of the Department of the Cumberland. His subsequent performance, however, led to his relief and allegations of "temporary insanity."

Sherman recovered and joined U.S. Grant as a division commander in the Battle of Shiloh in April 1862. For the next two years, Sherman's destiny was inexorably linked to that of Grant. He commanded a division in Grant's successful siege of Vicksburg and was soon elevated to command of the Department and Army of the Tennessee. In that capacity, he assisted Grant in raising the siege of Chattanooga in November 1863. When Grant was summoned east to assume command of all Union armies, Sherman inherited command of the western armies. In May 1864, Sherman initiated a campaign to seize Atlanta and destroy the Confederate Army of Tennessee. Atlanta fell in early September, but John Bell Hood's army escaped. Dispatching Major General George Thomas to run down Hood's army, Sherman then led his 62,000 regulars on a march to the sea. From Atlanta to Savannah, Sherman destroyed all military resources in his path. After capturing Savannah on December 20, he then turned north to wreak havoc in the Carolinas and link up with Grant in the trenches before Petersburg. He had reached Durham Station, North Carolina, when Lee finally surrendered. On April 26, Sherman accepted the surrender of the remnants of the old Army of Tennessee, now commanded by General Joseph E. Johnston.

Following the war, Sherman advocated a mild Reconstruction platform and fell from favor with the Radical Republicans who dominated Andrew Johnson's administration. Departing the nation's capital, he established his headquarters in St. Louis, Missouri. Upon Grant's election to the presidency, Sherman became commanding general of the U.S. Army, a post he retained until his retirement in 1883. A dedicated Indian fighter and an early prophet of institutionalized professional education in the army's officer corps, Sherman had a profound impact on the future professionalization of the army. Sherman died on February 14, 1891, from the effects of asthma. Next to Grant, Sherman was the North's greatest military hero. He mastered the intricacies of tactics and logistics better than any general of his age, but his most significant contribution lay in his clear understanding that warfare had entered the dimension of total war.

Edwin McMasters Stanton (1814–1869)

Edwin McMasters Stanton served Abraham Lincoln, as his second secretary of war, and President Andrew Johnson, in the same capacity.

Born in Steubenville, Ohio, in 1814, Stanton suffered from chronic asthma. He worked for several years in his father's business before joining the legal profession in 1836. A loyal member of the Democratic Party, he developed strong anti-slavery views. Upon the death of his wife, Stanton immersed himself in his business, and by 1856 he was one of the Midwest's most successful lawyers. Now immersed in national politics through his relations with several members of the Buchanan administration, Stanton became popular within Democratic Party circles in Washington, D.C. He served briefly as Buchanan's attorney general, but achieved national notoriety for his spirited legal defense of Daniel Sickles, who was acquitted of the murder of Barton Key in 1859 on grounds of temporary insanity. That defense became a landmark in legal circles.

Due to Stanton's organizational ability and political patronage, Lincoln appointed him secretary of war upon the resignation of Simon Cameron. It proved to be an inspired choice. Stanton ruthlessly eliminated fraud and abuse, supported the president's hard-line policies toward military action, and played an instrumental role in the appointment and removal of military commanders. Together with Quartermaster General Montgomery Meigs, Stanton mobilized the North's industrial might that provided the economic resources so vital to the conduct of war. His adept management of logistical support for Grant's 1864 campaigns also played a pivotal role in the ultimate victory of Union arms. Now a full-fledged member of the Republican Party, Stanton took control of the government after Lincoln's death and directly supervised the pursuit and capture of the conspirators involved in the Lincoln assassination plot. Years later, allegations that Stanton himself was involved in the plot proved largely unsubstantiated.

Under Andrew Johnson, Stanton remained in the forefront of Radical Republican efforts to reconstruct the South. Out of tune with Johnson's more moderate efforts, he was suspended by the president on August 11, 1867, thereby triggering the president's impeachment hearings under the Tenure of Office Act. After resigning his office on May 26, 1868, following Johnson's acquittal, Stanton supported Grant's successful presidential bid in 1868. For his support, Grant appointed Stanton to the U.S. Supreme Court in 1869, but Stanton succumbed to asthma, at the age of fifty-five, before he could assume his post.

Probably the most efficient of Lincoln's cabinet members, Stanton proved indispensable in the successful conduct of the war. Despite his actions during Johnson's administration, Stanton's place in the history of the republic remained secure. Under Lincoln's guiding hand, he had been the true organizer of victory.

Alexander H. Stephens (1812–1883)

Alexander Hamilton Stephens served as the first and only vice president of the Confederate States of America. A dedicated member of the Whig Party, he supported states' rights and served inconspicuously as Jefferson Davis's vice president for the duration of the Civil War.

Stephens was born in Georgia sometime in 1812. Orphaned at a relatively early age, he entered Franklin College and graduated first in his class in 1832. Politics became his primary interest, and he served six years in the Georgia state legislature. In the 1840s, Stephens strongly supported the Whig Party in the U.S. House of Representatives but opposed the annexation of Texas, and became an outspoken critic of President James K. Polk's expansionist policies. Following the Mexican War, Stephens joined the Democratic Party and supported popular sovereignty that found expression in the Kansas–Nebraska Act. In all, he spent sixteen years in Congress. A moderate Democrat, Stephens initially opposed secession, but once it had occurred, he helped draft the Confederate constitution in February 1861.

Elected vice president to balance the ticket and to present an image of a moderate government, Stephens delivered a milestone speech on March 21, 1861, in which he expressed his opinion that the cornerstone of the Confederate government rested on the great truth that the Negro was not equal to the white man. The speech alienated incoming President Jefferson Davis, and the relationship between the two leading Confederate politicians remained estranged for the remainder of the war. Stephens played no discernible role in the development and execution of Confederate strategy and, aside from leading several diplomatic teams to negotiate a peaceful resolution of the conflict, played no significant role in the fortunes of the Confederate republic. By 1863, tension between Stephens and Davis further reduced the vice president's effectiveness. With fellow Georgians Robert Toombs and Governor Joseph Brown, Stephens remained a vocal critic of the president for the duration of the war. In February 1865, Stephens led a three-man delegation to Hampton Roads, Virginia, where the Confederate delegation failed to extract any concessions from President Abraham Lincoln and Secretary of State William Seward.

Following the war, Stephens was imprisoned at Fort Warren, Massachusetts, and then returned to his congressional seat. He followed his election with a successful run for the U.S. Senate, then for governor of Georgia in 1882. In the interim, he wrote *A Constitutional View of the Late War Between the States*, a two-volume defense of Southern constitutionalism. He died in 1883, shortly after taking office as governor, a mere footnote in the history of the Confederacy.

Harriet Beecher Stowe (1811–1896)

Harriet Beecher Stowe was a political activist and the author of *Uncle Tom's Cabin*, one of the most influential books in American history. A diehard abolitionist, she led the call for the abolition of slavery and the advancement of women's rights.

Born in Litchfield, Connecticut, on June 14, 1811, Harriet Beecher was the daughter of abolitionist Lyman Beecher. Educated at Litchfield Female Academy and the Hartford Female Seminary, she demonstrated a unique literary talent at an early age and became one of the country's leading educational reformers. Already well known within Connecticut's literary circles, Stowe became swept up in the political furor originating from the enactment of a more forceful Fugitive Slave Act in 1850. Beginning in 1851, she published a series of articles centering on the evils of slavery. Having witnessed runaway slaves firsthand, albeit briefly, during a visit to Cincinnati, Ohio, Stowe struck a resonant chord among the evangelical readers schooled during the Second Great Awakening.

In 1852 Stowe published *Uncle Tom's Cabin, or Life Among the Lowly* in book form to protest the inherent cruelty and inhumanity of slavery. A central theme of the novel was the destruction of the family unit, one of the dominant themes in early Victorian fiction. The book was an instant success, selling in excess of 300,000 copies within a year, causing poet

Henry Wadsworth Longfellow to proclaim that there had never existed such a literary coup de main as *Uncle Tom's Cabin*. Nathaniel Hawthorne wholeheartedly concurred. Within a year the novel was equally popular across the Atlantic and had been transformed into a popular play. A volume that outlined the particulars of Stowe's research appeared in 1853. A decade later, President Abraham Lincoln echoed Longfellow's sentiments and congratulated the world-renowned author when he welcomed Stowe to the White House. Not surprisingly, the Northern public hailed Stowe's literary achievement as much as the Southern press decried its "untruths." Within three years over a dozen Southern novels sought to address the charges that Stowe had leveled against Southern civilization. Their efforts failed to dilute the intellectual fervor that *Uncle Tom's Cabin* had unleashed.

During the Civil War, Stowe remained an activist who campaigned relentlessly for the abolition of slavery. Writing in the *Atlantic Monthly* in 1862, she repeatedly urged Lincoln to take the necessary steps toward racial equality. On January 1, 1863, she openly wept for joy as the Emancipation Proclamation went into effect. With several sons in the Union Army, Stowe prayed earnestly for the cessation of hostilities and rejoiced at the success of Union arms in April 1865. Shaken by the events surrounding Lincoln's assassination, Stowe returned to teaching and spent the next decade advancing the cause of freedmen's education. She continued to write, but nothing rivaled the success of *Uncle Tom's Cabin*. In later years, Stowe argued for universal female suffrage. She suffered a debilitating stroke in 1889 and died seven years later. Some 150 years after its initial publication, *Uncle Tom's Cabin* remains a tribute to the author who defied gender stereotypes and penned the most influential book of her generation.

James Ewell Brown (Jeb) Stuart (1833–1864)

James Ewell Brown (Jeb) Stuart was a Confederate general and chief of cavalry for Robert E. Lee's Army of Northern Virginia. The most famous cavalryman of the war, he redefined cavalry tactics and provided invaluable intelligence to Lee through three years of war. His death in May 1864 proved an irreplaceable loss to the general and to the Confederacy.

Stuart was born at Laurel Hill, Virginia, on February 6, 1833. After graduating from West Point in 1854, he was commissioned a second lieutenant and served on the Texas frontier. Service in Kansas and the American West sharpened his skills as a cavalryman, and when John Brown seized the federal arsenal at Harpers Ferry in October 1859, Stuart served as an aide to Colonel Robert E. Lee in suppressing Brown's force. Resigning his commission to fight for the Confederacy in 1861, Stuart proved an able commander of cavalry. Advanced to the grade of brigadier general for his service during the First Battle of Manassas/Bull Run, he again performed heroically during the Peninsula Campaign of 1862. At Lee's suggestion, Stuart encircled Major General George B. McClellan's forces and provided intelligence that greatly contributed to the ultimate Confederate victory. Now a twenty-eight year-old major general, he achieved legendary status as a cavalry commander in the ensuing campaigns in northern Virginia and Maryland. Again at Fredericksburg, in December 1862, Stuart's horse artillery delayed the initial Union attack. At Chancellorsville the following May, it was Stuart who discovered the exposed right wing of the Union army that Stonewall Jackson successfully attacked on May 2. Following Jackson's wounding, Stuart assumed command of Jackson's corps and led it successfully for the remainder of the battle.

During Lee's second invasion of the North, Stuart failed badly and left Lee uninformed about the enemy's movements. The loss at Gettysburg was due in no small part to Stuart's inability to provide timely intelligence to Lee. In 1864, Stuart redeemed his image by screening Lee's force as it advanced to battle Grant in the Wilderness. When Grant dispatched General Philip Sheridan on a raid toward Richmond, Stuart countered and engaged Sheridan at Todd's Tavern on May 9 and at Yellow Tavern on May 11. During the latter engagement, Stuart was mortally wounded. Transferred to Richmond, he died the following day and was buried in Richmond's Hollywood Cemetery. Upon hearing of his demise, Lee wrote that Stuart had never brought him a piece of false information. One of the Confederacy's brightest stars, Stuart was dead at age thirty-one, but not before he was uniformly recognized as one of the war's premier commanders of mounted cavalry.

Abraham Lincoln, sixteenth president of the United States and commander in chief of all Union armies and navies. (Courtesy of the National Archives of the United States).

Jefferson Davis, West Point (1828) and president of the Confederate States of America. (Courtesy of the National Archives of the United States).

Lieutenant General Ulysses S. Grant, West Point (1843), newly appointed commander of all Union armies, outside City Point, Virginia, at the beginning of the Wilderness Campaign in May 1864. The conqueror of Fort Donelson, Vicksburg, and Chattanooga, Grant compelled Lee to surrender at Appomattox Courthouse on April 9, 1865. (Courtesy of the National Archives of the United States).

General Robert E. Lee, West Point (1829), general-in-chief of all Confederate armies. As commander of the Army of Northern Virginia, Lee twice invaded the North in an effort to secure Confederate independence. (Courtesy of the National Archives of the United States).

Major General William T. Sherman, West Point (1840), commander of all Union armies in the Department of the West. Sherman captured Atlanta in September 1864 and then marched to the sea, destroying all Confederate war matériel in his path. (Courtesy of the National Archives of the United States).

Lieutenant General Thomas J. "Stonewall" Jackson, West Point (1846), commander of the 2nd Corps, Army of Northern Virginia. Lee's "right arm" and most trusted subordinate, Jackson led the flank attack that crushed the Union army at Chancellorsville. His untimely death due to friendly fire proved an irreplaceable loss to the South as Lee began the Gettysburg Campaign. (Courtesy of the National Archives of the United States).

Interior view of Fort Sumter taken in the immediate aftermath of its surrender by Major Robert Anderson on April 14, 1861. (Courtesy of the National Archives of the United States).

Burnside's Bridge, over which the final Union attack occurred at the Battle of Antietam/ Sharpsburg on September 17, 1862. The Battle of Antietam marked the bloodiest day of the war. (Courtesy of the National Archives of the United States).

Battle of Champion Hills, Mississippi, May 16, 1863. Grant's defeat of the Confederate forces under John C. Pemberton led to the siege of Vicksburg, last Confederate bastion on the Mississippi River. Vicksburg surrendered on July 4, 1863. (Courtesy of the National Archives of the United States).

Abandoned Confederate position on Marye's Heights outside Fredericksburg, Virginia, during the Chancellorsville Campaign on May 3, 1863. (Courtesy of the National Archives of the United States).

One of Matthew Brady's cameramen took this photograph of Little Round Top outside Gettysburg, Pennsylvania. Little Round Top was the scene of intense fighting as Lee attempted to drive Major General George G. Meade's forces from the southern end of the Union line on July 2, 1863. (Courtesy of the National Archives of the United States).

The "Dictator," an 8.5-ton Union mortar that comprised a portion of the Union line in the siege of Petersburg in 1864. Grant began the siege in June 1864. The city finally fell when Lee abandoned the Petersburg trenches on April 2, 1865. (Courtesy of the National Archives of the United States).

PRIMARY DOCUMENTS OF THE WAR

Lincoln Takes a Stand Against a Divided Union

In 1858 a virtually unknown Illinois politician by the name of Abraham Lincoln challenged incumbent U.S. Senator Stephen A. Douglas for the U.S. Senate seat from the state of Illinois. Nominated by the Illinois Republican state convention, Lincoln delivered his "House Divided Against Itself" speech, in which he accepted the nomination of his party to oppose Douglas. Harking back to Daniel Webster's reply to Robert Hayne in an earlier crisis, Lincoln traced the evolution of slavery and attacked Douglas as the author of the Kansas–Nebraska Act. That legislation, coupled with the Supreme Court's Dred Scott Decision in 1857, in effect nullified the Missouri Compromise of 1820. In his opening paragraph, Lincoln stated his expectation that civil war would erupt between North and South and that the opponents of slavery would eventual triumph over the pro-slavery faction. Lincoln subsequently engaged Douglas in a series of seven debates that received national attention. The debates had national implications, for Lincoln attacked Douglas savagely on issues including the extension of slavery into the territories, the Kansas–Nebraska Act, the Dred Scott Decision, and popular sovereignty—issues that had shaken the Union for decades. The overriding theme of what became the most popular debates in American history was slavery. By design, the first speaker spoke for one hour, his opponent responded for an hour an a half, and the initial speaker used the final half-hour for rebuttal. Lincoln would eventually lose the election, but he emerged from the debates with a national reputation that would propel him into the White House two years later.

Document 1
Lincoln's "House Divided Against Itself" Speech, June 17, 1858

Mr. President and Gentlemen of the Convention:

If we could first know where we are, and whither we are tending, we could better judge what to do, and how to do it. We are now far into the fifth year since a policy was initiated with the avowed object and confident promise of putting an end to slavery agitation. Under the operation of that policy, that agitation has not only not ceased, but has constantly augmented. In my opinion, it will not cease until a crisis shall have been reached and passed. "A house divided against itself cannot stand." I believe this government cannot endure permanently half slave and half free. I do not expect the Union to be dissolved; I do not expect the house to fall; but I do expect it will cease to be divided. It will become all one thing, or all the other. Either the opponents of slavery will arrest the further spread of it, and place it where the public mind shall rest in belief that it is in the course of ultimate extinction, or its advocates will push it forward till it shall become alike lawful in all the States, old as well as new, North as well as South.

Have we no tendency to the latter condition?

Let any one who doubts, carefully contemplate that now almost complete legal combination—piece of machinery, so to speak—compounded of the Nebraska doctrine and the Dred Scott decision. Let him consider, not only what work the machinery is adapted to do, and how well adapted, but also let him study the history of its construction, and trace, if he can, or rather fail, if he can, to trace the evidences of design, and concert of action, among its chief architects, from the beginning.

. . . Our cause, then must be entrusted to, and conducted by, its own undoubted friends,—those whose hands are free, whose hearts are in the work, who do care for the result. Two years ago the Republicans of the nation mustered over thirteen hundred thousand strong. We did this under the single impulse of resistance to a common danger, with every external circumstance against us. Of strange, discordant, and even hostile elements we gathered from the four winds, and armed and fought the battle through, under the constant hot fire of a disciplined, proud, and pampered enemy. Did we brave all then to falter now,—now, when that same enemy is wavering, dissevered, and belligerent? The result is not doubtful. We shall not fail; if we stand firm, we shall not fail. Wise counsels may accelerate, or mistakes delay it, but, sooner or later, the victory is sure to come.

Source: John G. Nicolay and John Hay, *Abraham Lincoln: A History* (New York: The Century Company, 1890), vol. 2, 136–138.

The First Wave of Sucession

Lincoln's election as the nation's sixteenth president on November 6, 1860, triggered a series of events culminating in the secession of seven states of the Lower South. First to secede was South Carolina. The South Carolina legislature rapidly convened and called for a special convention to meet in Charleston on December 17 to consider the subject of disunion. Based on three decades of state resistance to federal laws, the issue of remaining in the Union was never in doubt. On the designated date, the convention unanimously voted for secession, signing the formal ordinance three days later, thus severing its ties with the Union. Eight years earlier, on April 26, 1852, the people of the state had declared that the "frequent violations of the Constitution of the United States, by the Federal Government" justified secession. Drawing upon the Declaration of Independence and the Articles of Confederation of 1778 that reserved to each state its sovereignty, freedom, and independence, the delegates voiced their opinion that the Constitution of the United States was a compact between two or more parties and that the failure of one of the "contracting parties to perform a material part of the agreement, entirely releases the obligation of the other." The convention in Charleston in 1860 merely confirmed the direction of South Carolina politics since the days of John C. Calhoun and Robert Hayne.

Following South Carolina's lead, Mississippi, Florida, Alabama, Georgia, Louisiana, and Texas quickly followed suit. The states agreed to send delegates to Montgomery, Alabama, no later than February 15 to form a new government. Thus the Confederate States of America was born, modeling its constitution on the federal constitution in most respects except that the Confederate constitution guaranteed the right to own slaves and granted its president a single term of six years. Following Lincoln's call for federal volunteers to suppress the rebellion, Virginia, Arkansas, North Carolina, and Tennessee passed similar ordinances and were admitted to the Confederacy.

Document 2
South Carolina's Ordinance Of Secession, December 20, 1860

AN ORDINANCE to dissolve the union between the State of South Carolina and other States united with her under the compact entitled "The Constitution of the United States of America."

We, the people of the State of South Carolina, in convention assembled, do declare and ordain, and it is hereby declared and ordained, that the ordinance adopted by us in convention on the twenty-third day of May, in the year of our Lord one thousand seven hundred and eighty-eight, whereby the Constitution of the United States of America was ratified, and also all acts and parts of acts of the General Assembly of this State ratifying amendments of the said Constitution, are hereby repealed; and that the union now subsisting between South Carolina and other States, under the name of the "United States of America," is hereby dissolved.

Done at Charleston the twentieth day of December, in the year of our Lord one thousand eight hundred and sixty.

Source: U.S. War Department, *War of the Rebellion: A Compilation of the Official Records of the Union and Confederate Armies,* Washington, DC: Government Printing Office, 1900. ser. IV, vol. 1, p. 1.

Jefferson Davis's Inaugural Address

On February 18, 1861, Jefferson Davis was formally inaugurated as the provisional president of the Confederate States of America in Montgomery, Alabama. Before a crowd estimated at 5,000, he contemplated the auspicious moment, noting that beyond the assemblage, "I saw troubles and thorns innumerable." In a clear voice he then delivered his address, reminding the crowd that like George Washington before him, he did not seek the post and he felt a degree of distrust in his own abilities. With God's help and the support of his fellow Confederates, however, he would rise to the challenge, but his fellow Southerners must be prepared to forgive his mistakes and tolerate his deficiencies. He sought perseverance so that the South would make permanent the provisional nature of its government. In an attempt to garner foreign recognition, Davis then turned toward Europe, as if to remind its nations that their textile markets were contingent on the free flow of Southern cotton. Most important, the newly elected president reminded the crowd that war with the United States, though not inevitable, was a distinct possibility and that the South had to prepare to meet Northern aggression.

Reaction to his speech was uniformly positive, even among Davis's rivals for the presidency. Caught up in the euphoria of the moment, William L. Yancey, an ardent secessionist who had introduced Davis to the Alabama delegation upon his arrival in Montgomery, proclaimed, "The man and the hour have met." His address completed, Davis turned to the business at hand and set out to establish a government for the Confederate States of America.

Document 3
Jefferson Davis's Inaugural Address, February 18, 1861

Gentlemen of the Congress of the Confederate States of America, Friends and Fellow-Citizens:

Called to the difficult and responsible station of Chief Executive of the Provisional Government which you have instituted, I approach the discharge of the duties assigned to me with an humble distrust of my abilities, but with a sustaining confidence in the wisdom of those who are to guide and to aid me in the administration of public affairs, and an abiding faith in the virtue and patriotism of the people.

Looking forward to the speedy establishment of a permanent government to take the place of this [government], and which by its greater moral and physical power will be better able to combat with the many difficulties which arise from the conflicting interests of separate nations, I enter upon the duties of the office to which I have been chosen with the hope that the beginning of our career as a Confederacy may not be obstructed by hostile opposition to our enjoyment of the separate existence and independence which we have asserted, and, with the blessing of Providence, intend to maintain. Our present condition, achieved in a manner unprecedented in the history of nations, illustrates the American idea that governments rest upon the consent of the governed, and that it is the right of the people to alter or abolish governments whenever they become destructive of the ends for which they were established.

The declared purpose of the compact of Union from which we have withdrawn was "to establish justice, insure domestic tranquility, provide for the common defense, promote the general welfare, and secure the blessings of liberty to ourselves and our posterity"; and when, in the judgment of the sovereign States now composing this Confederacy, it had been perverted from the purposes for which it was ordained, and had ceased to answer the ends for which it was established, a peaceful appeal to the ballot-box declared that so far as they were concerned, the government created by that compact should cease to exist. In this they merely asserted a right which the Declaration of Independence of 1776 had defined to be inalienable; of the time and occasion for its exercise, they, as sovereigns, were the final judges, each for itself. The impartial and enlightened verdict of mankind will vindicate the rectitude of our conduct, and He who knows the hearts of men will judge of the sincerity with which we labored to preserve the Government of our fathers in its spirit. The right solemnly proclaimed at the birth of the States, and which has been affirmed and reaffirmed in the bills of rights of States subsequently admitted into the Union of 1789, undeniably recognizes in the people the power to resume the authority delegated for the purposes of government. Thus the sovereign States here represented proceeded to form this Confederacy, and it is by abuse of language that their act has been denominated a revolution. They formed a new alliance, but within each State its government has remained, the rights of person and property have not been disturbed. The agent through whom they communicated with foreign nations is changed, but this does not necessarily interrupt their international relations.

. . . We have changed the constituent parts, but not the system of our Government. The Constitution formed by our fathers is that of these Confederate States, in their exposition of it, and in the judicial construction it has received, we have a light which reveals its true meaning. Thus instructed as to the just interpretation of the instrument, and ever remembering that all offices are but trusts held for the people, and that delegated powers are to be strictly construed, I will hope, by due diligence in the performance of my duties, though I may disappoint your expectations, yet to retain, when retiring, something of the good will and confidence which welcome my entrance into office.

It is joyous, in the midst of perilous times, to look around upon a people united in heart, where one purpose of high resolve animates and actuates the whole—where the sacrifices to be made are not weighed in the balance against honor and right and liberty and equality. Obstacles may retard, they cannot long prevent the progress of a movement sanctified by its justice, and sustained by a virtuous people. Reverently let us invoke the God of our fathers to guide and protect us in our efforts to perpetuate the principles which, by His blessing, they were able to vindicate, establish, and transmit to their posterity, and with a continuance of His favor, ever gratefully acknowledged, we may hopefully look forward to success, to peace, and to prosperity.

Source: U.S. War Department, *War of the Rebellion: A Compilation of the Official Records of the Union and Confederate Armies*, Washington, DC: Government Printing Office, 1900. ser. IV, vol. 1, 104–106.

A Northern Soldier Recalls the Battle of Antietam

In response to Lincoln's call for additional volunteers, George Thomas Stevens enlisted in the 77th New York Volunteer Regiment in November 1861. The Honorable James B. McKean, a former member of Congress, was appointed colonel and supervised the mustering of 1,000 officers and men at Saratoga Springs, New York, on November 23. Known as the Bemis Heights Battalion after the location of the decisive battle in the American Revolution, the regiment departed its home base on Thanksgiving Day. By the time they reached Washington, D.C., 100 men were sick. Within three months the regiment had joined the Army of the Potomac on the Peninsula and fought at Yorktown and the Seven Days' Campaign. September 1862 found the regiment at Antietam, where it participated in the bloodiest day's fighting in the Civil War. Following the battle, Stevens described the horrible scenes of one of the war's most decisive engagements in a letter to his family.

Document 4
Scenes on the Battlefield Of Antietam, September 17, 1862

The scene on the battlefield was past description. The mangled forms of our own comrades lay stretched upon the ground, side by side with those of the rebels. On almost every rod of ground over one hundred acres, the dead and wounded, some clad in the Union blue and some in confederate gray, were lying. A ghastly sight, presenting all the horrible features of death which are to be seen on such a field. At one point in our own front, for more than half a mile, the rebels lay so thickly as almost to touch each other. On the field where [Fighting Joe] Hooker's men had won and lost the field, the dead and dying were scattered thickly among the broken cornstalks, their eyes protruding and their faces blackened by the sun. Wherever the lines of battle had surged to and fro, these vestiges of the terrible work were left. In the edge of the wood, where the rebels had made a stand against Hooker's advancing divisions, the bodies lay in perfect line, as though they had fallen while on dress parade. Further to the left there was a narrow road, not more than fifteen feet wide, with high fences on either side. Here a regiment of rebels was posted; when our batteries getting an enfilading fire upon them, and the infantry at the same time opening a murderous fire, the regiment was literally destroyed; not more than twenty of their number escaping. Their bodies filled the narrow road. Some were shot while attempting to get over the fence; and their remains hung upon the boards. A more fearful picture than we saw here could not be conceived.

Broken caissons, wheels, dismounted guns, thousands of muskets, blankets, haversacks, and canteens, were scattered thickly over the field; and hundreds of slain horses, bloated and with feet turned toward the sky, added to the horror of the scene.

While the excitement of battle lasts, and we hear the roar of artillery, and the shock of contending armies, the terrible reality of the occasion hardly presents itself to our minds, and it is only when we survey the bloody field, strewed with the mangled, lifeless remains of friend and foe, or walk through the hospitals, where the unfortunate victims of battle writhe in the agony of their wounds, that we realize the terrible nature of a great battle.

Sickening as is the sight of the battlefield, the scenes about the hospitals are worse, except to those who are actually engaged in ministering to the relief of the wounded. To these the excitement and labor incident to their duties, crowd out the thoughts of the ghastly surroundings. They see only so many demands upon them for assistance, and have no time to indulge in sentimental emotions.

Here in the rear of the army for miles, was a succession of hospitals. Every house, and barn, and haystack, formed the nucleus of a hospital, where men, shot through the head, through the limbs, through the body; with every conceivable variety of wounds, lay groaning in anguish. Surgeons toiled day and night with never lagging zeal to relieve these sufferings, but all their labor could only afford slight relief. The labors of medical officers after a great battle are immense, and there is no respite. . . . While others find repose from the fatigues of battle in sleep, the surgeons are still at work; there is no sleep for them so long as work remains to be done.

Source: George Thomas Stevens, *Three Years in the Sixth Corps* (Albany, NY: S.R. Gray, 1866), 153–154.

Lincoln Discusses War Aims

By the summer of 1862 Abraham Lincoln had moved deliberately to abolish slavery in the rebellious states. Such an open declaration, however, at the time the Union faced military defeat, was deemed politically dangerous and a show of weakness. Moreover, Lincoln feared emancipation might drive the border states into the Confederacy. Various abolitionists remained undeterred and mounted increasing pressure on the president to move toward total emancipation. One such proponent was Horace Greeley, the editor of the *New York Tribune* and a frequent presidential critic, who assailed Lincoln for moving slowly on the issue of emancipation. In Greeley's opinion, Lincoln "was strangely and disastrously remiss in the discharge of his official and imperative duty with regard to the emancipating provisions" of the Confiscation Act. Only by emancipating the slaves would Lincoln answer the prayer of 20 million Americans.

In an oft-quoted response, Lincoln reminded Greeley that his paramount concern remained the preservation of the Union, not the emancipation of the slaves. Simultaneously, Lincoln stated that he "might move" toward emancipation if in his mind such action might help preserve the Union. Within months, of course, Lincoln moved toward issuing a preliminary emancipation proclamation, but he did so as a war measure to preserve the Union.

Document 5
Lincoln's Reply To Horace Greeley, August 22, 1862

Executive Mansion,
Washington, August 22, 1862
Hon. Horace Greeley:

Dear Sir, I have just read yours of the 19th addressed to myself through the *New York Tribune*. If there be in it any statements, or assumptions of fact, which I may know to be erroneous, I do not, now and here, controvert them. If there be in it any inferences which I may believe to be falsely drawn, I do not, now and here, argue against them. If there be perceptible in it an impatient and dictatorial tone, I waive it in deference to an old friend, whose heart I have always supposed to be right.

As to the policy I "seem to be pursuing," as you say, I have not meant to leave any one in doubt.

I would save the Union. I would save it the shortest way under the Constitution. The sooner the national authority can be restored; the nearer the Union will be "the Union as it was." If there be those who would not save the Union, unless they could at the same time save slavery, I do not agree with them. If there be those who would not save the Union unless they could at the same time destroy slavery, I do not agree with them. My paramount object in this struggle is to save the Union, and is not either to save or to destroy slavery. If I could save the Union without freeing any slave, I would do it, and if I could save it by freeing all the slaves, I would do it; and if I could save it by freeing some and leaving others alone, I would also do that. What I do about slavery, and the colored race, I do because I believe it helps to save the Union; and what I forbear, I forbear because I do not believe it would help to save the Union. I shall do less whenever I shall believe what I am doing hurts the cause, and I shall do more whenever I shall believe doing more will help the cause. I shall try to correct errors when shown to be errors; and I shall adopt new views so fast as they shall appear to be true views.

I have here stated my purpose according to my view of official duty; and I intend no modification of my oft-expressed personal wish that all men everywhere could be free.

Yours,

A. Lincoln

Source: John G. Nicolay and John Hay, *Abraham Lincoln: A History* (New York: The Century Company, 1890), vol. 6, 152–153.

Lincoln Frees The Slaves

With the war in its second year, Lincoln recognized the ever-changing nature of the conflict. Limited war had given way to total war with its accompanying dictates of military necessity and political expediency to achieve war aims. By the summer of 1862, Lincoln moved forcibly to abolish slavery within the parameters of the Constitution. Drafting an executive proclamation to abolish slavery, he viewed this action as a war measure meant to discourage foreign recognition of the Confederacy and to strike the center of the South's socioeconomic system. Emancipation was "a military necessity, absolutely essential to the preservation of the Union," since the slaves were "undeniably an element of strength to those who had their service." To those who would view his act unconstitutional, the president dismissed their arguments, stating that the Constitution invests the commander-in-chief with the law of war in time of war. As for the dissident Southerners who would claim that the president was usurping the Constitution, Lincoln replied that those "who have sought to throw off the Constitution . . . can not invoke its aid."

Lincoln informed his cabinet of his intention to emancipate the slaves in late July 1862. Merely waiting for a Northern victory to announce his proclamation, Lincoln weathered the Union defeat at Second Bull Run/ Manassas and the fate of Lee's first invasion of the North. When Lee recrossed the Potomac River following his defeat at Sharpsburg on September 17, Lincoln took the decisive step. The significance of the Emancipation Proclamation was not lost on its author: "If my name ever goes into history, it will be for this act."

Document 6
Emancipation Proclamation, January 1, 1863

By the President of the United States of America: A Proclamation

Whereas, on the twenty-second day of September, in the year of our Lord one thousand eight hundred and sixty-two, a proclamation was issued by the President of the United States, containing, among other things, the following, to wit: "That on the first day of January, in the year of our Lord one thousand eight hundred and sixty-three, all persons held as slaves within any State or designated part of a State, the people whereof shall then be in rebellion against the United States, shall be then, thenceforward, and forever free; and the military and naval authority thereof, will recognize and maintain the freedom of such persons, and will do no act or acts to repress such persons, or any of them, in any efforts they may make for their actual freedom.

"That the Executive will, on the first day of January aforesaid, by proclamation, designate the States and parts of States, if any, in which the people thereof, respectively, shall then be in rebellion against the United States and the fact that any State, or the people thereof, shall on that day be, in good faith, represented in the Congress of the United States by members chosen thereto at elections wherein a majority of the qualified voters of such State shall have participated, shall, in the absence of strong countervailing testimony, be deemed conclusive evidence that such State, and the people thereof, are not then in rebellion against the United States."

Now, therefore I, Abraham Lincoln, President of the United States, by virtue of the power in me vested as Commander-in-chief, of the Army and Navy of the United States in time of actual armed rebellion against the authority and government of the United States, and as a fit and necessary war measure for suppressing said rebellion, do, on this first day of January, in the year of our Lord one thousand eight hundred and sixty-three, and in accordance with my purpose so to do publicly proclaimed for the full period of one hundred days, from the day first above mentioned, order and designate as the States and parts of States wherein the people thereof respectively, are this day in rebellion against the United States, the following, to wit:

Arkansas, Texas, Louisiana, (except the Parishes of St. Bernard, Plaquemines, Jefferson, St. John, St. Charles, St. James Ascension, Assumption, Terrebonne, Lafourche, St. Mary, St. Martin, and Orleans, including the City of New Orleans), Mississippi, Alabama, Florida, Georgia, South Carolina, North Carolina, and Virginia, (except the forty-eight counties designated as West Virginia, and also the counties of Berkley, Accomac[k], Northampton, Elizabeth City, York, Princess Anne, and Norfolk, including the cities of Norfolk and Portsmouth, and which excepted parts, are for the present, left precisely as if this proclamation were not issued).

And by virtue of the power, and for the purpose aforesaid, I do order and declare that all persons held as slaves within said designated States, and parts of States, are, and henceforward shall be free; and that the Executive government of the United States, including the military and naval authorities thereof, will recognize and maintain the freedom of said persons.

And I hereby enjoin upon the people so declared to be free to abstain from all violence, unless in necessary self-defense; and I recommend to them that, in all cases when allowed, they labor faithfully for reasonable wages.

And I further declare and make known, that such persons of suitable condition, will be received into the armed service of the United States to garrison forts, positions, stations, and other places, and to man vessels of all sorts in said service. And upon this act, sincerely believed to be an act of justice, warranted by the Constitution, upon military necessity, I invoke the considerate judgment of mankind, and the gracious favor of Almighty God.

In witness whereof, I have hereunto set my hand and caused the seal of the United States to be affixed.

Done at the City of Washington, this first day of January, in the year of our Lord one thousand eight hundred and sixty-three, and of the Independence of the United States of America the eighty-seventh.

By the President: ABRAHAM LINCOLN
WILLIAM H. SEWARD, Secretary of State.

Source: John G. Nicolay and John Hay, *Abraham Lincoln: A History* (New York: The Century Company, 1890), vol. 6, 422–428.

The Battle of Little Round Top

The Battle of Gettysburg was the largest battle ever fought on the North American continent. For three days in early July 1863, Robert E. Lee's Army of Northern Virginia vigorously attacked George Gordon Meade's Army of the Potomac. On July 2, the most ferocious engagement occurred on the southern extremity of Meade's line around a rocky precipice known as Little Round Top. Holding the far left of the Union line was Colonel Joshua Lawrence Chamberlain's 20th Maine Volunteer Regiment. Chamberlain epitomized the citizen–soldier who fought the American Civil War. A professor of rhetoric at Bowdoin College in Maine, he took a sabbatical and offered his services to the governor of Maine in 1862. Receiving his baptism of fire at the Battle of Fredericksburg in December 1862, Chamberlain assumed command of the regiment on the eve of the Battle of Gettysburg. The regiment numbered 358 men, including roughly 120 soldiers from the 2nd Maine Regiment. Chamberlain positioned his men on the far left of the Union line. Following is a description of the engagement by Chamberlain, as reported three days following the battle that ended Lee's second invasion of the North. For conspicuous gallantry above and beyond the call of duty, Chamberlain later received the Congressional Medal of Honor for his actions on July 2.

Document 7
"Hold That Ground at all Hazards," July 2, 1863

The enemy's artillery got range of our column as we were climbing the spur, and the crashing of the shells among the rocks and the tree tops made us move lively along the crest. One or two shells burst in our ranks.

Passing to the southern slope of Little Round Top, Colonel Vincent [the brigade commander] indicated to me the ground my regiment was to occupy, informing me that this was the extreme left of our general line, and that a desperate attack was expected in order to turn that position, concluding by telling me I was to "hold that ground at all hazards." This was the last word I heard from him.

In order to commence by making my right firm, I formed my regiment on the right into line, giving such direction to the line as should best secure the advantage of the rough, rocky, and stragglingly wooded ground. The line faced generally toward a more conspicuous eminence southwest of ours, which is known as Sugar Loaf, or Round Top. Between this and my position intervened a smooth and thinly wooded hollow. . . . Mounting a large rock, I was able to see a considerable body of the enemy moving by the flank in rear of their line engaged, and passing from the direction of the foot of Great Round Top through the valley toward the front of my left. The close engagement not allowing any change of front, I immediately stretched my regiment to the left, by taking intervals by the left flank, and at the same time "refusing" my left wing, so that it was nearly at right angles with my right, thus occupying about twice the extent of our ordinary front, some of the companies being brought into single rank when the nature of the ground gave sufficient strength or shelter.

. . . The enemy's flanking column, having gained their desired direction, burst upon my left, where they evidently had expected an unguarded flank, with great demonstration. We opened a brisk fire at close range, which was so sudden and effective that they soon fell back among the rocks and low trees in the valley, only to burst forth again with a shout, and rapidly advanced, firing as they came. They pushed up to within a dozen yards of us before the terrible effectiveness of our fire compelled them to break and take shelter. They renewed the assault on our whole front, and for an hour the fighting was severe. Squads of the enemy broke through our line in several places, and the fight was literally hand-to-hand. The edge of the fight rolled backward and forward like a wave. The dead and wounded were now in our front and then in our rear. Forced from our position, we desperately recovered it, and pushed the enemy down to the foot of the slope.

. . . The enemy seemed to have gathered all their energies for their final assault. We had gotten our thin line into as good a shape as possible, when a strong force emerged from the scrub wood in the valley, and . . . we opened on them as well as we could with our scanty ammunition snatched from the field. It did not seem possible to withstand another shock like this now coming on. Our loss had been severe. One-half of my left wing had fallen, and a third of my regiment lay just behind us, dead or badly wounded. . . . My ammunition was soon exhausted. My men were firing their last shot and getting ready to "club" their muskets.

It was imperative to strike before we were struck by this overwhelming force in a hand-to-hand fight, which we could not probably have withstood or survived. At that crisis, I ordered the bayonet. The word was enough. It ran like fire along the line, from man to man, and rose into a shout, with which they sprang forward upon the enemy, now not 30 yards away. The effect was surprising; many of the enemy's first line threw down their arms and surrendered. An officer fired his pistol at my head with one hand, while he handed me his sword with the other. Holding fast by our right, and swinging forward our left, we made an extended "right wheel," before which the enemy's second line broke and fell back, fighting from tree to tree, many being captured, until we had swept the valley and cleared the front of nearly our entire brigade.

. . . Four hundred prisoners, including two field and seven line officers, were sent to the rear. . . . One hundred and fifty of the enemy were found killed and wounded in our front. . . . We went into the fight with 386, all told—358 guns. Every pioneer and musician who could carry a musket went into the ranks. Even the sick and foot-sore, who could not keep up in the march, came up as soon as they could find their regiments, and took their places in line of battle, while it was battle, indeed. Some prisoners I had under guard, under sentence of court-martial, I was obliged to put into the fight, and they bore their part well, for which I shall recommend a commutation of their sentence. The loss, so far as I can ascertain it, is 136—30 of whom were killed, and among the wounded are many mortally.

Joshua L. Chamberlain,
Colonel, Commanding Twentieth Maine Volunteers.

Source: U.S. War Department, *War of the Rebellion: A Compilation of the Official Records of the Union and Confederate Armies,* Washington, DC: Government Printing Office, 1889. ser. I, vol. 27, pt. 1, 622–626.

Lee Offers to Resign Following the Battle of Gettysburg

The failure of Lee's second invasion of the North, coupled with the fall of Vicksburg on July 4, 1863, cast a dark pall on Confederate military fortunes. Had General George Gordon Meade been a more capable military commander, he would not have allowed Lee's Army of Northern Virginia to escape to Virginia following its defeat at the Battle of Gettysburg. Not surprisingly, recriminations, some directed against Lee himself, for his army's failure appeared in numerous Southern newspapers in the aftermath of the campaign. Always a proud individual, Lee was stung by these criticisms. In his personal report of the battle he informed President Jefferson Davis that the army had achieved "a general success, though it did not win a victory." As for the failure of his final assault [Pickett's Charge], Lee noted that had he known the outcome, he would have pursued a different course, but "what the ultimate result would have been is not so clear to me."

Following a time-honored principle for military commanders who have suffered defeat in the field, Lee then wrote to Davis and offered to resign from command of the Army of Northern Virginia since "the general remedy for the want of success in a military commander" was relief from command. Already suffering from a heart condition that limited his mobility on the battlefield, Lee suggested that his replacement be a younger officer who might be "more capable of exertion." Davis replied a few days later, informing Lee that in his [Davis's] judgment, "to substitute . . . some one more fit to command, or who would possess more of the confidence of the army. . . is to demand an impossibility." Lee would remain in command and the war would continue.

Document 8
Lee's Letter to Jefferson Davis, August 8, 1863

Camp Orange, August 8, 1863
His Excellency JEFFERSON DAVIS
President of the Confederate States:

Mr. PRESIDENT: Your letters of July 28 and August 2 have been received, and I have waited for a leisure hour to reply, but I fear that will never come. I am extremely obliged to you for the attention given to the wants of this army, and the efforts made to supply them. Our absentees are returning, and I hope the earnest and beautiful appeal made to the country in your proclamation may stir up the virtue of the whole people, and that they may see their duty and perform it. Nothing is wanted but that their fortitude should equal their bravery to insure the success of our cause. We must expect reverses, even defeats. They are sent to teach us wisdom and prudence, to call forth greater energies, and to prevent our falling into greater disasters. Our people have only to be true and united, to bear manfully the misfortunes incident to war, and all will come right in the end.

I know how prone we are to censure and how ready to blame others for the non-fulfillment of our expectations. This is unbecoming in a generous people, and I grieve to see its expression. The general remedy for the want of success in a military commander is his removal. This is natural, and, in many instances, proper. For, no matter what may be the ability of the officer, if he loses the confidence of his troops, disaster must sooner or later ensue.

I have been prompted by these reflections more than once since my return from Pennsylvania to propose to Your Excellency the propriety of selecting another commander for this army. I have seen and heard of expression of discontent in the public journals at the result of the expedition. I do not know how far this feeling extends in the army. My brother officers have been too kind to report it, and so far the troops have been too generous to exhibit it. It is fair, however, to suppose that it does exist, and success is so necessary to us that nothing should be risked to secure it. I therefore, in all sincerity, request Your Excellency to take measures to supply my place. I do this with the more earnestness because no one is more aware than myself of my inability for the duties of my position. I cannot even accomplish what I myself desire. How can I fulfill the expectations of others? In addition I sensibly feel the growing failure of my bodily strength. I have not yet recovered from the attack I experienced the past spring. I am becoming more and more incapable of exertion, and am thus prevented from making the personal examinations and giving the personal supervision to the operations in the field which I feel to be necessary. I am so dull that in making use of the eyes of others, I am frequently misled. Everything, therefore, points to the advantages to be derived from a new commander, and I the more anxiously urge the matter upon Your Excellency from my belief that a younger and abler man than myself can readily be attained. I know that he will have as gallant and brave an army as ever existed to second his efforts, and it would be the happiest day of my life to see at its head a worthy leader—one that would accomplish more than I could perform and all that I have wished. I hope Your Excellency will attribute my request to the true reason, the desire to serve my country, and to do all in my power to insure the success of her righteous cause.

I have no complaints to make of any one but myself. I have received nothing but kindness from those above me, and most considerate attention from my comrades and companions in arms. To Your Excellency I am specially [sic] indebted for uniform kindness and consideration. You have done everything in your power to aid me in the work committed to my charge, without omitting anything to promote the general welfare. I pray that your efforts may at length be crowned with success and that you may long live to enjoy the thanks of a grateful people.

With sentiments of great esteem, I am, very respectfully and truly, yours,

R.E. LEE,
General

Source: U.S. War Department, *War of the Rebellion: A Compilation of the Official Records of the Union and Confederate Armies,* Washington, DC: Government Printing Office, 1897. ser. I, vol. 51, pt. 2, 752–753.

Care and Transportation of Wounded Soldiers

Of the roughly 620,000 Americans who died during the Civil War, fully two-thirds died of infection or disease. Astronomical as these figures were, they were a dramatic improvement over prior wars, in which the ratio of death by disease to death by battle often exceeded five or six to one. A medical revolution in which the new science of bacteriology was discovered and antiseptic surgery was introduced followed the war, but these innovations occurred too late to benefit the soldiers who fell in battle.

Edward Vollum, a medical inspector with the office of the surgeon general, U.S. Army, received orders to proceed to Gettysburg in the immediate aftermath of the battle and to report on the transportation of the wounded. He arrived at Gettysburg on July 8, 1863. Despite the efforts of the U.S. Sanitary Commission, a large voluntary association designed to ease the suffering, and the formation of a new ambulance corps, literally thousands of soldiers died due to inadequate medical treatment and inadequate transportation to larger hospitals. In his report, Vollum made a distinction between the U.S. Sanitary Commission and the senior officials of the railroad companies, who seemed more interested in making a financial profit from a government contract.

Document 9
Edward P. Vollum, A Medical Inspector, Visits Gettysburg, July 8, 1863
Washington, D.C., July 25, 1863

General: I have the honor to report that, pursuant to your orders of the 7th July, I proceeded on the same day to Gettysburg, Pa., for the purpose of reporting to Medical Inspector Cuyler, U.S. Army, for duty in connection with the transportation of the wounded at that place. I was detained a few hours, on the 8th, at Hanover, Pa., where I found about 150 wounded, chiefly from [Judson] Kilpatrick's cavalry, under charge of Assistant Surgeon Gardner, First [West] Virginia Cavalry. They were comfortably situated in a school-house and in dwellings. The inhabitants had furnished them with bunks, bedding, dressings, utensils, and food in sufficient quantity, the people in each street in the town furnishing food, delicacies, nurses, &c., two days at a time.

I arrived at Gettysburg about 7 p.m. on the 8th, and in consequence of some irregularity or delay in the railroad trains, there were about 2,000 slightly wounded men collected at a point a mile from town, where the trains stopped, without food, shelter, or attendance for the night. Fortunately, through the agents of the Sanitary Commission, these men were all fed, and some 300 sheltered that night. No system had as yet been adopted for the transportation of the wounded, nor had this been possible in the deranged condition of the railroad, though Surgeon J.D. Osborne, Fourth New Jersey... in charge of the hospitals at Gettysburg, was using his best endeavors to work through the confusion and crowds of wounded with which he was surrounded . . . the railroad authorities were perplexed, and deficient in motive power and rolling stock. The bridges put up since the rebel raids proved too weak excepting for the lightest engines, and for a second time some were carried away by the floods.

Medical Inspector Cuyler arrived on the 11th, when I reported to him for duty, and, by mutual arrangement, I continued in immediate charge of the transportation of the wounded which confined me to the railroad depot and city of Gettysburg. Every train of wounded was placed in charge of a medical officer. . . . Instruments, dressings, stimulants, &c.,

were furnished him, and he was instructed to announce his coming by telegraph, if possible, and to report in person to the medical director at the place of his destination. Each car was filled with a sufficient quantity of hay, and, on the longer routes, water-coolers, tin cups, bed-pans, and urinals were placed in them, and guarded on the route by some agents of the Sanitary Commission. In some instances, these conveniences were furnished by the medical department, but the demand for them by the hospitals often exhausted the supplies at the purveyors. Before leaving, the wounded were fed and watered by the Sanitary Commission, and often hundreds of wounded, laid over for a night or a part of a day, were attended and fed by the Commission, whose agents placed them in the cars.

Before the arrival of Medical Inspector Cuyler . . . I endeavored to make up the deficiencies in medical supplies at Gettysburg by telegraphing to Surgeon [Josiah] Simpson, U.S. Army, at Baltimore. In reply, he ordered liberal supplies of alcohol, solution chloride of soda, tincture of iron, creosote, nitric acid, permanganate of potassa [sic], buckets, tin cups, stretchers, bed-sacks, and stationery of all kinds for 10,000 men in field hospitals.

Very respectfully, your obedient servant,
EDW. P. VOLLUM, Medical Inspector, U.S. Army

P.S.—I neglected to comment in the proper place upon the utter indifference manifested by the railroad companies toward the sufferings and wants of our wounded at Gettysburg, Pa. I allude to those over whose roads our mangled soldiers traveled to various points from Gettysburg. The period of ten days following the battle . . . was the occasion of the greatest amount of human suffering known to this nation since its birth, and, as was natural and unavoidable among a Christian people, benevolent societies, Sanitary and Christian Commissions, express companies, fire organizations, bands of generous people of all denominations, and individuals from great distances, all came forward with their offerings, sympathy, and personal services. . . . The railroad companies, who got the only profit of the battle, and who had the greatest opportunities of ameliorating the sufferings of the wounded, alone stood aloof and rendered no aid. Their trains were allowed to go off without a single individual attached to them in any way authorized to minister to the wounded.

There was no check-line or means of stopping the train in case of necessity; no way provided for passing from car to car. The cars—ordinary stock and freight cars—were always unclean; no one connected with the companies to clean them; the dung of cattle and litter from freight often remaining to be removed by any extemporized means at hand. There was no water, or vessels to contain it, no lanterns, no straw—absolutely nothing but the bare cars, filthy from the business of transporting freight and cattle. The only agents of the railroad companies that appeared upon this memorable scene were those sent especially to look after their pecuniary interests, and I can testify to their zeal in getting the actual numbers transported and securing the proper certificates therefore, but beyond this they did nothing.

Source: U.S. War Department, *War of the Rebellion: A Compilation of the Official Records of the Union and Confederate Armies,* Washington, DC: Government Printing Office, 1897. ser. I, vol. 27, pt. 1, 25–28.

Lincoln Redefines the War at Gettysburg

On November 19, 1863, President Abraham Lincoln accepted an invitation to deliver a "few appropriate remarks" at the dedication of a national cemetery on the site of the Gettysburg battlefield. For some time Lincoln had been looking for an opportunity to issue a public statement to explain to the American people the significance of the Civil War and to bolster their morale for the great task remaining before them. Contrary to popular opinion, the president did not write the address on the back of an envelope while en route to Gettysburg. Rather, he wrote a portion of the initial draft over the course of two weeks prior to November 19, then applied the finishing touches on the eve of the address. Five manuscript copies of the Gettysburg Address in Lincoln's own hand have survived, but there are no doubt others that the president provided for his friends. All contain minor differences, but the copy he gave Colonel Alexander Bliss remains the most widely accepted version of his remarks.

A crowd in excess of 6,000 attended the dedication of the cemetery and heard Lincoln's remarks. The featured speaker was Edward Everett, the former governor of Massachusetts and the nation's most noted orator. Everett spoke for nearly two hours, and following a brief introduction, Lincoln rose to speak. In less than two minutes, he redefined the war aims and called for a new birth of freedom. Rededicating the nation to the unfinished work that lay before it, Lincoln transformed the war from merely a struggle to preserve the Union to the creation of a new nation based on equality and liberty. Lincoln viewed the address as a "flat failure." "That speech won't scour," he told his friend Ward Hill Lamon, but history has judged his remarks to be the greatest speech in American history.

Document 10
The Gettysburg Address, November 19, 1863

Four score and seven years ago our fathers brought forth on this continent a new nation, conceived in liberty and dedicated to the proposition that all men are created equal. Now we are engaged in a great civil war, testing whether that nation or any nation, can long endure. We are met on a great battlefield of that war. We have come to dedicate a portion of that field as a final resting-place for those who here gave their lives that that nation might live. It is altogether fitting and proper that we should do this. But in a larger sense, we cannot dedicate, we cannot consecrate, we cannot hallow this ground. The brave men, living and dead who struggled here have consecrated it far above our poor power to add or detract. The world will little note nor long remember what we say here, but it can never forget what they did here.

It is for us the living rather to be dedicated here to the unfinished work which they who fought here have thus far so nobly advanced. It is rather for us to be here dedicated to the great task remaining before us— that from these honored dead we take increased devotion to that cause for which they gave that last full measure of devotion—that we here highly resolve that these dead shall not have died in vain, that this nation under God shall have a new birth of freedom, and that government of the people, by the people, for the people shall not perish from the earth.

Source: John G. Nicolay and John Hay, *Abraham Lincoln: A History* (New York: The Century Company, 1890), vol. 8, 200–201.

The Evolution Toward Total War

By late 1864, the war had taken a sinister turn. Limited war had given way to total war, involving the full resources of North and South. No general better personified this transition than William Tecumseh Sherman, commanding the western armies of the United States. While Grant and Meade battled Lee in Virginia, Sherman conducted a successful campaign that brought him to the outskirts of Atlanta in midsummer. After a bloody and brutal campaign that witnessed thousands of casualties, Atlanta surrendered to Sherman on September 2. Sherman's armies occupied the city and delivered an ultimatum to the civil authorities, directing them to evacuate the city. The city authorities appealed directly to Sherman, urging him to be more lenient to Atlanta's inhabitants. Their request evoked an angry reply by Sherman, who defined war in its harshest terms. Years later Sherman would proclaim, "War is hell," but in 1864 he limited his discourse to "War is cruelty and you cannot refine it." The outcome remained the same—there would be no leniency from Sherman. The South had initiated the war; now it must suffer the consequences until the Confederacy yielded to federal authority. In November 1864, Sherman led his armies from Atlanta to Savannah, destroying all war resources in his path. The war had entered a new stage.

Document 11
General Sherman's Letter to the City Council Of Atlanta, September 12, 1864

James M. Calhoun, Mayor, E.E. Rawson, and S.C. Wells, representing City Council of Atlanta:

Gentlemen: I have your letter of the 11th, in the nature of a petition to revoke my orders removing all the inhabitants from Atlanta. I have read it carefully, and give full credit to your statements of the distress that will be occasioned, and yet shall not revoke my orders, because they were not designed to meet the humanities of the case, but to prepare for the future struggles in which millions of good people outside of Atlanta have a deep interest. We must have peace, not only at Atlanta, but in all America. To secure this, we must stop the war that now desolates our once happy and favored country. To stop war, we must defeat the rebel armies which are arrayed against the laws and Constitution that all must respect and obey. To defeat those armies, we must prepare the way to reach them in their recesses, provided with the arms and instruments which enable us to accomplish our purpose. Now, I know the vindictive nature of our enemy, that we may have many years of military operations from this quarter; and, therefore, deem it wise and prudent to prepare in time. The use of Atlanta for warlike purposes is inconsistent with its character as a home for families. There will be no manufactures, commerce, or agriculture here, for the maintenance of families, and sooner or later want will compel the inhabitants to go. Why not go now, when all the arrangements are completed for the transfer, instead of waiting till the plunging shot of contending armies will renew the scenes of the past month? Of course, I do not apprehend any such thing at this moment, but you do not suppose this army will be here until the war is over. I cannot discuss this subject with you fairly, because I cannot impart to you what we propose to do, but I assert that our military plans make it necessary for the inhabitants to go away, and I can only renew my offer of services to make their exodus in any direction as easy and comfortable as possible.

You cannot qualify war in harsher terms than I will. War is cruelty, and you cannot refine it; and those who brought war into our country deserve all the curses and maledictions a people can pour out. I know I had no hand in making this war, and I know I will make more sacrifices today than any of you to secure peace. But you cannot have peace and a division of our country. If the United States submits to a division now, it will not stop, but will go on until we reap the fate of Mexico, which is eternal war. The United States does and must assert its authority, wherever it once had power; for, if it relaxes one bit to pressure, it is gone, and I believe that such is the national feeling. This feeling assumes various shapes, but always comes back to that of Union. Once admit the Union, once more acknowledge the authority of the national Government, and, instead of devoting your houses and streets and roads to the dread uses of war, I and this army become at once your protectors and supporters, shielding you from danger, let it come from what quarter it may. I know that a few individuals cannot resist a torrent of error and passion, such as swept the South into rebellion, but you can point out, so that we may know those who desire a government, and those who insist on war and its desolation.

You might as well appeal against the thunder-storm as against these terrible hardships of war. They are inevitable, and the only way the people of Atlanta can hope once more to live in peace and quiet at home, is to stop the war, which can only be done by admitting that it began in error and is perpetuated in pride.

We don't want your negroes, or your horses, or your houses, or your lands, or any thing you have, but we do want and will have a just obedience to the laws of the United States. That we will have, and, if it involves the destruction of your improvements, we cannot help it.

You have heretofore read public sentiment in your newspapers that live by falsehood and excitement; and the quicker you seek for truth in other quarters, the better. I repeat then that, by the original compact of the Government, the United States had certain rights in Georgia, which have never been relinquished and never will be; that the South began war by seizing forts, arsenals, mints, custom-houses, etc. long before Mr. Lincoln was installed, and before the South had one jot or tittle of provocation. I myself have seen in Missouri, Kentucky, Tennessee, and Mississippi, hundreds and thousands of women and children fleeing from your armies and desperadoes, hungry and with bleeding feet. In Memphis, Vicksburg, and Mississippi, we fed thousands upon thousands of the families of rebel soldiers left on our hands, and whom we could not see starve. Now that war comes home to you, you feel very different. You deprecate its horrors, but did not feel them when you sent car-loads of soldiers and ammunition, and moulded [sic] shells and shot, to carry war into Kentucky and Tennessee, to desolate the homes of hundreds and thousands of good people who only asked to live in peace at their old homes, and under the Government of their inheritance. But these comparisons are idle. I want peace, and believe it can only be reached through union and war, and I will ever conduct war with a view to perfect and early success.

But, my dear sirs, when peace does come, you may call on me for anything. Then will I share with you the last cracker, and watch with you to shield your homes and families against danger from every quarter.

Now you must go, and take with you the old and feeble, feed and nurse them, and build for them, in more quiet places, proper habitations to shield them against the weather until the mad passions of men cool down, and allow the Union and peace once more to settle over your old homes at Atlanta. Yours in haste,

W. T. Sherman, Major General commanding.

Source: William T. Sherman, *Memoirs of General William T. Sherman* (New York: Charles L. Webster, 1892), vol. 2, 125–127.

Civil War Prisons

The conditions of prisons remained a monumental problem throughout the war. The two most notorious prisons were at Andersonville (Georgia) and Elmira (New York). Though conditions in the prison camps were less than desirable, Confederate captives generally fared better than their Union counterparts in the South. The most controversial issues surrounding the camps centered on Confederate treatment of black prisoners.

Although humanitarian efforts to accelerate the exchange of prisoners mounted, the separate treatment of black and white soldiers by Confederate captors halted most exchange programs until late in the war. Exact numbers of deaths in prisons remain surrounded by controversy, but the most accepted figures are that roughly 15 percent of Northern prisoners died in Southern camps and 12 percent of Southern prisoners died in the Northern camps.

Exacerbating the conditions in prison camps and hospitals throughout the South was the fact that the South was starving to death by 1864. Despite their best efforts, Southern commandants could not afford to feed prisoners more than the South could feed its own soldiers. Nowhere was this more evident than at Andersonville, a prison camp designed to hold 10,000 inmates. By late 1864, the camp held 45,000 prisoners, making Andersonville one of the largest cities in the Confederacy. Of these, 13,000 prisoners died, nearly 29 percnt of the captives. Upon his capture in April 1865, the camp's commandant, Henry Wirz, petitioned Major General J. H. Wilson, U.S. Army, for leniency prior to his case being brought to trial before a Union military commission. Wirz was subsequently found guilty of war crimes and hanged on November 10, 1865.

Document 12
The Commandant at Andersonville Requests Leniency, May 7, 1865
Maj. Gen. J. H. Wilson, U.S. Army,
Commanding, Macon, GA.:

GENERAL: It is with great reluctance that I address you these lines, being fully aware how little time is left you to attend to such matters as I now have the honor to lay before you; and if I could see any other way to accomplish my object I would not intrude upon you. I am a native of Switzerland, and was before the war a citizen of Louisiana, by profession a physician. Like hundreds and thousands of others I was carried away by the maelstrom of excitement and joined the southern Army. I was very severely wounded at the battle of Seven Pines, near Richmond, VA., and have nearly lost the use of my right arm. Unfit for field duty, I was ordered to report to Brevet Brigadier General J. H. Winder, in charge of Federal prisoners of war, who ordered me to take charge of a prison in Tuscaloosa, Ala. My health failing me, I applied for a furlough and went to Europe, from whence I returned in February, 1864. I was then ordered to report to the commandant of military prisons at Andersonville, GA., who assigned me to the command of the interior of the prison. The duties I had to perform were arduous and unpleasant, and I am satisfied that no man can or will justly blame me for things that happened here and which were beyond my power to control. I do not think that I ought to be held responsible for the shortness of rations, for the over-crowded state of the prison (which was in itself a prolific source of the fearful mortality), for the inadequate supplies of clothing, want of shelters, etc. Still I now bear the odium, and men who were prisoners here seem disposed to wreak their vengeance upon me for what they have suffered, who was only the medium, or, I may better say the tool in the hands of my superiors. This is my condition. I am a man with a family; I lost all my property when the Federal army besieged Vicksburg; I have no means at present to go any place, and even if I had I know of no place where I could go. My life is in danger, and I most respectfully ask of you help and relief. If you will be so generous as to give me some sort of a safe-conduct, or, what I should greatly prefer, a guard to protect myself and family against violence, I shall be thankful to you, and you may rest assured that your protection will not be given to one who is unworthy of it. My intention is to return with my family to Europe so soon as I can make the arrangements.

In the meantime I have the honor, general, to remain,

Very respectfully, your obedient servant,
HY. WIRZ,
Captain, S.S. Army

Source: U.S. War Department, *War of the Rebellion: A Compilation of the Official Records of the Union and Confederate Armies*. Washington, DC: Government Printing Office, 1899. ser. II, vol. 8, 537–538.

Lincoln Offers a Plan for Reconciliation

By the time Lincoln delivered his second inaugural address, the Civil War was drawing to a close. Splintered on all sides, the Confederacy had but one month to live. Facing the conclusion of the struggle that had consumed his efforts over the past four years, Lincoln turned to reconciliation and offered a prescription to reunite North and South. Placing the war into perspective, the president recalled the dark days of 1861, when the North accepted war rather than let the Union be destroyed. He then turned to slavery, what he termed the real "cause of the war," and invoked the Bible in condemning the institution as an "offense" against humanity, one for which God was now exacting retribution. He then concluded on a more conciliatory note, calling for a combined effort "to bind up the nation's wounds" in order to secure "a just and lasting peace."

Lincoln considered his second inaugural the greatest speech he ever delivered. Said Lincoln one week later, "I expect the latter to wear as well—perhaps better than anything I have produced." Contemporary observers were mixed in their reactions. Washington's *National Intelligencer* labeled Lincoln's remarks "equally distinguished for patriotism, statesmanship, and benevolence." Abolitionist Frederick Douglass declared that "The address sounded more like a sermon than a state paper." In a larger sense, Lincoln's second inaugural address, like the Gettysburg Address delivered just sixteen months earlier, has resonated through the ages and left a legacy of humanity and decency for ages hence.

Document 13
Lincoln's Second Inaugural Address, March 4, 1865

Fellow Countrymen:

At this second appearing, to take the oath of the presidential office, there is less occasion for an extended address than there was at the first. Then a statement, somewhat in detail, of a course to be pursued, seemed fitting and proper. Now, at the expiration of four years, during which public declarations have been constantly called forth on every point and phase of the great contest which still absorbs the attention, and engrosses the energies of the nation, little that is new could be presented. The progress of our arms, upon which all else chiefly depends, is as well known to the public as to myself; and it is, I trust, reasonably satisfactory and encouraging to all. With high hope for the future, no prediction in regard to it is ventured.

On the occasion corresponding to this four years ago, all thoughts were anxiously directed to an impending civil war. All dreaded it—all sought to avert it. While the inaugural address was being delivered from this place, devoted altogether to saving the Union without war, insurgent agents were in the city seeking to destroy it without war—seeking to dissolve the Union, and divide effects, by negotiation. Both parties deprecated war; but one of them would make war rather than let the nation survive; and the other would accept war rather than let it perish. And the war came.

One eighth of the whole population were colored slaves, not distributed generally over the Union, but localized in the Southern part of it. These slaves constituted a peculiar and powerful interest. All knew that this interest was, somehow, the cause of the war. To strengthen, perpetuate, and extend this interest was the object for which the insurgents would rend the Union, even by war; while the government claimed no right to do more than to restrict the territorial enlargement of it. Neither party expected for the war, the magnitude, or the duration, which it has already attained. Neither anticipated that the cause of the conflict might cease with, or even before, the conflict itself should cease. Each looked for an easier triumph, and a result less fundamental and astounding. Both read the same Bible, and pray to the same God; and each invokes His aid against the other. It may seem strange that any men should dare to ask a just God's assistance in wringing their bread from the sweat of other men's faces; but let us judge not that we be not judged. The prayers of both could not be answered; that of neither has been answered fully. The Almighty has His own purposes. "Woe unto the world because of offenses! For it must needs be that offenses come; but woe to that man by whom the offense cometh!" If we shall suppose that American Slavery is one of those offenses which, in the providence of God, must needs come, but which, having continued through His appointed time, He now wills to remove, and that He gives to both North and South, this terrible war, as the woe due to those by whom the offense came, shall we discern therein any departure from those divine attributes which the believers in a Living God always ascribe to Him? Fondly do we hope—fervently do we pray—that this mighty scourge of war may speedily pass away. Yet, if God wills that it continue, until all the wealth piled by the bondman's two hundred and fifty years of unrequited toil shall be sunk, and until every drop of blood drawn with the lash, shall be paid by another drawn with the sword, as was said three thousand years ago, so still it must be said "the judgments of the Lord, are true and righteous altogether."

With malice toward none; with charity for all; with firmness in the right, as God gives us to see the right, let us strive on to finish the work we are in; to bind up the nation's wounds; to care for him who shall have borne the battle, and for his widow, and his orphan—to do all which may achieve and cherish a just, and a lasting peace, among ourselves, and with all nations.

Source: John G. Nicolay and John Hay, *Abraham Lincoln: A History* (New York: The Century Company, 1890), vol. 10, 143–145.

The Confederacy Enlists Black Soldiers

With Grant preparing for his final assault at Petersburg and Sherman leading his army into South Carolina, the days of the Confederacy were numbered. In a final effort to starve off military disaster, General Robert E. Lee petitioned Davis and the Confederate Congress for additional troops. There were no troops to be found, so Lee asked that slaves be armed to defend the Confederacy. Lee's prestige carried the day. The Confederate Congress reluctantly approved the recruitment of black soldiers on March 13, 1865, by a vote of 40–37 in the House of Representatives and 9–8 in the Senate. Robert Toombs, former governor of Georgia, disapproved, stating: "The day you make soldiers of them is the beginning of the end of the revolution. If slaves will make good soldiers, our whole theory of slavery is wrong."

Document 14
An Act to Increase the Military Force of the Confederate States, March 13, 1865

AN ACT to increase the military force of the Confederate States.

The Congress of the Confederate States of America do enact, That, in order to provide additional forces to repel invasion, maintain the rightful possession of the Confederate States, secure their independence, and preserve their institutions, the President be, and he is hereby, authorized to ask for and accept from the owners of slaves, the services of such number of able-bodied negro men as he may deem expedient, for and during the war, to perform military service in whatever capacity he may direct. . . .

Sec. 2. That the General-in-Chief be authorized to organize the said slaves into companies, battalions, regiments, and brigades, under such rules and regulations as the Secretary of War may prescribe, and to be commanded by such officers as the President may appoint.

Sec. 3. That while employed in the service the said troops shall receive the same rations, clothing, and compensation as are allowed to other troops in the same branch of the service.

Sec. 4. That if, under the previous sections of this act, the President shall not be able to raise a sufficient number of troops to prosecute the war successfully and maintain the sovereignty of the States and the independence of the Confederate States, then he is hereby authorized to call on each State, whenever he thinks it expedient, for her quota of 300,000 troops, in addition to those subject to military service under existing laws, or so many thereof as the President may deem necessary to be raised from such classes of the population, irrespective of color, in each State, as the proper authorities thereof may determine: *Provided* that not more than twenty-five per cent, of the male slaves between the ages of eighteen and forty-five, in any State, shall be called for under the provisions of this act.

Sec. 5. That nothing in this act shall be construed to authorize a change in the relation which the said slaves shall bear toward their owners, except by consent of the owners and of the States in which they may reside, and in pursuance of the laws thereof.

Approved March 13, 1865

Source: U.S. War Department, *War of the Rebellion: A Compilation of the Official Records of the Union and Confederate Armies,* Washington, DC: Government Printing Office, 1900. ser. IV, vol. 3, 1161.

Lee's Farewell Address to the Army of Northern Virginia

After four years of war, General Robert E. Lee surrendered the Army of Northern Virginia to Lieutenant General Ulysses S. Grant at Appomattox Courthouse on April 9, 1865. Following the surrender, Lee returned to his lines, where he was met by tearful veterans who had followed their beloved commander since the dark days of June 1862 through the Seven Days, Second Manassas, Sharpsburg, Fredericksburg, Chancellorsville, Gettysburg, the Wilderness, Petersburg, and Appomattox. Telling his men to return home and to be good citizens, Lee retreated to his tent to be alone and to contemplate the magnitude of the day's events. He then instructed Colonel Charles Marshall to draft a farewell address to the army. On April 10, Marshall forwarded the draft to Lee, who immediately struck out a paragraph that he calculated would generate ill feeling and made some minor editorial revisions, before signing a revised copy.

Lee's farewell order remains a model of brevity and clarity. Acknowledging the tremendous sacrifices of the soldiers in his command and the hopelessness of continuing the struggle, Lee accepted total responsibility for surrendering the Army of Northern Virginia to avert further bloodshed. Carefully outlining the principal components of the terms Grant had outlined the previous day, the commanding general then acknowledged his personal gratitude to the veterans of the army who had remained steadfast to the last. Defeat of the army, said Lee, was the result not of failed valor, but due to the overwhelming resources of the enemy. "Consciousness of duty faithfully performed" became the Army of Northern Virginia's lasting tribute from their beloved commander, who had led them from the Seven Days' Campaign to Appomattox. Bidding his men an affectionate farewell, Lee departed Appomattox two days later and returned to Richmond.

Document 15
Lee's General Order No. 9
Headquarters, Army of Northern Virginia, April 10, 1865

After four years of arduous service, marked by unsurpassed courage and fortitude, the Army of Northern Virginia has been compelled to yield to overwhelming numbers and resources. I need not tell the brave survivors of so many hard-fought battles, who have remained steadfast to the last, that I have consented to the result from no distrust of them. But, feeling that valor and devotion could accomplish nothing that could compensate for the loss that must have attended the continuance of the contest, I determined to avoid the useless sacrifice of those whose past services have endeared them to their countrymen.

By terms of the agreement officers and men can return to their homes and remain until exchanged. You will take with you the satisfaction that proceeds from the consciousness of duty faithfully performed, and I earnestly pray that a merciful God will extend to you His blessing and protection.

With an increasing admiration of your constancy and devotion to your country, and a grateful remembrance of your kind and generous considerations for myself, I bid you all an affectionate farewell.

R. E. Lee, General

Source: U.S. War Department, *War of the Rebellion: A Compilation of the Official Records of the Union and Confederate Armies,* Washington, DC: Government Printing Office, 1894. ser. I, vol. 46, pt. 1, 1267.

How the North Won the Civil War
At the beginning of the war President Abraham Lincoln had determined that victory was possible only with the destruction of the enemy's armies. Unfortunately, successive Union commanders had failed to act in

unison and had directed their efforts toward the capture of Confederate cities rather than the destruction of the South's armies. In March 1864, Lincoln brought Grant to Washington, D.C., and appointed him commander of all armies of the United States. Within a month Grant devised a strategy that called for all Union armies to commence an offensive campaign the first week in May and aimed at the destruction of Robert E. Lee's Army of Northern Virginia and Joseph E. Johnston's Army of Tennessee. Subsidiary enemy armies would be attacked on the periphery of the Confederacy, and for the first time in the war, the Union armies would march simultaneously.

As senior commander, Grant positioned himself with Major General George Meade's Army of the Potomac, but he gave wide latitude to his principal commanders to direct their armies within the parameters of his broad strategy. Within one year of the commencement of Grant's operations, the various Confederate armies ceased to exist as effective fighting forces. With Lee's surrender at Appomattox Courthouse on April 9, 1865, the Civil War was effectively over, the various remaining Southern armies surrendering over the course of the next month. Free to concentrate on the demobilization of the Union armies and the compilation of the historical record, Grant submitted his final report to the secretary of war, in which he outlined the war-winning strategy he had developed and personally supervised to achieve strategic victory for the armies of the United States.

Document 16
Report of Lieutenant General U. S. Grant, of the United States Armies—1864–1865 July 22, 1865

Headquarters, Armies of the United States,
Washington, D.C., July 22, 1865
Hon. E. M. Stanton, Secretary of War

Sir:—I have the honor to submit the following report of the operations of the Armies of the United States from the date of my appointment to command the same.

From an early period in the rebellion I had been impressed with the idea that active and continuous operations of all the troops that could be brought into the field, regardless of season and weather, were necessary to a speedy termination of the war. The resources of the enemy and his numerical strength were far inferior to ours; but as an offset to this, we had a vast territory, with a population hostile to the government, to garrison, and long lines of river and railroad communications to protect, to enable us to supply the operating armies.

The armies in the East and West acted independently and without concert, like a balky team, no two ever pulling together, enabling the enemy to use to great advantage his interior lines of communication for transporting troops from East to West, reinforcing the army most vigorously pressed, and to furlough large numbers, during seasons of inactivity on our part, to go to their homes and do the work of producing, for the support of their armies. It was a question whether our numerical strength and resources were not more than balanced by these disadvantages and the enemy's superior position.

From the first, I was firm in the conviction that no peace could be had that would be stable and conducive to the happiness of the people, both North and South, until the military power of the rebellion was entirely broken.

I therefore determined, first, to use the greatest number of troops practicable against the armed force of the enemy; preventing him from using the same force at different seasons against first one and then another of our armies, and the possibility of repose for refitting and producing necessary supplies for carrying on resistance. Second, to hammer continuously against the armed force of the enemy and his resources, until by mere attrition, if in no other way, there should be nothing left to him but an equal submission with the loyal section of our common country to the constitution and laws of the land.

These views have been kept constantly in mind, and orders given and campaigns made to carry them out. Whether they might have been better in conception and execution is for the people, who mourn the loss of friends, fallen, and who have to pay the pecuniary cost, to say. All I can say is, that what I have done has been done conscientiously, to the best of my ability, and in what I conceived to be for the best interests of the whole country.

[Grant next reviewed the current disposition of armies and his specific orders to individual commanders to act in unison toward the destruction of Confederate armies.] The enemy had concentrated the bulk of his forces east of the Mississippi into two armies, commanded by Generals R. E. Lee and J. E. Johnston, his ablest and best generals. The army commanded by Lee occupied the south bank of the Rapidan, extending from Mine Run westward, strongly entrenched, covering and defending Richmond, the rebel capital, against the Army of the Potomac. The army under Johnston occupied a strongly entrenched position at Dalton, Georgia, covering and defending Atlanta, Georgia, a place of great importance as a railroad center, against the armies under Major General W. T. Sherman. . . . These two armies, and the cities covered and defended by them, were the main objective points of the campaign.

[Grant next reviewed the conduct of the respective campaigns culminating in the destruction and the surrender of the Confederate armies.] It has been my fortune to see the armies of both the West and the East fight battles, and from what I have seen I know there is no difference in their fighting qualities. All that it was possible for men to do in battle they have done. The Western armies commenced their battles in the Mississippi Valley, and received the final surrender of the remnant of the principal army opposed to them in North Carolina. The armies of the East commenced their battles on the river from which the Army of the Potomac derived its name, and received the final surrender of their old antagonists at Appomattox Court House, Virginia. The splendid achievements of each have nationalized our victories, removed all sectional jealousies (of which we have unfortunately experienced so much), and the cause of crimination and recrimination that might have followed had either section failed in its duty. All have a proud record, and all sections can well congratulate themselves and each other for having done their full share in restoring the supremacy of law over every foot of territory belonging to the United States. Let them hope for perpetual peace and harmony with that enemy, whose manhood, however mistaken the cause, drew forth such Herculean deeds of valor.

I have the honor to be,
Very respectfully, your obedient servant,
U. S. Grant,
Lieutenant General

Source: U. S. Grant, *Personal Memoirs of U. S. Grant* (New York: Charles L. Webster, 1886), vol. 2, 555–632.

GLOSSARY OF SELECTED TERMS

Abolitionist. Any proponent for the abolition of slavery. Prominent abolitionists included Frederick Douglass, Harriet Beecher Stowe, John Brown, and Horace Greeley.

Army of Northern Virginia. The main Confederate army in the Eastern Theater. Commanded by General Robert E. Lee, the Army of Northern Virginia was formed on June 1, 1862, and was surrendered to Lieutenant General Ulysses S. Grant on April 9, 1865. The army fought a series of battles and campaigns against the Army of the Potomac, including the Seven Days' Campaign, Second Manassas, Sharpsburg, Fredericksburg, Chancellorsville, Gettysburg, the Wilderness Campaign, Petersburg, and Appomattox.

Army of the Potomac. The main Union army in the Eastern Theater. Organized by Major General George B. McClellan, the Army of the Potomac battled the Army of Northern Virginia from 1861 to 1865. Principal commanders included Major Generals McClellan, Ambrose Burnside, Joseph Hooker, and George G. Meade. During the final year of the war, Lieutenant General Ulysses S. Grant accompanied the Army of the Potomac on its operations, but Meade technically remained in command.

Blockade. The isolation of an enemy area or harbor by troops or warships to prevent the free movement of supplies, men, and matériel into or out of a designated area. According to international law, the proclamation of a blockade is a formal act of war against a sovereign nation.

Border States. Usually associated with those slave states which remained in the Union and that bordered the northern tier of the seceding states. These states included Delaware, Maryland, Kentucky, and Missouri.

Campaign. A series of battles designed to achieve the goal of an army commander.

Cavalry. Commonly referred to as horse soldiers or the mounted arm of an army. Cavalry operations included raids, reconnaissance, screening the main army, intelligence-gathering, and fighting. Confederate cavalry commanders included J.E.B. Stuart, Nathan B. Forrest, and John Hunt Morgan. Principal Union commanders included Major Generals Phillip Sheridan, Alfred Pleasanton, John Buford, and George A. Custer.

Company. A unit of 100 officers and men that formed the basic combat unit of an army. Companies were usually raised within a single county or adjacent counties, and officers were usually elected by the soldiers.

Confederacy. Any voluntary association of states in a federal union, but with each state retaining its sovereignty.

Conscription. Another name for the draft. The Confederacy initiated the draft with the passage of the Conscription Act of 1862, and the Union followed suit with the Enrollment Act of 1863. Both legislative acts were designed to encourage enlistments and to increase the size of the respective armies.

Contraband. According to the laws of war, contraband included property subject to confiscation if its use aided the enemy. Categories included locomotives and railroad lines, supply wagons, and agricultural products, and later expanded to include liberated or escaped slaves.

Copperheads. A term used to describe Northern "Peace Democrats" who opposed the war and the Lincoln administration's prosecution of the war. Their principal strength lay in the states of the Old Northwest Territory. The most visible Copperhead was Clement Vallandigham, whose opposition to the war led to his conviction by a military tribunal and his expulsion to the Confederacy. Union battlefield victories in 1864–1865 led to the decline of Copperhead influence, but Lincoln remained cognizant of the dangers from what he termed the "fire in the rear."

Corps. The organization in an army that includes two or more divisions. Confederate corps usually were larger than Union corps. In the Confederate Army, corps were commanded by lieutenant generals, whereas major generals usually commanded Union corps.

Division. The principal fighting organization in an army. Numbering 3000–5000 men, a division consisted of two or more brigades and was commanded by a brigadier general or a major general.

Eastern Theater. A general term most closely associated with the Virginia/Maryland/Pennsylvania Theater of operations. In the broadest sense the Eastern Theater included all operations conducted east of the Appalachian Mountains.

Emancipation. To free from bondage.

Flotilla. Any grouping or assembly of ships, usually smaller than a battle fleet. Typical Civil War flotillas included a mixture of wooden ships and ironclads, and conducted operations on the internal waterways of the Confederacy or engaged in blockade duty. Flotillas are distinct from sea-going fleets, which encompass a greater number of larger ships.

Infantry. Foot soldiers, the major fighting element of an army.

Ironclads. Iron-plated ships that first saw combat service in the Civil War. The initial battle of the ironclads occurred off Hampton Roads, Virginia, in an indecisive battle between the *USS Monitor* and the *CSS Virginia* on March 9, 1862. The introduction of ironclads revolutionized naval warfare and immediately made wooden vessels obsolete.

Regiment. An infantry unit encompassing ten companies and consisting of approximately 1000 officers and men at the beginning of the Civil War. Most regiments were commanded by a colonel or lieutenant colonel appointed by the governor of the state in which the regiment was raised. When joined with other regiments, they formed a brigade. Artillery and cavalry brigades generally consisted of twelve companies.

Secession. According to the Southern states, the constitutional right of a state to voluntarily leave the Union. Lincoln's 1860 election to the presidency led to the secession of South Carolina, followed by six other states in the Lower South. Lincoln's call for 75,000 volunteers to suppress the rebellion in April 1861 led to the secession of four more states of the Upper South.

Strategy. The use of military engagement for the purpose of the war. Strategy involves the application of tactics and battles to achieve a specific objective in war.

Tactics. The movement and engagement of specific units on a battlefield to achieve the objectives of strategy.

Western Theater. A general term most closely associated with military operations west of the Appalachian Mountains. Union and Confederate strategists subdivided the Western Theater into separate departments according to state lines and geographic regions.

SELECTED ANNOTATED BIBLIOGRAPHY

PRINT SOURCES
Official Government Documents and Reference Books

Commager, Henry Steele, ed. *The Civil War Archive: The History of the Civil War in Documents*. New York: Black Dog and Leventhal Publishers, 1950. A compilation of primary documents that outline the history of the Civil War.

Heidler, David S., and Jeanne T. Heidler, eds. *Encyclopedia of the American Civil War*. New York: W. W. Norton, 2000. Undoubtedly the most comprehensive reference book on the Civil War. Volume concentrates on the political, social, and military history of the conflict and contains a detailed bibliography.

United States Congress. *Journal of the Congress of the Confederate States of America*. 7 vols. Washington, DC: Government Printing Office, 1905. The official journal of the Confederacy's Congress from the beginning to the end of the war.

United States Department of War. *The War of the Rebellion: A Compilation of the Official Records of the Union and Confederate Armies*. 70 vols. in 128 parts. Washington, DC: Government Printing Office, 1880–1901. Volumes contain official records, reports, and correspondence relating to the Union and Confederate armies. Also available on CD-ROM.

United States Navy Department. *Official Record of the Union and Confederate Navies in the War of the Rebellion*. 31 vols. Washington, DC: Government Printing Office, 1894–1927. Volumes contain official records, reports, and correspondence relating to the Union and Confederate navies. Also available on CD-ROM.

General Histories of the War

Beringer, Richard, et al. *Why the South Lost the Civil War*. Athens: University of Georgia Press, 1986. A provocative book by several authors that calls into question the inevitability of the Confederacy's defeat. The book offers several interpretations of why the South lost the Civil War.

Catton, Bruce. *Bruce Catton's Civil War*. New York: Fairfax Press, 1984. A one-volume history that contains the complete and unabridged *Mr. Lincoln's Army*, *Glory Road*, and *A Stillness at Appomattox*.

Cowley, Robert, ed. *With My Face to the Enemy*. New York: G. P. Putnam's Sons, 2001. An anthology of essays by the leading historians of the Civil War that were originally published in *MHQ: The Quarterly Journal of Military History* and address virtually every aspect of the nation's bloodiest conflict.

Davis, William C. *A Government of Our Own*. New York: The Free Press, 1994. A superb history of the making of the Confederacy by one of the Civil War's premier historians.

————. *An Honorable Defeat*. New York: Harcourt, 2001. An excellent history of the last days of the Confederate government that focuses on the dissolution of the Confederacy and the postwar battle to preserve the Lost Cause for Confederate posterity.

————. *Look Away: A History of the Confederate States of America*. New York: The Free Press, 2002. A retelling of the history of the Confederacy that presents a comprehensive view of Confederate national experience beyond the battlefield.

Foote, Shelby. *The Civil War: A Narrative*. 3 vols. New York: Random House, 1963. An excellent historical narrative that includes numerous anecdotes, maps, and analyses of the leading figures and events of the Civil War.

Grimsley, Mark. *The Hard Hand of War: Union Military Policy Toward Southern Civilians, 1861–1865*. Cambridge, MA: Cambridge University Press, 1995. A controversial interpretation of the civil–military treatment of Southern civilians by Union commanders during the Civil War. Grimsley argues that Union armies gradually adopted measures that were expressly intended to demoralize Southern civilians and to ruin the Confederate economy.

McPherson, James M. *Battle Cry of Freedom*. New York: Oxford University Press, 1988. The standard one-volume history of the Civil War that brought its author the Pulitzer Prize. The book is a volume in the *Oxford History of the United States*.

Nevins, Allan. *Ordeal of the Union*. 8 vols. New York: Scribner's, 1947–1971. A definitive history that spans the spectrum of American politics from the 1840s to the conclusion of the Civil War.

Owsley, Frank. *King Cotton Diplomacy*. Chicago: University of Chicago Press, 1931. Somewhat dated, but still the most comprehensive analysis of the foreign relations of the Confederate States of America.

Starr, Stephen Z. *The Union Cavalry in the Civil War*. 3 vols. Baton Rouge: Louisiana State University Press, 1985. Author traces the evolution of Union cavalry into the development of a highly effective fighting force that proved vastly superior to its Confederate counterpart.

Ward, Geoffrey E., with Ric Burns and Ken Burns. *The Civil War: An Illustrated History*. New York: Alfred A. Knopf, 1990. The companion volume to the Public Broadcasting service television series of the same name.

Weigley, Russell F. *A Great Civil War*. Bloomington: Indiana University Press, 2000. The best single-volume military and political history of the Civil War.

Woodward, C. Vann, ed. *Mary Chesnut's Civil War*. New Haven, CT: Yale University Press, 1981. Superb examination of life on the Confederate home front by one of the South's leading diarists.

Wartime Leaders

Buell, Thomas B. *The Warrior Generals: Combat Leadership in the Civil War*. New York: Crown, 1997. A provocative analysis of Civil War leadership that focuses on three opposing pairs of generals: Ulysses S. Grant and Robert E. Lee, George Thomas and John Bell Hood, and Francis C. Barlow and John Brown Gordon.

Connelly, Thomas L. *Army of the Heartland: The Army of Tennessee, 1861–1862*. Baton Rouge: Louisiana State University Press, 1967. This book, which examines the history of the Confederate Army of the West, is by one of the South's premier military historians. Connelly argues that the Army of the West faced obstacles of a different nature than the Army of Northern Virginia, and that it was shaped by the influence of the Confederate heartland and a succession of commanders who left their influences upon the army but failed to temper the newly shaped force.

———. *Autumn of Glory: The Army of Tennessee, 1862–1865*. Baton Rouge: Louisiana State University Press, 1971. The second volume of Connelly's superb history of the Confederate Army of Tennessee. This volume analyzes the factors that contributed to the final destruction of the South's principal army in the West.

———. *The Marble Man: Robert E. Lee and His Image in American Society*. Baton Rouge: Louisiana State University Press, 1977. Connelly is the first author to analyze critically the image of Lee from its origins among Lost Cause writers from Reconstruction to the 1961–1965 Civil War centennial.

Connelly, Thomas L., and Barbara L. Bellows. *God and General Longstreet*. Baton Rouge: Louisiana State University Press, 1982. An excellent analysis of the literature of the Lost Cause in Southern memory. This book examines the evolution of the Inner Lost Cause, the heart of which was the canonization of Robert E. Lee and the lasting bond between Southern piety and Confederate memory.

Davis, Burke. *They Called Him Stonewall.* New York: Rinehart, 1954. An extremely positive portrayal of the genral whom Lee called his right arm.

————. *Jeb Stuart: The Last Cavalier.* New York: Rinehart, 1957. A very flattering portrayal of the Confederate cavalry leader who commanded the cavalry arm of the Army of Northern Virginia.

Davis, William C. *Jefferson Davis: The Man and His Hour.* New York: HarperCollins, 1991. Premier biography of the president of the Confederacy by one of the finest Civil War historians. Author posits that Davis prolonged the life of the Confederacy beyond what any likely competitors could legitimately have been expected to achieve.

Donald, David Herbert. *Lincoln.* London: Jonathan Cape, 1995. The best single-volume biography of Abraham Lincoln, and one that brought its author the Pulitzer Prize.

————. *"We Are Lincoln's Men": Abraham Lincoln and His Men.* New York: Simon and Schuster, 2003. Donald superbly analyzes Lincoln's relationship with asmall group of people who thought of themselves as his special friends. Friends included the president's law partners, his private secretaries, and his secretary of state.

Freeman, Douglas S. *R. E. Lee.* 4 vols. New York: Scribner's, 1934–1935. Laudatory portrayal of the Confederate general that brought its author the Pulitzer Prize for biography.

————. *Lee's Lieutenants.* 3 vols. New York: Scribner's, 1942–1944. A classic study of the command in Robert E. Lee's Army of Northern Virginia.

Gallagher, Gary W. *Lee and His Army in Confederate History.* Chapel Hill: University of North Carolina Press, 2001. An intriguing analysis of the relationship between Lee's operations and Confederate morale, the quality and nature of his generalship, and how postwar historiography shaped the interpretation of Lee and the Lost Cause.

Glatthaar, Joseph T. *Partners in Command.* New York: The Free Press, 1994. A critical analysis of the relationship between civil–military leaders and among army commanders and their principal subordinates.

Henderson, C. F. R. *Stonewall Jackson and the American Civil War.* 2 vols. New York: Grosset & Dunlap, 1898. Somewhat dated, but still the best biography of the commander of the 2nd Corps of the Army of Northern Virginia.

Hirshson, Stanley P. *The White Tecumseh.* New York: John Wiley, 1997. An insightful biography of Major General William T. Sherman that offers a refreshing perspective on a deeply troubled man who emerged as Grant's principal military protégé.

Keneally, Thomas. *American Scoundrel: The Life of the Notorious Civil War General Dan Sickles.* New York: Nan A. Talese, 2002. Biography of the self-proclaimed "Hero of Gettysburg" that focuses primarily on July 2, 1863, and Sickles's battle in the Peach Orchard.

McFeely, William S. *Grant: A Biography*. New York: W. W. Norton, 1981. Controversial biography that claims Grant possessed no artistic or intellectual uniqueness, but was merely an ordinary American who finally reached his fulfillment in war because it was the only field available in which he had not failed.

Nolan, Alan T. *Lee Considered*. Chapel Hill: University of North Carolina Press, 1991. Extremely critical perspective on the generalship of Robert E. Lee that questions Lee's military genius.

Oates, Stephen B. *A Woman of Valor: Clara Barton and the Civil War*. New York: Free Press, 1994. A biography of one of the war's great humanitarians, written by the biographer of Nat Turner, John Brown, and Abraham Lincoln.

Perret, Geoffrey. *Ulysses S. Grant: Soldier and President*. New York: Random House, 1997. A pro-Grant biography that opines that Grant's military genius lay in his ability to teach an army how to fight modern war.

Robertson, James I., Jr. *Stonewall Jackson: The Man, the Soldier, the Legend*. New York: Macmillan, 1997. The most complete and comprehensive modern biography of Lieutenant General Thomas J. Jackson, Lee's right arm.

Sandberg, Carl. *Abraham Lincoln: The War Years*. 4 vols. New York: Harcourt, Brace, 1939. Still the finest and most comprehensive biography of the nation's sixteenth president.

Trulock, Alice Rains. *In the Hands of Providence*. Chapel Hill: University of North Carolina Press, 1992. The most comprehensive biography of Joshua L. Chamberlain from his birth through the Civil War to a postwar life that included political and academic careers.

Wert, Jeffry D. *Custer: The Controversial Life of George Armstrong Custer*. New York: Simon and Schuster, 1996. The first complete biography of the controversial cavalry commander in the last twenty years of his life. Book covers Custer as the Union's youngest general up to his defeat at the Little Big Horn in 1876.

Memoirs

Alexander, Edward Porter. *Fighting for the Confederacy: The Personal Recollections of General Edward Porter Alexander*. Edited by Gary W. Gallagher. Chapel Hill: University of North Carolina Press, 1989. The memoirs of Lieutenant General James Longstreet's chief of artillery. The book contains provocative insights into the third day of the Battle of Gettysburg and the roles of Lee and Longstreet.

Chamberlain, Joshua Lawrence. *"Bayonet! Forward": My Civil War Reminiscences.* Gettysburg, PA: Stan Clark Military Books, 1994. A reprint of Chamberlain's original memoir that covers his military career from the Battle of Fredericksburg to the grand review of the Army of the Potomac.

Chesnut, Mary. *A Diary from Dixie.* New York: Gramercy Books, 1905 (1997). First-rate republication of the Civil War's most celebrated journal.

Davis, Jefferson. *The Rise and Fall of the Confederate Government.* 2 vols. New York: D. Appleton, 1881. Davis's postwar memoir of the Confederate government that seeks to exonerate Southerners of treason by proposing legalistic constitutional arguments of the righteousness of the Confederate cause.

Douglas, Henry Kyd. *I Rode with Stonewall.* Chapel Hill: University of North Carolina Press, 1968. The memoirs of the youngest member of Stonewall Jackson's staff, from the raid on Harpers Ferry to the hanging of the Lincoln conspirators. This edition is a reprint of the original narrative published by Douglas's nephew in 1940.

Grant, Ulysses S. *Personal Memoirs of U. S. Grant.* 2 vols. New York: Charles L. Webster, 1886. Arguably the finest wartime memoir in American history.

Longstreet, James. *From Manassas to Appomattox.* Secaucus, NJ: The Blue and Grey Press, 1984. Personal memoirs from the commander of the 1st Corps of the Army of Northern Virginia.

Sherman, William T. *Memoirs of General William T. Sherman.* New York: Charles L. Webster, 1891. The personal memoirs of the Union commander in the West that trace his battle exploits from Manassas to the end of the war.

Watkins, Sam R. *Co. Aytch: A Side Show of the Big Show.* New York: Simon and Schuster, 1997. A reprint of Watkins's original memoir published in 1882. Watkins served in the Confederate Army of Tennessee and presents a vivid view of the war from an enlisted soldier's perspective.

Strategy and Tactics

Griffith, Paddy. *Battle Tactics of the Civil War.* New Haven, CT: Yale University Press, 1989. Excellent analysis of Civil War tactics that concludes that the Civil War was not the first modern war, but a continuation of the less sophisticated Napoleonic wars.

Jones, Archer. *Civil War Command and Strategy.* New York: The Free Press, 1992. A detailed analysis of the conduct and character of the Civil War that concludes that few battles had strategic significance.

McWhiney, Grady, and Perry D. Jamieson. *Attack and Die.* Tuscaloosa: University of Alabama Press, 1982. A critical analysis of Confederate military tactics and the Southern military tradition that resulted in disproportionate casualties as a result of a military culture that failed to adapt to changing technological innovations.

Williams, T. Harry. *Lincoln and His Generals*. New York: Alfred A. Knopf, 1952. Somewhat dated, but still one of the premier analyses of the wartime relationship between Abraham Lincoln and his senior military commanders. Book traces the evolution of Union military strategy by focusing on Lincoln's search for a military commander to implement his grand strategy.

Woodworth, Steven E. *Jefferson Davis and His Generals*. Lawrence: University Press of Kansas, 1990. A critical review of the failure of Confederate strategy in the West.

————. *Davis and Lee at War*. Lawrence: University Press of Kansas, 1995. An examination of the development of Confederate strategy in the East that focuses on the wartime relationship between President Jefferson Davis and Robert E. Lee.

Battles and Campaigns

Coddington, Edwin B. *The Gettysburg Campaign: A Study in Command*. New York: Scribner's, 1984. The most detailed single-volume analysis of command on both sides during the three-day battle. Author argues that the real meaning of Meade's victory emerged only with the passage of time.

Detzer, David. *Allegiance: Fort Sumter, Charleston, and the Beginning of the Civil War*. New York: Harcourt, 2001. Use of primary sources gives a rare insight into the lives of Charleston's leading citizens and the events that precipitated the outbreak of the Civil War.

Ferris, Norman B. *The Trent Affair: A Diplomatic Crisis*. Knoxville: University of Tennessee Press, 1977. A concise treatment of one of the first diplomatic imbroglios of the Civil War, surrounding the *USS San Jacinto*'s seizure of the British mail steamer *Trent* and its two Confederate agents.

Hennessy, John J. *Return to Bull Run*. New York: Simon and Schuster, 1993. A comprehensive account of the campaign of Second Manassas that contrasts the splendid performance of Robert E. Lee's Army of Northern Virginia with the mediocre action of Major General John Pope's Army of Virginia.

McPherson, James M. *Crossroads of Freedom: Antietam*. New York: Oxford University Press, 2002. A concise volume in the series Pivotal Moments in American History. Author argues persuasively that no other campaign in the war had such momentous, multiple consequences as the Battle of Antietam.

Murfin, James V. *The Gleam of Bayonets*. New York: Bonanza Books, 1965. An analysis of the Battle of Antietam and Robert E. Lee's Maryland Campaign of September 1862.

Reardon, Carol. *Pickett's Charge in History and Memory*. Chapel Hill: University of North Carolina Press, 1997. An excellent account of Pickett's Charge that questions the conventions of history. Written by one of the premier military historians of the battle, the book concludes that most of what history tells us is "true" about the Confederate attack may not rest on a strong foundation of fact.

Sears, Stephen W. *To the Gates of Richmond.* New York: Ticknor & Fields, 1992. An examination of Major General George B. McClellan's failed Peninsula Campaign that also witnessed the emergence of Robert E. Lee as the Confederacy's finest army commander.

———. *Chancellorsville.* Boston: Houghton Mifflin, 1996. A detailed account of the battle that the author claims witnessed the most intense and concentrated few hours of fighting of the entire war.

———. *Gettysburg.* Boston: Houghton Mifflin, 2003. Controversial interpretation of the climactic battle. Sears argues that the campaign marked a major departure in the career of Robert E. Lee.

Trudeau, Noah Andre. *Gettysburg: A Testing of Courage.* New York: HarperCollins, 2002. An indispensable account of the most crucial battle of the war. Appendices include biographical sketches of key leaders and a detailed breakdown of casualties by brigade.

Wert, Jeffry D. *Gettysburg: Day Three.* New York: Simon and Schuster, 2002. Best new book on the Battle of Gettysburg's third day, with particular emphasis on Pickett's Charge.

Novels

Crane, Stephen. *The Red Badge of Courage: An Episode of the American Civil War.* New York: D. Appleton, 1896. Perhaps the greatest novel ever written on the Civil War. Crane uses the figure of Henry Flemming to examine the psychological turmoil that grips ordinary soldiers as they endure combat for the first time.

Hale, Edward E. *The Man Without a Country.* New York: Buccaneer Books, 1976. Originally published in serial form during the Civil War. The author uses a fictitious character who betrayed his country to dissuade voters from electing a well-known Copperhead as governor of Ohio.

Shaara, Jeff. *Gods and Generals.* New York: Ballantine Books, 1996. The prequel to *The Killer Angels,* written by Michael Shaara's son. Set against the background of the first two years of the Civil War, this novel develops the characters who later appear in his father's epic work.

———. *The Last Full Measure.* New York: Ballantine Books, 1996. The moving sequel to the Pulitzer Prize-winning classic *The Killer Angels.* In the final volume of the Civil War trilogy by Michael and Jeff Shaara, Lee, Grant, and Joshua L. Chamberlain form the trio whose fates are inextricably linked during the last two years of the Civil War.

Shaara, Michael. *The Killer Angels*. New York: Ballantine Books, 1974. The Pulitzer Prize-winning novel that focuses on the Gettysburg campaign. Shaara manages to capture the essence of war, leadership under fire, and the human drama that characterized this nation's greatest conflict.

Stowe, Harriet Beecher. *Uncle Tom's Cabin: Or Life Among the Lowly*. Boston: John P. Jewett, 1852. Stowe's classic novel that heightened the sectional tension between North and South on the eve of the Civil War. The central theme of the book is slavery as a manifestation of evil.

WEB SITES AND CD-ROM

http://memory.loc.gov/ammem/cwphome.html. Site contains the majority of Matthew Brady's photographs and is the most extensive collection of Civil War photographs available on the Web.

http://scriptorium.lib.duke.edu/collections/civil-war-women.html. The Duke University Library site features three significant sets of manuscripts that portray key aspects of women's experience in the American Civil War. Site contains thirteen documents from the well-known Confederate spy Rose O'Neal Greenhow; the journal of sixteen-year-old Alice Williamson, a Confederate partisan; and documents of Sarah E. Thompson, an active Unionist in the South.

http://www.abrahamlincoln.org. Educational Web site containing five Web sites and lesson plans on various aspects of the Lincoln presidency. Web sites include "Mr. Lincoln and Freedom," "Mr. Lincoln and Friends," "Mr. Lincoln and the Founders," "Mr. Lincoln and New York," and "Mr. Lincoln's White House."

http://www.dean.usma.edu/history/web03/atlases/atlas%20home.htm. Contains the complete list of Civil War maps used at the U.S. Military Academy at West Point.

http://www.nara.gov/education/teaching/usct/home.html. This Web site addresses the fight for equal rights and the history of black soldiers in the Civil War.

http://www2.cr.nps.gov/abpp/battles/tvii.htm. Created by the American Battlefield Protection Program of the National Park Service, this site contains brief summaries of both major and minor Civil War battles.

The Civil War CD-ROM, ISBN 1-878208-76-4. CD contains the *Official Records of the War of the Rebellion,* Frederick H. Dyer's *A Compendium of the War of the Rebellion*, William F. Fox's *Regimental Losses in the American Civil War (1861–1865)*, and *Military Operations of the Civil War: A Guide Index to the Official Records of the Union and Confederate Armies*, edited by National Archives historians.

Thomas, William G., and Alice E. Carter. *The Civil War on the Web*. Wilmington, DE: Scholarly Resources, 2001. The very best single-volume guide to the Web sites on the Civil War. The book contains a CD-ROM with reviews and ratings of the most popular sites and a topical index to facilitate research.

INDEX